DOCUMENT ANALYSIS
AND
TEXT RECOGNITION
Benchmarking State-of-the-Art Systems

SERIES IN MACHINE PERCEPTION AND ARTIFICIAL INTELLIGENCE*

ISSN: 1793-0839

Editors: **H. Bunke** (University of Bern, Switzerland)
P. S. P. Wang (Northeastern University, USA)
Joseph Lladós (Autonomous University of Barcelona, Spain)

This book series addresses all aspects of machine perception and artificial intelligence. Of particular interest are the areas of pattern recognition, image processing, computer vision, natural language understanding, speech processing, neural computing, machine learning, hardware architectures, software tools, and others. The series includes publications of various types, for example, textbooks, monographs, edited volumes, conference and workshop proceedings, PhD theses with significant impact, and special issues of the International Journal of Pattern Recognition and Artificial Intelligence.

Published

Series in Machine Perception and Artificial Intelligence – Vol. 82

DOCUMENT ANALYSIS
AND
TEXT RECOGNITION

Benchmarking State-of-the-Art Systems

Editors

Volker Märgner
Technische Universität Braunschweig, Germany

Umapada Pal
Indian Statistical Institute, India

Apostolos Antonacopoulos
University of Salford, UK

World Scientific

NEW JERSEY · LONDON · SINGAPORE · BEIJING · SHANGHAI · HONG KONG · TAIPEI · CHENNAI

Published by

World Scientific Publishing Co. Pte. Ltd.

5 Toh Tuck Link, Singapore 596224

USA office: 27 Warren Street, Suite 401-402, Hackensack, NJ 07601

UK office: 57 Shelton Street, Covent Garden, London WC2H 9HE

Library of Congress Cataloging-in-Publication Data
Names: Märgner, Volker, editor. | Pal, Umapada, editor. | Antonacopoulos, Apostolos, editor.
Title: Document analysis and text recognition : benchmarking state-of-the art systems /
    Volker Märgner (Technische Universität Braunschweig, Germany), Umapada Pal
    (Indian Statistical Institute, India), Apostolos Antonacopoulos (University of Salford, UK).
Description: New Jersey : World Scientific, [2017] | Series: Series in machine perception and
    artificial intelligence ; volume 82 | Includes bibliographical references.
Identifiers: LCCN 2017027906 | ISBN 9789813229266 (hardcover : acid-free paper)
Subjects: LCSH: Optical character recognition. | Mathematical notation--Data processing. |
    Arabic alphabet--Data processing. | Graphology--Data processing. |
    Content analysis (Communication)--Data processing.
Classification: LCC TA1640 .D586 2017 | DDC 006.4/24--dc23
LC record available at https://lccn.loc.gov/2017027906

British Library Cataloguing-in-Publication Data
A catalogue record for this book is available from the British Library.

For any available supplementary material, please visit
http://www.worldscientific.com/worldscibooks/10.1142/10689#t=suppl

Desk Editor: Suraj Kumar

Typeset by Stallion Press
Email: enquiries@stallionpress.com

Printed in Singapore

Foreword

Over the past five decades, slow and steady progress has been made in the general domain of document image analysis. In the early days, optical character recognition (OCR) was embraced by the pattern recognition community as an example of a task that could demonstrate quick and useful progress in the field. It was pseudobinary, the pattern set was fixed as a collection of machine printed, uniformly spaced symbols, and there were real applications for office automation and data entry. The late Professor Azriel Rosenfeld was often quoted as saying in the early 1960s that the leaders of the field had expected the problem to be solved within "a few years at most." By the mid-1960s, the realization had hit that the problem was a bit more difficult than originally anticipated due to unexpected variations in many applications, but the progress of the pattern recognition community put the problem on a trajectory to be solved in principle "by the end of the decade." That time too came and went, and the pattern continued — a few more years.... While we still work on similar problems today, the field has evolved, and we are now addressing much more difficult problems than the one first envisioned as a simple pattern matching task.

In the early days, there was very little work, which formally evaluated progress. Little was known about the algorithms that industry used in their systems, about the exact types of data they were interested in, or about the accuracy they were obtaining on real-world data sets. This was one disadvantage of having a problem that came out of industry, rather than an academic problem that evolved into something with industrial potential. One could imagine character recognition rates for isolated symbols, but as experts know today, that is only the tip of the iceberg.

Document analysis is inherently an applied problem and as such deserves formal, well defined, and rigorous methods for evaluation. Evaluation itself serves three primary purposes: to compare various systems to each other to determine which one is best for a given task, to measure the results of an individual systems against a known requirement, and to measure general progress of the field over time. Each of these purposes has its own impact on the community, and it is essential for us as researchers to embrace them and continue to keep the bigger picture in mind (what is the bigger picture?), not just evaluation data sets and protocols that make our individual technology look the best.

Academically, the first formal data sets that moved beyond the task of OCR were produced by the University of Washington in the early 1990s. Since that time, numerous additional data sets have been released by researchers as part of their own projects, while others have been released solely to present a challenge to the community. Some have survived over time, others have not, but the fact is clear that we have learned from successive releases and continue to provide more comprehensive resources that benefit not only our own ability to publish, but also to advance the field.

Fast forward to the early 2000s when our community started to embrace more formal competitions. Data sets and competitions have been the key to the advancement of many human-language-technology-related fields, including information retrieval, speech recognition, and computer vision. By having data sets which are large and address the real challenges of the field, researchers can measure progress and compare approaches in a systematic way. By having software and systems readily available that allow us to run these evaluations, and having metrics which are agreed upon, we can give our researchers a target for success.

Attached to various conferences and workshops in the document analysis community, the editors of this book, Volker Märgner, Umapada Pal, and Apostolos Antonacopoulos have done just that. They have provided a structure in the community and, among others, have been instrumental in providing a history of evaluations that often run for many years, and demonstrate progress. These pioneers continue to ensure that the research in our field is moving in the right direction. Without such leadership, we would be destined to make small incremental and often wavering progress.

We especially owe a great deal of gratitude to each and every competition organizer highlighted in this book. There is a tremendous amount of work that goes into each event — creating data, defining and implanting metrics, providing interaction with performers, comparing results, and ultimately publishing the successes (and possibly shortcomings) of the event. They have worked countless hours to help the field by providing a structured resource, and we are very thankful for their work.

In the future, I encourage the field to continue to be proactive in organizing these competitions. Furthermore, I hope that there will evolve a more formal approach to ensuring that each provides publically available data, releases software, and archives results in a way that researchers continually have resources to measure their progress. Furthermore, I encourage the community to take the task of evaluation seriously, and require evaluation on publically available data sets and demonstration of progress against the state of the art, for any papers published in the field. This type of requirement is evident in many of the top computer vision-related domains, and will certainly serve the document analysis community well.

I hope that you as a reader of this material can make use of the valuable information provided here and, where possible, are able to contribute back to the field.

Again, kudos to Volker, Umapada, and Apostolos for a job well done and for providing such a valuable resource for the community. Keep up the good work, gentlemen.

Dr David Doermann
University of Maryland, College Park

About the Editors

Volker Märgner is currently retired from the position of Academic Director at the Technische Universität Braunschweig, where he received diploma (Dipl.-Ing.) and doctorate (Dr.-Ing.) degrees in electrical engineering in 1974 and 1983, respectively. Until he retired in March 2015, he was a member of the research and teaching staff at the Institute for Communications Technology. He lectured courses in image processing and pattern recognition. His main areas of research are image processing andpattern recognition. Since his retirement, he has been working on historical manuscript processing as part of a team at the "Centre for the Study of Manuscripts Cultures" at Universität Hamburg.

During his active time in Braunschweig, he developed the IFN/ENIT database of handwritten Arabic words in 2002 in cooperation with ENIT in Tunis and organizeda series of competitions on Arabic handwriting recognition within the ICDAR and ICFHR conferences since 2005. He has carried out research on image pre-processing and pattern recognition-methods and their application to industrial quality control as well as to the recognition of cursive handwriting in contemporary or historical documents. He developed a recognizer for printed German text and for German handwritten words. Robust pre-processing and feature extraction with an HMM-based recognizer are the key features of this solution. Since 1991, he was also working on Arabic text recognition, at first in printed text and thereafter for handwritten Arabic words. This work was done in close cooperation with ENIT and ENIS in Tunisia. He worked on the task of system evaluation, in particular on the evaluation of document segmentation results. He has published more than 100 papers, including journal papers and book chapters. He is a member of program committees of conferences and workshops. He is a reviewer for international journals, including IEEE-PAMI, IJDAR, and PR, and he is amember of VDE/VDI, DAGM, IAPR (TC10, TC11), and IEEE.

Apostolos Antonacopoulos leads the Pattern Recognition and Image Analysis (PRImA) research lab at the School of Computing, Science and Engineering at the University of Salford, UK where he currently holds the post of Professor of Pattern Recognition. He has worked and published extensively on various problems in Document Analysis and Understanding (Image Enhancement, Segmentation, Recognition, Performance Evaluation) as well as on other applications of Pattern Recognition and Image Analysis. He has co-edited the first Special Issue (IJDAR) on Historical Document Analysis as well as the first book on Web Document Analysis. Professor Antonacopoulos was the co-organiser of the very first competition in the context of the International Conference on Document Analysis and Recognition (ICDAR) in 2001 and regularly co-organises benchmarking challenges and competitions on several topics in this field.

Umapada Pal has been a Faculty member of Computer Vision and Pattern Recognition Unit (CVPRU) of the Indian Statistical Institute, Kolkata from January 1997, and at present he is Professor and Head of CVPRU. His fields of research interest include different pattern recognition problems like Digital Document Processing, Optical Character Recognition, Camera/video text processing, Biometrics, Document Retrieval, keyword spotting etc. He has published 320 research papers in various international journals, conference proceedings and edited volumes. Because of his significant impact in the Document Analysis research, in 2003 he received "ICDAR Outstanding Young Researcher Award" from International Association for Pattern Recognition (IAPR). During 2005–2006, Dr. Pal received a JSPS fellowship from Japan government. In 2008, 2011 and 2012, Dr. Pal received visiting fellowship from Spanish, French and Australian government, respectively. Dr. Pal has been serving as General/Program/Organizing Chair of many conferences including

International Conference on Document Analysis and Recognition (ICDAR), International Conference on Frontiers of Handwritten Recognition (ICFHR), International Workshop on Document Analysis and Systems (DAS), Asian Conference on Pattern recognition (ACPR) etc. Also, he has served as a program committee member of more than 60 international events. He was the co-organiser of some competitions in the context of the International Conference on Document Analysis and Recognition (ICDAR) and Biometric areas. He has many international research collaborations and, at present, is supervising PhD students of 5 foreign universities. He is currently serving as an Associate Editor of the *ACM Transactions on Asian and Low-Resource Language Information Processing* (TALLIP), *Pattern Recognition* (PR), *Pattern recognition Letters* (PRL), *International Journal of Document Analysis and Recognition* (IJDAR), *IET Biometrics*, and *Electronic Letters on Computer Vision and Image Analysis* (ELCVIA). He has also served as a guest editor of several special issues. He is a Fellow of IAPR.

List of Contributors

Sheraz Ahmed German Research Center for Artificial Intelligence (DFKI) GmbH, Trippstadter Straße 122, 67663 Kaiserslautern, Germany
Email: Sheraz.Malik@dfki.de

Sameh Awaida Computer Engineering Department, Qassim University, Saudi Arabia
Email: s.awaida@qu.edu.sa

Andreas Dengel German Research Center for Artificial Intelligence (DFKI) GmbH, Trippstadter Straße 122, 67663 Kaiserslautern, Germany
Email: Andreas.Dengel@dfki.de

Markus Diem Computer Vision Lab, TU Wien, Favoritenstr. 9/183, 1040 Vienna, Austria
Email: diem@caa.tuwien.ac.at

Antoine Doucet Doucet Laboratoire Informatique, Image et Interaction (L3i), University of La Rochelle, France
Email: antoine.doucet@univ-lr.fr

Stefan Fiel Stefan Fiel Institute of Computer Aided Automation, Computer Vision Lab, TU Wien, Favoritenstr. 9/183, 1040 Vienna, Austria
Email: fiel@caa.tuwien.ac.at

Utpal Garain Computer Vision and Pattern Recognition Unit (CVPRU), Indian Statistical Institute, 203, B.T. Road, Kolkata 700 108, India
Email: utpal@isical.ac.in

Basilis Gatos Institute of Informatics and Telecommunications, National Center for Scientific Research "Demokritos", GR-153 10 Agia Paraskevi, Athens, Greece
Email: bgat@iit.demokritos.gr

Florian Kleber Computer Vision Lab, TU Wien, Favoritenstr. 9/183, 1040 Vienna, Austria
Email: kleber@caa.tuwien.ac.at

Marcus Liwicki University of Fribourg, Department of Informatics, Bd de Pérolles 90, 1700 Fribourg, Switzerland
Email: marcus.liwicki@unifr.ch

Georgios Louloudis Computational Intelligence Laboratory, Institute of Informatics and Telecommunications, National Center for Scientific Research "Demokritos", GR-153 10 Agia Paraskevi, Athens, Greece
Email: louloud@iit.demokritos.gr

Muhammad Imran Malik National University of Sciences and Technology, Sector H-12, Islamabad, Pakistan
Email: malik.imran@seecs.edu.pk

Harold Mouchère UBL/University of Nantes/LS2N, Rue Christian Pauc, 44306 Nantes, France
Email: harold.mouchere@univ-nantes.fr

Verónica Romero Pattern Recognition and Human Language Technologies Research Center, Universitat Politècnica de València, Valencia, Spain
Email: vromero@prhlt.upv.es

Joan Andreu Sánchez Pattern Recognition and Human Language Technologies Research Center, Universitat Politècnica de València, Valencia, Spain
Email: jandreu@prhlt.upv.es

Fouad Slimane MEDIA research lab, Ecole Polytechnique Fédérale de Lausanne (EPFL), Lausanne, Switzerland
Email: fouad.slimane@gmail.com

Nikolaos Stamatopoulos Computational Intelligence Laboratory, Institute of Informatics and Telecommunications, National Center for Scientific Research "Demokritos", GR-153 10 Agia Paraskevi, Athens, Greece
Email: nstam@iit.demokritos.gr

Alejandro H. Toselli Pattern Recognition and Human Language Technologies Research Center, Universitat Politècnica de València, Valencia, Spain
Email: ahector@prhlt.upv.es

Christine Vanoirbeek MEDIA research lab, Ecole Polytechnique Fédérale de Lausanne (EPFL), INF 218 Station 14, CH-1015 Lausanne, Switzerland
Email: christine.vanoirbeek@epfl.ch

Christian Viard-Gaudin UBL/University of Nantes/LS2N, Rue Christian Pauc, 44306 Nantes, France
Email: Christian.viard-gaudin@univ-nantes.fr

Enrique Vidal Pattern Recognition and Human Language Technologies Research Center, Universitat Politècnica de València, Valencia, Spain
Email: evidal@prhlt.upv.es

Richard Zanibi Document and Pattern Recognition Lab (dprl), Department of Computer Science, Rochester Institute of Technology, NY, USA
Email: rlaz@cs.rit.edu

Contents

Introduction

Document analysis is of growing interest since the mass digitization of any kind of document started. As not only contemporary but also historical documents, printed or even handwritten, are digitized, more complex processing is needed for the analysis of the scanned text pages. The development of such processing urgently needs a method or device to measure the system quality.

For several years, researchers have worked on this problem, as can be seen, for instance, in conferences in the field of document analysis such as the *International Conference on Document Analysis and Recognition* (ICDAR), the *International Conference on Frontiers in Handwriting Recognition* (ICFHR), the *International Workshop on Document Analysis Systems* (DAS) where benchmarks are used for different types of document analysis systems. The reader may examine the proceedings of those conferences to find a number of benchmarking efforts, often called competitions.

Motivated by the usefulness of benchmarks, this book presents a number of different benchmarking efforts carried out as part of document-analysis-based conferences or workshops, thus constituting the state of the art in different fields of document analysis systems. Each chapter is written by organizers of a competition, presenting not only the results and details of the metrics used for the comparison of the systems quality but also the lessons learned. The book contains the following four parts.

Part I: Logical Structure and Segmentation
This part contains two chapters. In Chapter 1, Doucet *et al.* present the background and results of a book structure extraction competition where systems for the extraction of the logical structure of digitized books are tested. Chapter 2 by Stamatopoulos *et al.* is concerned with the problem of segmentation of handwritten text into text lines and words.

Part II: Digits and Mathematical Expressions
Part II also consists of two chapters. In Chapter 3, Diem *et al.* present the results of competitions on offline recognition methods for handwritten digits and digit strings. Mouchére *et al.* present and evaluate in Chapter 4 some systems for the analysis of handwritten mathematical expressions.

Part III: Writer Identification and Signature Verification
Louloudis *et al.* treat the problem of writer identification in Chapter 5 from a more general point of view. Slimane tackles the writer identification of Arabic handwritten text on two different data sets in Chapter 6. In the third chapter of this part, Malik *et al.* describe recent developments and perspectives in the field of signature verification and present results of competitions in Chapter 7.

Part IV: Text Recognition
The last part treats two diverse topics from the field of text recognition. In Chapter 8, Sánchez *et al.* present work from the subfield of historical handwritten text recognition, discussing the results of a competition using the tranScriptorium data set. Chapter 9 by Slimane is on a different aspect of the recognition problem. The data set used is of printed low-resolution and low-size Arabic text. In that way, it tackles the challenges of size and resolution, in general, and the connected characters in Arabic text, in particular.

Volker Märgner
Umapada Pal
Apostolos Antonacopoulos

Part I
Logical Structure and Segmentation

Chapter 1

Logical Structure Extraction from Digitized Books

Antoine Doucet

1.1 Introduction

Mass digitization projects, such as the Million Book Project, efforts of the Open Content Alliance, and the digitization work of Google, are converting whole libraries by digitizing books on an industrial scale [5]. The process involves the efficient photographing of books, page-by-page, and the conversion of the image of each page into searchable text through the use of optical character recognition (OCR) software.

Current digitization and OCR technologies typically produce the full text of digitized books with only minimal structure information. Pages and paragraphs are usually identified and marked up in the OCR, but more sophisticated structures, such as chapters, sections, etc., are not recognized. In order to enable systems to provide users with richer browsing experiences, it is necessary to make such additional structures available, for example, in the form of XML markup embedded in the full text of the digitized books.

The Book Structure Extraction competition aims to address this need by promoting research into automatic structure recognition and extraction techniques that could complement or enhance current OCR methods and lead to the availability of rich structure information for digitized books. Such structure information can then be used to aid user navigation inside books as well as to improve search performance [35].

The chapter is structured as follows. We start by placing the competition in the context of the work conducted at the Initiative for the Evaluation of XML Retrieval (INEX) Evaluation Forum [22]. We then describe the setup of the competition, including its goals and the task that has been set for its participants. The book collection used in the task is also detailed. The ground-truth-creation process and its outcome are next described, together with the corresponding evaluation metrics used and the final results, alongside brief descriptions of the participants' approaches. We conclude with a summary of the competition and how it could be built upon.

1.1.1 *Background*

Motivated by the need to foster research in areas relating to large digital book repositories (see e.g., [21]), the Book Track was launched in 2007 [22] as part of the INEX. Founded in 2002, INEX is an evaluation forum that investigates focused retrieval approaches [14] where structure information is used to aid the retrieval of parts of documents, relevant to a search query. Focused retrieval over books presents a clear benefit to users, enabling them to gain direct access to those parts of books (of potentially hundreds of pages in length) that are relevant to their information needs.

One major limitation of digitized books is the fact that their structure is physical, rather than logical. Following this, the evaluation and relevance judgments based on the book corpus have essentially been based on whole books and selections of pages. This is unfortunate considering that books seem to be the key application field for structured information retrieval (IR). The fact that, for instance, chapters, sections, and paragraphs are not readily available has been a frustration for the structured IR community gathered at INEX, because it does not allow us to test the techniques created for collections of scientific articles and for Wikipedia.

Unlike digitally born content, the logical structure of digitized books is not readily available. A digitized book is often only split into pages with possible paragraphs, lines, and word markup. This was also the case for the 50,000 digitized book collection of the INEX Book Search track [22]. The use of more meaningful structure, e.g., chapters, table of contents (ToC), bibliography, or back-of-book index, to support focused retrieval has been explored for many years at INEX and has been shown to increase retrieval performance [35].

To encourage research aiming to provide the logical structure of digitized books, we created the Book Structure Extraction competition, which we later brought to the community of document analysis.

Starting from 2008, within the second round of the INEX Book Track, we entirely created the methodology to evaluate the Structure Extraction process from digitized books: problem description, submission procedure, annotation procedure (and corresponding software), metrics, and evaluation.

1.1.2 Context and Motivation

The overall goal of the INEX Book Track is to promote interdisciplinary research investigating techniques for supporting users in reading, searching, and navigating the full texts of digitized books and to provide a forum for the exchange of research ideas and contributions. In 2007, the Track focused on IR tasks [24].

However, since the collection was made of digitized books, the only structure that was readily available was that of pages, each page being easily identified from the fact that it corresponds to one and only one image file, as a result of the scanning process. In addition, a few other elements can easily be detected through OCR, as we can see with the DjVu file format (an example of which is given in Figure 1.1). This markup denotes pages, words (detected as regions of text separated by horizontal space), lines (regions of text separated by vertical space), and "paragraphs" (regions of text separated by a significantly wider vertical space than other lines). Those paragraphs, however, are only defined as internal regions of a page (by definition, they cannot span over different pages).

Hence, there is a clear gap to be filled between research in structured IR, which relies on a logical structure (chapters, sections, etc.), and the digitized book collection, which contains only the physical structure. From

```
<DjVuXML>
<BODY>
 <OBJECT data="file..." [...]>
 <PARAM name="PAGE" value="[...]">
 [...]
 <REGION>
  <PARAGRAPH>
  <LINE>
   <WORD coords="[...]"> Moby </WORD>
   <WORD coords="[...]"> Dick </WORD>
   <WORD coords="[...]"> Herman </WORD>
   <WORD coords="[...]"> Melville </WORD>
   [...]
  </LINE>
  [...]
  </PARAGRAPH>
  </REGION>
  [...]
 </OBJECT>
 [...]
</BODY>
</DjVuXML>
```

Figure 1.1. A sample DjVu XML document.

a cognitive point of view, retrieving book pages may be sensible with a paper book, but it is nonsense with a digital book. The BookML format, of which we give an example in Figure 1.2, is a better attempt to grasp the logical structure of books, but it remains clearly insufficient.

1.1.2.1 *Structured Information Retrieval Requires Structure*

In the context of e-readers, even the concept of a page actually becomes questionable: What are pages if not a practical arrangement to avoid printing a book on a single 5 squared meter sheet of paper? For the moment, it seems, however, that users are still attached to the concept of a page, mostly as a convenient marker of "where did I stop last?", but when they can actually bookmark any word, line, or fragment of the book, how long will users continue to bookmark pages?

It is important to remember that books as we know them are only a step in the history of reading devices, starting from the papyrus, a very long scroll containing a single sequence of columns of text, used during 3 millennia until the Roman codex brought up the concept of a page.

```
<document>
  <page pageNumber="I-N" label="PT_CHAPTER" [...]>
    <region regionType="text" [...]>
      <section label=SEC_BODY" [...]>
        <line [...]>
          <word val="Moby" [...]/>
          <word val="Dick" [...]/>
        </line>
        <line [...]>
          <word val="Herman" [...]/>
          <word val="Melville" [...]/>
        </line>    [...]
      </section>   [...]
    </region>      [...]
  </page>          [...]
</docment>
```

Figure 1.2.   A sample BookML document.

The printing press in the 15th century allowed the shift from manual to mechanical copying, bringing books to the masses [36]. Because of reading devices, after switching from papyrus to paper, we are now living another dramatic change from the paper to the digital format; it is to be expected that the unnecessary implications of the paper format will disappear in the long run. All physical structure is bound to disappear or become widely unstable. For instance, should pages remain, the page content will vary widely every time the font size is changed, something that most e-readers allow.

What shall remain, however, is the logical structure, whose reason to be is not practical motivations but an editorial choice of the author to structure his works and to facilitate the readers' access. Unfortunately, it is exactly this part of the structure that the digitized book collection of INEX missed. On one hand, it seemed to be an ideal framework for structured IR, while on the other, the collection's logical structure was hardly usable. This motivated the design of the Book Structure Extraction competition, to bridge the gap between the digitized books and the (structured) IR research community.

1.1.2.2 *Context*

In 2008, during the second year of the INEX Book Track, the Book Structure Extraction task was introduced [25] and set up with the aim to evaluate automatic techniques for deriving structure from the OCR texts and page images of digitized books.

The first round of the Structure Extraction task was "beta" run in 2008 and permitted to set up appropriate evaluation infrastructure, including guidelines, tools to generate ground-truth data, evaluation measures, and a first test set of 100 books built by the organizers. The second round was run both at INEX 2009 [26] and additionally at the *International Conference on Document Analysis and Recognition* (ICDAR) [9] where it was accepted as an official competition. This allowed us to reach the document analysis community and bring a bigger audience to the effort while inviting competitors to present their approaches at the INEX workshop. This further allowed one to build up on the established infrastructure with an extended test set and a procedure for collaborative annotation that greatly reduced the effort needed for building the ground-truth. The competition was run again in 2010 at INEX [27] and in 2011 and 2013 at ICDAR [11, 12] (INEX runs every year, whereas ICDAR runs every second year).

In the next section, we will describe the full methodology that we put in place from scratch to evaluate the performance of Book Structure Extraction systems, as well as the challenges and contributions that this work involved.

1.2 Book Collection

The INEX Book Search corpus contains 50,239 digitized, out-of-copyright books, provided by Microsoft Live Search and the Internet Archive [22]. It consists of books of different genres, including history books, biographies, literary studies, religious texts and teachings, reference works, encyclopedias, essays, proceedings, novels, and poetry.

Each book is available in three different formats: image files as portable document format (PDF), DjVu XML containing the OCR text and basic structure markup as illustrated in Figure 4.1, and BookML, containing a more elaborate structure constructed from the OCR and illustrated in Figure 1.2.

DjVu format. An <OBJECT> element corresponds to a page in a digitized book. A page counter, corresponding to the physical page number, is embedded in the @value attribute of the <PARAM> element, which has the @name="PAGE" attribute. The logical page numbers (as printed inside the book) can be found (not always) in the header or the footer part of a page. Note, however, that headers/footers are not explicitly recognized in the OCR, i.e., the first paragraph on a page may be a header and the last one or more paragraphs may be part of a footer. Depending on the book, headers may include chapter/section titles and logical page numbers (although due to OCR error, the page number is not always present).

Inside a page, each paragraph is marked up. It should be noted that an actual paragraph that starts on one page and ends on the next is marked up as two separate paragraphs within two page elements. Each paragraph element consists of line elements, within which each word is marked up separately. Coordinates that correspond to the four points of a rectangle surrounding a word are given as attributes of word elements.

BookML format. The OCR content of the books has further been converted from the original DjVu format to an XML format, referred to as BookML, developed by the Document Layout Team of Microsoft Development Center, Serbia. BookML provides richer structure information, including markup for ToC entries. Most books also have an associated metadata file (*.mrc), which contains publication (author, title, etc.) and classification information in the MAchine-Readable Cataloging (MARC) record format.

The basic XML structure of a typical book in BookML (ocrml.xml) is a sequence of pages containing nested structures of regions, sections, lines, and words (Figure 1.2).

BookML provides a rich set of labels indicating structure information and additional marker elements for more complex texts, such as a ToC. For example, the label attribute of a section indicates the type of semantic unit that the text contained in the section is likely to be a part of, e.g., a table of contents (SEC_TOC), a header (SEC_HEADER), a footer (SEC_FOOTER), or the body of the page (SEC_BODY).

The original corpus totals 400 GB, while the reduced version is only 50 GB (and 13 GB compressed). The reduced version was created by removing the word tags and their attributes (coordinates, etc.) and propagating the values of the val attributes as content into the parent line elements.

1.3 Setting Up the Competition

The goal of the competition was to evaluate and compare automatic techniques for deriving structure information from digitized books, which could then be used to aid navigation inside the books.

More specifically, the task that participants face is to construct hyperlinked ToCs for a collection of digitized books. As the name "Structure Extraction competition" suggests, the long-term goal of this effort is to extract the whole logical structure of documents, but the extraction of ToC has been planned as a significant milestone, unexpectedly difficult to reach. The next steps will be discussed in perspectives.

To evaluate the quality of extracted ToCs, we had to construct an appropriate book collection, define a format for ToCs, define metrics to compare extracted ToCs to a ground-truth, and last but not least, define ways to build such a ground-truth in a reasonable time, while still constructing a ground-truth that is large enough to allow for significant results, but without compromising quality and consistency.

1.3.1 *Defining the Evaluation Corpus*

In 2009, 2011, and 2013, the Book Structure Extraction evaluation corpus consisted of 1,000 distinct book subsets of the Book Search Track's 50,239 book corpus. Therefore, it consisted of a representative set of books of different genres, including history books, biographies, literary studies, religious texts and teachings, reference works, encyclopedias, essays, proceedings, novels, and poetry.

To facilitate the separate evaluation of Structure Extraction techniques that are based on the analysis of book pages that contain the printed ToC versus techniques that are based on deriving structure information from the full book content, we made sure to include 200 books that did not contain a printed ToC into the total set of 1,000. To do this, we used the BookML format where pages that contain the printed ToC (the so-called ToC pages) are explicitly marked up. We then selected a set of 800 books with detected ToC pages, and added a set of 200 books without any detected ToC pages into the full test set of 1,000 books. Please note that this ratio of 80.20% of books with and without printed ToCs is proportional to that observed over the whole corpus of 50,239 books.

1.3.2 *Sample Research Questions*

To motivate the community of researchers, we provided a sample of open research questions that the competition shall help address. Example research questions whose exploration is facilitated by this competition include, but are not limited to:

- Can a ToC be extracted from the pages of a book that contains the actual printed ToC (where available) or could it be generated more reliably from the full content of the book?
- Can a ToC be extracted only from textual information or is page layout information necessary?
- What techniques provide reliable logical page number recognition and extraction and how logical page numbers can be mapped to physical page numbers?

1.3.3 *Task Description*

Given the OCR text and the PDF of a sample set of 1,000 digitized books of different genre and style, the task was to build hyperlinked ToCs for each book in the test set. The OCR text of each book is stored in the DjVu XML format (see once more Figure 1.1). Participants could employ any techniques and could make use of either or both the OCR text and the PDF images to derive the necessary structure information and generate the ToCs. Giving the possibility of using the OCR text (DjVu format) was meant to facilitate access for participants with no experience of OCR, and let them start from a preprocessed common-ground format. Participating systems were expected to output an XML file (referred to as a "run") containing the generated hyperlinked ToC for each book in the test set. The document type definition (DTD) of a run is given in Figure 1.3.

1.3.4 *Annotation of ToCs: Methodology and Software*

Naturally, comparing the submitted runs to a ground-truth necessitates the construction of such a ground-truth. Given the burden that this task may represent, we chose to split it between participating institutions, and

```
<!ELEMENT bs-submission
    (source-files, description, book+)>
<!ATTLIST bs-submission
    participant-id CDATA #REQUIRED
    run-id CDATA #REQUIRED
    task (book-toc) #REQUIRED
    toc-creation (automatic |
        semi-automatic) #REQUIRED
    toc-source (book-toc | no-book-toc |
        full-content | other) #REQUIRED>
<!ELEMENT source-files EMPTY>
<!ATTLIST source-files
    xml (yes|no) #REQUIRED
    pdf (yes|no) #REQUIRED>
<!ELEMENT description (#PCDATA)>
<!ELEMENT book (bookid, toc-entry+)>
<!ELEMENT bookid (#PCDATA)>
<!ELEMENT toc-entry(toc-entry*)>
<!ATTLIST toc-entry
    title (#PCDATA) #REQUIRED
    page  (#PCDATA) #REQUIRED>
```

Figure 1.3.   DTD of the XML output (run) that participating systems were expected to submit to the competition, containing the generated hyperlinked ToC for each book in the test set.

rather than forcing participants to perform annotations (which may trigger hasty and careless work), we encouraged them with an incentive: we limited the distribution of the resulting ground-truth set to those who contributed a minimum number of annotations. This was pretty much in line with INEX practice. However, placing the burden on participants is evidently a hindrance, and so the effort must be as limited as possible. This section describes the ground-truth annotation process we designed and its outcomes.

1.3.4.1 *Annotation Process*

The process of manually building the ToC of a book is very time-consuming. Hence, to make the creation of the ground-truth for 1,000 digitized books

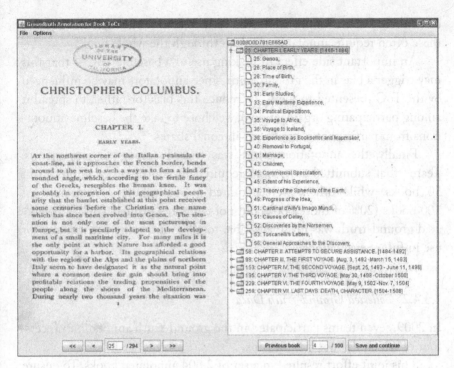

Figure 1.4.   A screenshot of the ground-truth annotation tool.

feasible, we resorted to (1) facilitating the annotation task with a dedicated tool, (2) making use of a baseline annotation as starting point and employing human annotators to make corrections, and (3) sharing the workload.

An annotation tool was specifically designed and implemented by the organizers for this purpose. The tool takes as input a generated ToC and allows annotators to manually correct any mistakes. A screenshot of the tool is shown in Figure 1.4. In the application window, the right-hand side displays the baseline ToC with clickable (and editable) links. The left-hand side shows the current page and allows one to navigate through the book. The JPEG image of each visited page was downloaded from a former INEX server at www.booksearch.org.uk and locally cached to limit bandwidth usage.

Using the submitted ToCs as starting points of the annotation process greatly reduces the required effort, since only the missing entries need to be entered. Others simply need to be verified and/or edited, although even these often require annotators to skim through the whole book.

An important side effect of making use of a baseline ToC is that this may trigger a bias in the ground truth, since annotators may be influenced by the ToC presented to them. To reduce this bias (or rather, to spread it among participating organizations), we chose to take the baseline annotations from participant submissions in equal shares.

Finally, the annotation effort was shared among all participants. Teams that submitted runs were required to contribute a minimum of 50 books, while others were required to contribute a minimum of 100 books (20% of those books did not contain a printed ToC). The created ground-truth was made available to all contributing participants for use in future evaluations.

1.3.4.2 *Collected Ground-truth Data*

In 2009, seven teams participated in the ground-truth annotation process, four of which did not submit runs.

This joint effort resulted in a set of 2,004 annotated books. To ensure the quality and internal consistency of the collected annotations, each of the annotated ToCs was reviewed by the organizers, and a significant number had to be removed. Any ToC with annotation errors was then removed. Most of the time, errors were due to failure to follow the annotation guidelines or incomplete annotations.

Following this cleansing step, 527 annotated books remain to form the ground-truth file that was distributed to each contributing organization. Around 97 of the annotated books are those for which no ToC pages were detected.

In 2011, the output was very similar with six teams participating to the annotation phase, two of which did not submit run, and a total number of 513 annotated books brought out to form the 2011 ground-truth.

In 2013, there were again six participating teams; this time all submitted runs. In 2013, we were able to outsource the evaluation, thanks to partial funding from the Seventh Framework Programme (FP7) of the European Union (EU) Commission. This allowed one to annotate a total of 967 books using the Aletheia tool [4].

1.3.5 *Validation of the Annotation Procedure*

To validate the methodology, and as the evaluation is based on manually built ground-truth, it was crucial to validate the approach by verifying the consistency of the gathered ToC annotations.

To do this, we assigned the same set of books to two different institutions. This resulted in 61 books being annotated twice. We measured annotator agreement by using one of these sets as a run and the other as the ground-truth and calculating our official evaluation metrics. The result of this comparison is given in Table 1.1.

We can observe an agreement rate of over 70% for complete entries based on the *F*-measure. It is important to observe that most of the disagreements stem from title matching, which makes us question whether the 20% tolerance utilized when comparing title strings with the Levenshtein distance may need to be increased, so as to lower the impact of annotator disagreement on the evaluation results. However, this requires further investigation because an excessive increase would lead to uniform results (more duly distinct titles would be deemed equivalent).

1.3.6 *Metrics*

The automatically generated ToCs submitted by participants were evaluated by comparing them to a manually built ground-truth. The evaluation required the definition of a number of basic concepts.

Table 1.1. The score sheet measuring annotator agreement for the 61 books that were assessed independently by two distinct institutions.

	Precision (%)	Recall (%)	*F*-measure (%)
Titles	83.51	83.91	82.86
Levels	74.32	75.00	74.04
Links	82.45	82.87	81.83
Complete, except depth	82.45	82.87	81.83
Complete entries	73.57	74.25	73.31

Definitions. We define the atomic units that make up a ToC as ToC entries. A ToC entry has the following three properties: title, link, and depth level. For example, given a ToC entry corresponding to a book chapter, its title is the chapter title, its link is the physical page number at which the chapter starts in the book, and its depth level is the depth at which the chapter is found in the ToC tree, where the book represents the root.

Given the above definitions, the task of comparing two ToCs (i.e., comparing a generated ToC to one in the ground-truth) can be reduced to matching the titles, links, and depth levels of each ToC entry. This is, however, not a trivial task as we explain next.

Matching titles. A ToC title may take several forms, and it may only contain, e.g., the actual title of a chapter, such as "His Birth and First Years," or it may also include the chapter number as "3. His Birth and First Years" or even the word "chapter" as "Chapter 3. His Birth and First Years". In addition, the title that is used in the printed ToC may differ from the title, which then appears in the book content. It is difficult to differentiate between the different answers as all of them are in fact correct titles for a ToC entry.

Thus, to take into account not only OCR errors but also the fact that many similar answers may be correct, we adopt vague title matching in the evaluation. We say that two titles match if they are "sufficiently similar," where similarity is measured based on a modified version of the Levenshtein algorithm (where the cost of alphanumeric substitution, deletion, and insertion is 10, and the cost of nonalphanumeric substitution, deletion, and insertion remains 1) [32].

Two strings A and B are "sufficiently similar" if

$$D = \frac{\text{Levenshtein Dist} * 10}{\text{Min}(\text{length}(A), \text{lengh}(B))}$$

is less than 20% and if the distance between their first and last (up to) five characters is less than 60%.

Matching links. A link is said to be correctly recognized if there is an entry with matching title linking to the same physical page in the ground-truth.

Matching depth levels. A depth level is said to be correct if there is an entry with matching title at the same depth level in the ground-truth.

Matching complete ToC entries. A ToC entry is entirely correct if there is an entry with matching title and same depth level, linking to the same physical page in the ground-truth.

Measures. For a given book ToC, we can then calculate precision and recall measures [34] for each property separately and for complete entries. Precision is defined as the ratio of the total number of correctly recognized ToC entries and the total number of ToC entries in a generated ToC, and recall as the ratio of the total number of correctly recognized ToC entries and the total number of ToC entries in the ground-truth. The F-measure is then calculated as the harmonic mean of precision and recall. Each of these values was computed separately for each book and then averaged over the total number of books (macro-average).

The measures were computed over the two subsets of the 1,000 books, as well as the entire test set to calculate overall performance. The two subsets, originally comprising of 800 and 200 books, respectively, that do and do not have a printed ToC, allowed us to compare the effectiveness of techniques that do or do not rely on the presence of printed ToC pages in a book.

Results. For each submission, a summary was provided in two tables, presenting general information about the run as well as a corresponding score sheet (see an example in Table 1.2).

1.3.6.1 *Alternative Measure and Discussion*

Participants were encouraged to propose alternative metrics, and thus the XRCE link-based measure [6] was introduced to complement the official measures with the aim to take into account the quality of the links directly, rather than conditionally to the title's validity.

Indeed, the official measure works by matching ToC entries primarily based on their title. Hence, the runs that incorrectly extract titles will be penalized with respect to all the measures presented in the score sheet of Table 1.2. For instance, a system that incorrectly extracts titles, while correctly identifying links will obtain very low scores (possibly 0%). The XRCE link-based measure permits one to evaluate the performance of systems works by matching ToC entries primarily based on links rather than titles.

Table 1.2.   An example score sheet summarizing the performance evaluation of the "MDCS" run.

	Precision (%)	Recall (%)	*F*-measure (%)
Titles	57.90	61.07	58.44
Levels	44.81	46.92	45.09
Links	53.21	55.53	53.62
Complete, except depth	53.21	55.53	53.62
Complete entries	41.33	42.83	41.51

The "complete entries" measure, used as a reference in most of this chapter, is a global, cumulative measure. Because an entry must be entirely correct, i.e., title, link, etc., to be counted as a correct entry, an error in any of the criteria implies a complete error.

While the various measures presented previously have in common a sensitivity to errors in the titles of ToC entries, the alternative measure in turn is strongly dependent on the correctness of page links.

We do not claim that success with respect to one metric is more important than that with another, but believe that the measures presented should be seen as complementary. Depending on the application or situation, one metric may be preferred over another. For example, if navigation is key, then being able to land the user on a page where a chapter starts may be more important than getting the title of the chapter right.

One of our goals in the future is to provide a toolbox of metrics, to be used by researchers enabling them to analyze and better understand the outcome of each of their approaches. The current version of this toolkit is available on the competition's website.

1.3.7 *Approaches Presented*

Throughout the campaigns of the Book Structure Extraction competition, several approaches have been presented. They can be categorized into three families.

ToC recognition and analysis. Most of the approaches of the state of the art rely on the detection of ToC pages within the book, and their detailed analysis for listing all ToC entries and linking them to the corresponding pages. To extract ToC entries and link them to the right page, the most effective technique to date remains the one developed by Dresevic *et al.* [13] which consists in recognizing ToC pages and then processing them so as to extract all ToC entries using a supervised method relying on pattern occurrences from an external training set. However, it is worth noting that the approach of Gander *et al.* [16] performs better for the sole ToC entry extraction (not taking page-linking into account). This rule-based technique is meant to mimic the ToC reading behavior of users, incorporating fuzzy logic so as to handle variations in the style of books.

Further work was presented by Wu *et al.* [37] who introduced a taxonomy of ToC styles requiring distinct system behavior: "flat," "ordered," and "divided" ToC. The reported scores seem to overcome the state of the art, although unfortunately they are reported over a combination of data sets, with no direct mention of the prior results of the Book Structure Extraction competition, which renders comparison difficult.

Book content analysis. Rather than searching for ToC pages as a prior, Giguet and Lucas [20] search for chapter beginnings through the book content, using a 4-page window and aiming to spot large whitespaces as strong indicators of the end of a chapter and the beginning of a new one. Unlike most other approaches, their method is fully unsupervised.

Hybrid approaches. Given that 20% of the books of the book collection have no physical ToC, the combination of techniques using ToC recognition and book content analysis seems a reasonable solution. Liu *et al.* [33] proposed exactly that, relying on the book content when no ToC was detected, which allowed for improvement over using ToC recognition only. Still, their method fell short of outperforming the top ToC page-based approaches [13, 16]. Surprisingly, no approach has been presented, fully combining the features of ToC pages and the book content.

1.3.8 *Summary*

Starting from scratch, a complete framework was created for the evaluation of Structure Extraction from digitized books.

Unlike book retrieval, where adjustments had to be made to existing IR evaluation techniques, everything had to be done to be able to evaluate Book Structure Extraction. Hence, every step of the competition setup is a contribution: the problem definition, the compilation of the collection, the task description and submission procedure, the definition of evaluation metrics, the annotation format and procedure, etc.

Clearly, in a similar fashion as with book retrieval, the most important challenge is (and remains) to be able to annotate such massive collections. Being able to do it was the first challenge that we have managed to address. The next challenge is to increase significantly the amount of collected ground-truth. One obvious way, in the light of the latest development in Book Search, is to rely on crowdsourcing.

The setup of this competition, initially sketched and tested on a low scale in INEX 2008, was validated by the community for the first time when the competition was accepted by the ICDAR 2009 Program Committee as a conjoint event between INEX and ICDAR. The contributions were recognized through the publication of papers, the main one being an article in the *International Journal of Document Analysis and Recognition* (IJDAR) describing the framework in 2010 [10].

However, the most crucial acknowledgment is that of participants of the Structure Extraction competition. Around 22 institutions have expressed interest, 10 have participated to the ground-truth creation, and 8 submitted runs. This adhesion to the competition is not only supportive, but it is also the only way that we could provide a decent-sized collection to the community.

Standalone test data. Indeed, to facilitate the participation of other institutions in the future, it was decided in 2010 to always make available the second to last ground-truth set. We then distributed the initial set of 100 ToCs built during the first Book Structure Extraction task at INEX 2008 [25]. Following this, as soon as the 2011 competition started, the data collected in 2009 (527 book ToCs) was made available online. Similarly, for the ICDAR 2013 competition, the 2011 ground-truth set was released (until then, its access remained restricted to sufficient contributors of the 2011 ground-truth set). Finally, thanks to dedicated funding for its construction, the 2013 ground-truth was openly distributed from the start, providing an additional 967 annotated books.

Effectively, these ground-truth sets, distributed together with the document collection and the evaluation software, are forming standalone evaluation packages, freely available to the research community on the competition's website.[a]

ICDAR competition and INEX workshop. A strength of the conjoint organization between INEX and ICDAR is the effective bridging of two communities: the competition was labeled by and presented at ICDAR, but at the same time, participants were invited to write papers presenting their approaches at the INEX workshop, a selection of which have been published by *Springer Lecture Notes in Computer Science* (LNCS) within the INEX workshop proceedings (see, e.g., [6–8, 20, 31, 33]).

The respective ICDAR and INEX schedules facilitated this, since the ICDAR result deadline is around the middle of the year, whereas the INEX workshop is generally held in December, with paper submission deadlines at the end of October.

Future of the Structure Extraction competition. The data sets are now freely available. This was requested by several participants intending to run further experiments, as well by several other institutions which were still developing their Structure Extraction systems at submission time.

Another important reason to open access to the data set is the current results, indicating that much could still be improved upon, especially in the case of books that do not contain ToC pages. This underlines how much remains to be done in the field of Book Structure Extraction.

The possible directions of future rounds of the Structure Extraction competition are discussed in Section 1.5. Before that, we will summarize related publications and put them in context.

1.4 Related Publications

The general background of the INEX workshop is best summarized in INEX reports published within INEX workshops [24–30] and the SIGIR Forum [1, 2, 22], the biannual publication of the ACM Specific Interest Group on Information Retrieval (SIGIR). The evolution of the share of

---

[a] http://pageperso.univ-lr.fr/antoine.doucet/structureExtraction/training.

the reports dealing with the Book Track is a good indicator of its growing importance within the INEX Framework.

The initial setup of the book retrieval task was presented within INEX 2007 [24], while a more extensive standalone description was published in the SIGIR Forum in 2008 [22]. A number of potential new user tasks were exposed in a short position paper presented at the European Conference on Digital Libraries (ECDL) 2008 [23]. This is where the idea of the Structure Extraction was proposed for the first time. The later rounds of the Book Track introduced new tasks as well as variations of existing ones. All these tasks, as well as the participants' approaches, are described in the corresponding Book Track overviews [23–30].

The Structure Extraction competition is also briefly overviewed within each of these papers. However, extensive description and discussion are rather found in publications of the document analysis community. Indeed, following the acceptance of the 1st, 2nd, and 3rd Structure Extraction competitions at the International Conference on Document Analysis and Recognition (ICDAR), respectively, in 2009, 2011, and 2013, their setups, overviews, and results were published in corresponding ICDAR proceedings [9, 11, 12]. The contribution to the evaluation of Book Structure Extraction was most extensively described in a longer article, published in the IJDAR in 2011 [10].

In addition, selected papers describing participant approaches were published yearly within the INEX workshop proceedings by Springer, as different volumes of the LNCS series [15, 17–19]. These volumes contain descriptions of participant approaches to both the book search and the Structure Extraction task.

1.5 Conclusions and Perspectives

Starting from the distribution of a digitized book collection in 2007 and the subsequent very first Book Search Track run at INEX [24], progress has been steady. We have designed techniques to gather a sufficient number of relevance assessments and evaluate Book IR. We also fostered renewed interest and designed evaluation methods for the problem of the extraction of the logical structure from digitized books, opening the way for applications of structured IR in a motivating application setting.

The number of registered participants of the Book Track has grown from 27 in 2007 to 54 in 2008, and 84 in 2009 and 2010. In 2011, at the 10th anniversary of INEX, the Book Track became the main track of INEX, replacing the *ad hoc* track which evaluated structured IR with collections of scientific articles (IEEE) and Wikipedia articles, from 2002 to 2010. For both the Book Search and the Structure Extraction tasks, participants have been invited to present their approaches at the INEX workshop, with proceedings published by Springer LNCS.

Starting form 2012, the INEX workshop, with the Book Track as its main track, will be co-located with the Cross-Language Evaluation Forum (CLEF), which recently grew from a forum on cross-language evaluation to a full-scale conference focused on multilingual and multi-modal information access.

A number of improvements shall be considered for the future of the Book Structure Extraction task, e.g., crowdsourcing the ground-truth of Book Structure. In spite of the tremendous efforts of participants to build the ground-truth, we shall experiment with crowdsourcing methods in the future. This may offer a natural solution to the evaluation challenge posed by the massive data sets handled in digitized libraries. The step was successfully made in the Book Search task, and it is now natural for the Structure Extraction competition to follow a similar path.

Investigating the usability of the extracted ToCs also seems worthwhile. In particular, we will explore the use of qualitative evaluation measures in addition to the current precision/recall measures. This would enable us to better understand what properties make a ToC useful and which are important to users engaged in reading or searching. Such insights are expected to contribute to future research into providing better navigational aids to users of digital book repositories. This effort shall be led through crowdsourcing.

Both these extensions offer interesting questions in terms of quality control, a key issue to make the output of crowdsourcing useful. These shall be relevant internship topics for Master students.

Further structure. As the name "Book Structure Extraction" competition suggests, ToCs are not the sole objective, but rather a first milestone that proves to be far more difficult to reach than expected.

In the future, however, we plan to expand the task to include the identification of more exhaustive structure information, e.g., header/footer, bibliography, etc.

Human–computer interaction (HCI). An important fact about e-readers is that they deprive readers from a lot of context. Being returned only a fragment of text is not the same as being given a pointer into a printed book. The ability to search for keywords within an eBook is depriving readers from context that is intrinsically available with paper books [3]. This poses many questions in HCI.

References

1. P. Bellot, T. Chappell, A. Doucet, S. Geva, S. Gurajada, J. Kamps, G. Kazai, M. Koolen, M. Landoni, M. Marx, A. Mishra, V. Moriceau, J. Mothe, M. Preminger, G. Ramírez, M. Sanderson, E. Sanjuan, F. Scholer, A. Schuh, X. Tannier, M. Theobald, M. Trappett, A. Trotman, and Q. Wang, Report on INEX 2012. *SIGIR Forum*, vol. 46, no. 2, pp. 50–59, December 2012.
2. P. Bellot, A. Doucet, S. Geva, S. Gurajada, J. Kamps, G. Kazai, M. Koolen, A. Mishra, V. Moriceau, J. Mothe, M. Preminger, E. SanJuan, R. Schenkel, X. Tannier, M. Theobald, M. Trappett, A. Trotman, M. Sanderson, F. Scholer, and Q. Wang, Report on INEX 2013. *SIGIR Forum*, vol. 47, no. 2, pp. 21–32, January 2013.
3. R. Chartier and A. Paire, *Pratiques de la lecture/sous la direction de Roger Chartier et à l'initiative d'Alain Paire*. Payot & Rivages, Paris, 2003. (Publication originale chez Rivages en, 1985.)
4. C. Clausner, S. Pletschacher, and A. Antonacopoulos, "Aletheia — an advanced document layout and text ground-truthing system for production environments," in *Proceedings of the 11th International Conference on Document Analysis and Recognition* (ICDAR'2011), IEEE, Beijing, China, pp. 48–52, September 2011.
5. K. Coyle, "Mass digitization of books," *Journal of Academic Librarianship*, vol. 32, no. 6, pp. 641–645, 2006.
6. H. Déjean and J.-L. Meunier, "XRCE participation to the 2009 book structure task," in *Focused Retrieval and Evaluation: 8th International Workshop of the Initiative for the Evaluation of XML Retrieval* (INEX'2009), *Lecture Notes in Computer Science*, vol. 6203, pp. 160–169. Berlin, Heidelberg, Springer, 2010.

7. H. Déjean and J.-L. Meunier, "Reflections on the INEX structure extraction competition," in *Proceedings of the 9th IAPR International Workshop on Document Analysis Systems Series* (DAS'2010). New York, NY, ACM, pp. 301–308, 2010.

8. H. Déjean, "Using page breaks for book structuring," in *Focused Retrieval of Content and Structure: 10th International Workshop of the Initiative for the Evaluation of XML Retrieval* (INEX'2011), *Lecture Notes in Computer Science*, vol. 7424, pp. 57–67, Berlin, Heidelberg, Springer, 2012.

9. A. Doucet, G. Kazai, B. Dresevic, A. Uzelac, B. Radakovic, and N. Todic, "ICDAR 2009 Book Structure Extraction Competition," in *Proceedings of the 10th International Conference on Document Analysis and Recognition (ICDAR'2009)*, IEEE, Barcelona, Spain, pp. 1408–1412, July 2009.

10. A. Doucet, G. Kazai, B. Dresevic, A. Uzelac, B. Radakovic, and N. Todic, "Setting up a competition framework for the evaluation of structure extraction from OCR-ed books," *International Journal of Document Analysis and Recognition*, vol. 14, no. 1, pp. 45–52 (Special Issue on Performance Evaluation of Document Analysis and Recognition Algorithms), 2011.

11. A. Doucet, G. Kazai, and J.-L. Meunier, "ICDAR 2011 Book Structure Extraction Competition," in *Proceedings of the 11th International Conference on Document Analysis and Recognition* (ICDAR'2011), IEEE, Beijing, China, pp. 1501–1505, September 2011.

12. A. Doucet, G. Kazai, S. Colutto, and G. Mühlberger, "Overview of the ICDAR 2013 Competition on Book Structure Extraction," in *Proceedings of the 12th International Conference on Document Analysis and Recognition* (ICDAR'2013), Washington DC, USA, pp. 1438–1443, August 25–28, 2013.

13. B. Dresevic, A. Uzelac, B. Radakovic, and N. Todic, "Book layout analysis: TOC structure extraction engine," in S. Geva, J. Kamps, and A. Trotman, Eds. *Advances in Focused Retrieval* (INEX'2008), *Lecture Notes in Computer Science Series*, vol. 5613, pp. 164–171. Berlin, Heidelberg, Springer-Verlag, 2009.

14. N. Fuhr, N. Gövert, G. Kazai, and M. Lalmas, Eds., in *Proceedings of the 1st Workshop of the Initiative for the Evaluation of XML Retrieval* (INEX'2002), Schloss Dagstuhl, Germany, December 9–11, 2002.

15. N. Fuhr, J. Kamps, M. Lalmas, and A. Trotman, Eds., "Focused access to XML documents," in *6th International Workshop of the Initiative for the Evaluation of XML Retrieval* (INEX'2007), Dagstuhl Castle, Germany, December 17–19, 2007. (*Selected Papers, Lecture Notes in Computer Science*, vol. 4862, New York, NY, Springer, 2008.)

16. L. Gander, C. Lezuo, and R. Unterweger, "Rule based document understanding of historical books using a hybrid fuzzy classification system," in

Proceedings of the 2011 Workshop on Historical Document Imaging and Processing (HIP'2011). New York, NY, ACM, pp. 91–97, 2011.

17. S. Geva, J. Kamps, and A. Trotman, Eds., "Advances in focused retrieval," in *7th International Workshop of the Initiative for the Evaluation of XML Retrieval* (INEX'2008), Dagstuhl Castle, Germany, December 15–18, 2008. (*Revised and Selected Papers, Lecture Notes in Computer Science*, vol. 5631. New York, NY, Springer, 2009.)

18. S. Geva, J. Kamps, and A. Trotman, Eds., "Focused retrieval and evaluation," in *8th International Workshop of the Initiative for the Evaluation of XML Retrieval* (INEX'2009), Brisbane, Australia, December 7–9, 2009. (*Revised and Selected Papers, Lecture Notes in Computer Science*, vol. 6203. New York, NY, Springer, 2010.)

19. S. Geva, J. Kamps, R. Schenkel, and A. Trotman, Eds., "Comparative evaluation of focused retrieval," in *9th International Workshop of the Inititative for the Evaluation of XML Retrieval* (INEX'2010), Vught, The Netherlands, December 13–15, 2010. (*Revised and Selected Papers, Lecture Notes in Computer Science*, vol. 6932. Berlin, Heidelberg, Springer, 2011.)

20. E. Giguet and N. Lucas, "The book structure extraction competition with the resurgence software at CAEN university," in S. Geva, J. Kamps, and A. Trotman, Eds. *Focused Retrieval and Evaluation, Lecture Notes in Computer Science Series*, vol. 6203, pp. 170–178, Berlin, Heidelberg, Springer, 2010.

21. P. Kantor, G. Kazai, N. Milic-Frayling, and R. Wilkinson, Eds., BooksOnline'08: in *Proceedings of the 2008 ACM Workshop on Research Advances in Large Digital Book Repositories*. New York, NY, ACM, 2008.

22. G. Kazai and A. Doucet, "Overview of the INEX 2007 Book Search Track" (Book Search'07), *ACM SIGIR Forum*, vol. 42, no. 1, pp. 2–15, 2008.

23. G. Kazai, A. Doucet, and M. Landoni. "New tasks on collections of digitized books," in *Proceedings of the 12th European Conference on Research and Advanced Technology for Digital Libraries* (ECDL'2008). Berlin, Heidelberg, Springer-Verlag, pp. 410–412, 2008.

24. G. Kazai and A. Doucet, "Overview of the INEX 2007 Book Search Track (Book Search'07)," in *Focused Access to XML Documents: 6th International Workshop of the Initiative for the Evaluation of XML Retrieval* (INEX'2007), *Lecture Notes in Computer Science*, vol. 4862, pp. 148–161. Berlin, Heidelberg, Springer, 2008.

25. G. Kazai, A. Doucet, and M. Landoni, "Overview of the INEX 2008 Book Track," in S. Geva, J. Kamps, and A. Trotman, Eds. *Advances in Focused Retrieval* (INEX'2008), *Lecture Notes in Computer Science*, vol. 5613. Berlin, Heidelberg, Springer-Verlag, 2009.

26. G. Kazai, A. Doucet, M. Koolen, and M. Landoni, "Overview of the INEX 2009 Book Track," in *Advances in Focused Retrieval: 8th International Workshop of the Initiative for the Evaluation of XML Retrieval* (INEX'2009), *Lecture Notes in Computer Science*, vol. 6203, pp. 145–159. Berlin, Heidelberg, Springer, in press, 2010.

27. G. Kazai, M. Koolen, J. Kamps, A. Doucet, and M. Landoni, "Overview of the INEX 2010 Book Track: Scaling up the evaluation using crowdsourcing," in *Advances in Focused Retrieval: 9th International Workshop of the Initiative for the Evaluation of XML Retrieval* (INEX'2010), *Lecture Notes in Computers Science*, vol. 6932 pp. 98–117. Berlin, Heidelberg, Springer, 2011.

28. G. Kazai, J. Kamps, M. Koolen, and N. Milic-Frayling, "Crowdsourcing for book search evaluation: Impact of quality on comparative system ranking," in *Proceedings of the 34th Annual International ACM SIGIR Conference on Research and Development in Information Retrieval.* New York, NY, ACM, 2011.

29. G. Kazai, M. Koolen, J. Kamps, A. Doucet, and M. Landoni, "Overview of the INEX 2011 Books and Social Search Track," in *Focused Retrieval of Content and Structure: 10th International Workshop of the Initiative for the Evaluation of XML Retrieval* (INEX'2011), Lecture Notes in Computer Science, vol. 7424, pp. 1–29. Berlin, Heidelberg, Springer, 2012.

30. M. Koolen, G. Kazai, M. Preminger, and A. Doucet, "Overview of the INEX 2013 Social Book Search Track," in *Information Access Evaluation Meets Multilinguality, Multimodality, and Visualization: 4th International Conference on the Cross-Language Evaluation Forum* (CLEF'2013), Valencia, Spain, pp. 1–26, September 23–26, 2013.

31. G. Lazzara, R. Levillain, T. Géraud, Y. Jacquelet, J. Marquegnies, and A. Crepin-Leblond, "The scribo module of the OLENA platform: A free software framework for document image analysis," in *Proceedings of the 11th International Conference on Document Analysis and Recognition* (ICDAR'2011), IEEE, Beijing, China, pp. 252–258, September 2011.

32. V. I. Levenshtein, "Binary codes capable of correcting deletions, insertions and reversals," *Soviet Physics Doklady*, vol. 10, no. 8, pp. 707–710, 1966.

33. J. Liu, C. Liu, X. Zhang, J. Chen, and Y. Huang, "TOC Structure Extraction from OCR-ed books," in, S. Geva, J. Kamps, and R. Schenkel, Eds. *Focused Retrieval of Content and Structure: 10th International Workshop of the Initiative for the Evaluation of XML Retrieval* (INEX'2011), *Lecture Notes in Computer Science Series*, vol. 7424, pp. 80–89. Berlin, Heidelberg, Springer, 2012.

34. C. J. Van Rijsbergen, *Information Retrieval*, 2nd Edition. London, Butterworths, 1979.

35. R. Van Zwol and T. Van Loosbroek, "Effective use of semantic structure in XML retrieval," in G. Amati, C. Carpineto, and G. Romano, Eds. *Advances in Informal Retrieval* (ECIR'2007), *Lecture Notes in Computer Science Series*, vol. 4425, pp. 621–628. Berlin, Heidelberg, Springer, 2007.

36. C. Vandendorpe. Du papyrus à l'hypertexte. *Essai sur les mutations du texte et de la lecture*. Boréal, Montréal, 1999. nt2 hypertexte.

37. Z. Wu, P. Mitra and C. Lee Giles. "Table of contents recognition and extraction for heterogeneous book documents," in *Proceedings of the 12th International Conference on Document Analysis and Recognition* (ICDAR'2013), Washington, DC, USA, pp. 1205–1209, August 25–28, 2013.

Chapter 2

Handwriting Segmentation

Nikolaos Stamatopoulos, Georgios Louloudis,
and Basilis Gatos

2.1 Introduction

Document image segmentation is the process of dividing a document image into its base text components (blocks, text lines, words, characters). One of the most important and challenging tasks of document image analysis is the segmentation of handwritten document images into text lines and words. The overall performance of a character recognition or a word-spotting system strongly relies on the results of the text line and word segmentation process. Although the text line and word segmentation process for machine-printed documents, especially modern, is usually considered as a solved problem, the segmentation of handwritten document images presents significant challenges and is still considered as an open problem.

Different types of challenges are encountered in the handwritten text line and word segmentation processes. Concerning text line segmentation, difference in the skew angle between text lines, curvilinear text lines, variation in interline gaps, and overlapping and touching text lines that frequently appear in handwritten document images are some of the challenging issues. Furthermore, the appearance of accents in some languages (e.g., Greek) increases segmentation complexities. Regarding word segmentation, the challenges include the appearance of skew along a single text line, the existence of slant, the nonuniform spacing of words, as well as the existence of punctuation marks.

Over the last decade, a wide variety of segmentation methods for handwritten document images has been reported in the literature [5–35]. Moreover, four handwriting segmentation competitions have been organized in the context of the ICDAR and ICFHR conferences (ICDAR 2007, ICDAR 2009, ICFHR 2010, and ICDAR 2013) [1–4] in order to address the need for objective, comparative, and detailed evaluation under realistic circumstances and standard data sets. In this chapter, the evaluation results of the handwriting segmentation competitions are summarized in terms of a detailed description of the benchmarking data sets and the evaluation protocol used. Moreover, a brief description of the participating methods complemented by recently published (RP) methods which report on the competition's data are presented.

2.2 General Approaches

A wide variety of text line and word segmentation techniques for handwritten documents have been reported in the literature, which take into account the different types of challenges as described in the introduction of this chapter. Text line segmentation techniques can be categorized into five major groups: (i) projection based methods, (ii) smearing methods, (iii) grouping methods, (iv) methods based on Hough transform, and finally (v) other methods that cannot be clearly classified in a specific category.

Projection-based methods are among the most popular techniques for document image segmentation. A projection profile is a histogram of all foreground pixels of a document image along the horizontal direction. The detection of text lines is performed by analyzing this histogram with the purpose to detect hills corresponding to text lines and valleys corresponding to the areas between the text lines. Projection-based methods are commonly used for printed documents in which text lines are well separated, do not present significant overlap, and rarely touch each other. However, there are several techniques adapted to handwritten documents [5].

Smearing methods such as fuzzy RLSA (run-length smoothing algorithm) [6] and adaptive RLSA [7], are based on examining the white runs in a specified direction and are usually followed by connected component (CC) analysis. Several smearing methods are adapted to work on grayscale images and can efficiently handle cases of overlapping text lines as well as documents containing text lines with variable sizes. One of the major drawbacks, however, is the inability of smearing methods to handle the variability in interword distances.

Grouping methods are bottom-up approaches, which group low-level elements of the image such as pixels or related components [8]. Grouping rules, such as the geometric relationship between the elements, make these methods suitable for handling curvilinear text lines. The initialization step for grouping methods plays an important role and a wrong decision may result in segmentation errors.

Methods based on Hough transform are also bottom-up approaches since a set of points, such as the gravity centers or minima points of the CCs, comprise the input for them. The result of such a segmentation method corresponds to a set of lines that fit best to the input set of points [9]. The Hough transform has been used in many fields of document image analysis, such as skew detection, line detection, and text line segmentation, since its major advantage concerns its ability to detect skewed text lines. Although the problem of text lines presenting variability in their skew angles can be efficiently addressed with the use of Hough-based methods, the presence of different skew angles along the same text line cannot be treated well.

Finally, there are methods, which are based on the calculation of an energy map in order to detect paths that pass across text lines [10] as well as on the probabilistic Viterbi algorithm [11]. As a result, they can generate nonlinear segmentation paths to separate overlapping or touching neighboring text lines.

Concerning word segmentation, there are several segmentation methods based on the analysis of the geometric relationship of adjacent components within a text line. The first step of these approaches usually concerns the **calculation of the distance** of adjacent components. Many distance metrics have been proposed in the literature such as the bounding box, the Euclidean distance, the run-length distance, and the convex hull distance [12]. The second step of a word segmentation method deals with the **classification** of the previously calculated distances as an interword or intraword distance. There are mainly three categories that these classification methods lie in: methods processing only the local calculated distances, methods making use of all distances of a text line and, finally, methods that take into account all the estimated distances of the document image using a clustering technique [13]. The major difficulty of word segmentation methods is their sensitivity to the writing style, e.g., a simple extension of the horizontal part of character "t" may connect adjacent words.

2.3 Methods Participating in the Competitions

A brief description of the different segmentation methods, which participated in the handwriting segmentation competitions are given in this section.

2.3.1 *Participating Methods in the ICDAR 2007 Competition*

Five research groups submitted their methodologies to the ICDAR 2007 handwriting segmentation competition. A brief description of these methods is provided in this section.

BESUS method (CST Department of the Bengal Engineering and Science University in Shibpur in association with the ECS Unit of the Indian Statistical Institute in Kolkata, India): The text line segmentation technique is based on morphological operations and statistical values such as the mean line width and mean gap in order to merge adjacent components of the same text line [14]. A recursive procedure is applied until the width of all line separators produced is smaller than these values. Once the text lines have been detected, word segmentation is accomplished by classifying the gaps produced by the vertical projections as interword or intraword gaps using the mean value and the standard deviation.

DUTH-ARLSA method (Democritus University of Thrace in Xanthi, Greece): It is based on an adaptive run-length smoothing algorithm (ARLSA) [15] and it can be summarized in three steps. A CC analysis is performed and two types of obstacles are detected: column (left and right margins or between columns) and text (between text lines) obstacles. At a next step, the ARLSA algorithm is performed, in which additionally smoothing constraints are set with respect to the geometrical properties of neighboring CCs. Finally, for each text line, the mean value of the distances between the CCs is used as a threshold for detecting word gaps.

ILSP-LWSeg method (Institute for Language and Speech Processing in Athens, Greece): This method is based on [16]. For the text line segmentation task, the first-order statistics of the height and foreground density of the "within" and "between" line classes are estimated using the vertical profile as well as a smoothed version of it by employing a noncausal filtering on neighboring projections. Finally, combining the results of the Viterbi algorithm on the original and the smoothed profiles, the candidate line separators for each zone are obtained. Concerning the word segmentation, the initial candidate word boundaries are estimated by the local minima of the horizontal projection, and the strokes that are closest are grouped into two separate sets. As a metric of separability between the two sets, the negative logarithm of the objective function of a soft-margin Support Vector Machine (SVM) is adopted, in which the two classes are modeled by the expectation–maximization (EM) algorithm and the threshold is defined as the equiprobable point.

PARC method (Perceptual Document Analysis Area of the Palo Alto Research Center, USA): The text line segmentation method is based on CC analysis using several heuristic rules and thresholds. In this process, multi-line components are broken up, while ambiguous assignments are left out. Concerning the word segmentation method, a trained classifier is used in order to classify the distances of adjacent CCs as interword or intraword distances.

UoA-HT method (University of Athens, Greece): It is based on an efficient Hough transform (HT) mapping [17]. The CC space is partitioned into three subdomains depending on the CCs' height and width.

The CCs that correspond to the majority of the characters are partitioned to equally sized blocks, and the gravity center of each block is fed to the Hough transform procedure. A post-processing step is used in order to correct possible split or missed text lines and, finally, to separate vertically connected characters. Concerning word segmentation, the Euclidean distance of adjacent CCs is used and the threshold is calculated by the median of horizontal white run-lengths in the row with the maximum number of black to white transitions multiplied by a factor.

2.3.2 *Participating Methods in the ICDAR 2009 Competition*

Twelve research groups submitted their methodologies to the ICDAR 2009 handwriting segmentation competition, whereas four of them included only a text line segmentation method. A brief description of these methods is provided in this section.

CASIA-MSTSeg method (Institute of Automation of Chinese Academy of Sciences in Beijing, China): This method is based on [18]. The CCs are split based on several geometric constraints and then grouped into a tree structure by the minimal spanning tree (MST) algorithm in which the distance metric is designed by supervised learning. Text lines are extracted from the tree by dynamically cutting selected edges. Concerning word segmentation, for each gap between adjacent CCs in a text line, 11 geometric features are extracted and fed to an SVM classifier for classifying gaps into intraword or interword gaps.

CMM method (Center of Mathematical Morphology in Paris School of Mines, France): The first labeling of the image is applied using the minimum number of horizontal intersections with the text. Components with several labels or with labels that have to be merged are then handled based on several rules. For word segmentation, the average distance between the bounding boxes of the CCs of each text line is computed. A distance is considered to be an interword distance if it is larger than a threshold.

CUBS method (Center for Unified Biometrics and Sensors, University at Buffalo in New York, USA): The text line segmentation algorithm is based on an improved directional run-length analysis [19–20]. Concerning word segmentation, at each background pixel location, a horizontal background run including the location is traced and the run-length is saved in a new image buffer for each pixel location. A simple thresholding of the new buffer reveals word primitives. Then, the distances between the consecutive word primitives are computed using the convex hull distance. A threshold for grouping of the word primitives is calculated based on the mean and variance of the distances.

ETS method (Ecole de technologie superieure of the University of Quebec in Montreal, Canada): Both text line and word segmentation methods are based on text smearing and morphological operations. Most of the involved operations take into account the local text line orientation. This has the benefit of greatly reducing the frequency of accidental line merging. The text is smeared using a modified version of Weickest's coherence-enhancing diffusion filter, while the smeared image is binarized using Otsu's algorithm.

ILSP-LWSeg-09 method (Institute for Language and Speech Processing in Athens, Greece): This method is an extension of the previous method submitted in the ICDAR 2007 competition [5] (see Section 2.3.1). Text-line detection makes use of the Viterbi algorithm and candidate-line separators are obtained and combined by minimizing a function which exploits the distance between the separators and the local foreground density. For word segmentation, the negative logarithm of the objective function of a soft-margin linear SVM is used as a metric of separability.

JadavpurUniv method (CSE Dept., Jadavpur University, Kolkata, India): Text line segmentation is based on CC labeling and on comparison of components in a neighborhood. The dimensional features of the components are analyzed to determine the style of handwriting and threshold values are set for interword spacing in case of both isolated and cursive handwriting. Words are then identified on the basis of the difference in intraword and interword spacing.

LRDE method (EPITA Research and Development Laboratory in Le Kremlin-Bicetre, France): The input image is subsampled in both dimensions, while turning it into a grayscale image and an anisotropic Gaussian filtering is applied (mainly horizontal). The morphological watershed transform is computed, leading to a partition of the image into regions. Finally, a simple merging procedure is run on the region adjacency graph in order to obtain the text lines. Word segmentation is based on attribute morphological closing as well as on morphological watershed transform.

PAIS method (ECNU-SRI Joint Lab for Pattern Analysis and Intelligence System, Shanghai, China): The image is vertically divided into several strips. Potential text lines are detected using the horizontal projection values of each strip in order to estimate the average distance between the adjacent text lines. The text lines are then finalized by applying the knowledge of estimated line distance and reasonable black-to-white traversal numbers. Concerning word segmentation, the number of possible words is estimated by the black-to-white traversal numbers. A gap is considered as an interword gap if it is larger than a threshold calculated by estimating the number of possible words.

AegeanUniv method (University of Aegean, Samos, Greece) (*text line segmentation only*): This method is based on [21–22]. The document image is vertically separated into three areas, and for each area, a horizontal projection profile is calculated. The valleys with minima less than a threshold are considered to be likely beginners of line segments. Sequentially, the area is examined pixel by pixel until an entire white path is outlined.

PortoUniv method (Faculdade de Engenharia, University of Porto, Portugal) (*text line segmentation only*): This method is based on [23]. The image is handled as a graph and the text lines as connected paths between the two lateral margins of the image. The paths to look for are the shortest ones between the two lateral margins while paths through black pixels are favored. An efficient dynamic programming approach is used to find the minimum paths.

PPSL method (University of Mysore, India) (*text line segmentation only*): The text page is vertically crumbled into few strip-like structures. In order to get potential piece-wise separation line (PPSL) between two consecutive lines, the white/black spaces in each strip are analyzed. Next, such PPSLs are concatenated or extended in both directions to produce the complete segmentation lines based on the distance analysis of each PPSL with left and right neighboring PPSLs.

REGIM method (University of Sfax, Tunisia, in association with University of Le Havre, France) (*text line segmentation only*): The method is based on three distinct steps. The first step includes the document decomposition into columns and blocks covering all textual elements. The second step concerns the classification of the generated blocks using several statistical parameters. Finally, the third step detects the text line detections based on a fuzzy base line determination using a fuzzy C-means algorithm.

2.3.3 Participating Methods in the ICFHR 2010 Competition

Five research groups participated in the competition with seven different algorithms (two participants submitted two algorithms each). Six submissions included both text line and word segmentation algorithms, while one submission included only a text line segmentation method. A brief description of these methods is provided in this section.

NifiSoft method (NifiSoft, Saint-Etienne, France):

a. Text line segmentation is performed by adaptively thresholding a double-smoothed version of the original image. The size of the thresholding window is chosen in such a way that it maximizes the number of vertical lines that intersect with each CC at exactly two transition pixels. However, some lines might be split into several CCs which are subsequently merged using standard proximity rules. These rules are combined using a logistic regression classifier. Word segmentation is performed by thresholding a smoothed version of a generalized chamfer distance in which the horizontal distance is slightly favored. The global threshold is determined using logistic regression according to the distance, size, and proportion features of each text line.

b. The text line segmentation method remains the same, while concerning word segmentation, the distance between each pair of neighboring CCs is estimated using the Voronoi diagram. The global threshold is also determined in the same way.

IRISA method (IRISA Laboratory, IMADOC team, Université de Rennes I, France): A generic grammatical description of the organization of a page into text lines and words using two levels of resolution has been realized [24]. The localization of the text lines is realized using a low-resolution image. Then, an analysis in the resolution of the initial image enables us to associate each CC with a text line. Finally, conflicting CCs are detected when two text lines overlap. In that case, the grammatical level demands a re-segmentation of the CCs. Concerning word segmentation, the distances between CCs are computed using a Voronoi graph and a k-means algorithm enables the separation to interword and intraword distances.

CUBS method: This method is described in Section 2.3.2.

TEI method (Technological Educational Institution of Athens, Greece): Text line segmentation is based on an improved shredding technique [25]. The image is separated in horizontal strips along the white most paths (local minima tracers) of a pyramid blur of the binary image. The main innovation in this method is the complex shape of the blurring filter. Concerning word segmentation, for each detected text line the bounding box of all components are filled and then a vertically smearing is applied in order to produce a sequence of shapes which are called "syllables". Features for each gap along two consecutive "syllables" are extracted by considering various geometrical aspects of the gaps as well as the histogram of the gap's size within a particular image. A ten-layer feed-forward Neural Network with identical parameters was trained using the experimental data set.

ILSP method (Institute for Language and Speech Processing in Athens, Greece):

a. This method is described in Section 2.3.2.
b. The second submitted text line segmentation method is based on [26]. The basic steps are the following: (i) a low resolution image is

produced by applying dilation and sub-sampling, (ii) binary rank-order filtering is used in order to enhance the text line structures and (iii) dilations and generalized foreground rank openings are applied successively to join close and horizontally overlapping regions while preventing a merge in the vertical direction. Then, the image is over-sampled to its original resolution and the CCs of the resulting image correspond to the text lines of the initial document image. Finally, each CC of the initial document image is assigned to the text line that intersects, whereas if it intersects with more than one text lines it is segmented using the local ridges produced with the application of the watershed algorithm.

2.3.4 *Participating Methods in the ICDAR 2013 Competition*

Nine research groups participated in the competition with eleven different algorithms (two participants submitted two algorithms each). Nine submissions included both text line and word segmentation algorithms while two submissions included only a text line segmentation method. Brief descriptions of the methods are given in this section.

CUBS method: This method is described in Section 2.3.2.

GOLESTAN method (Electrical Engineering Department, Golestan University in Iran):

a. The text line segmentation method is based on a 2D Gaussian filter in which the size, the standard deviation, as well as the block size are calculated for each image. The filtered image is divided into a number of overlapped blocks. The filtered block is binarized using an adaptive threshold with respect to the estimated local skew angle. Binarized blocks are concatenated to get the overall path of text lines. Finally, the text lines are extracted by thinning the background of the path image. A similar approach is used to extract words from each text line in which ascenders and descenders are eliminated and an adaptive thresholding is used to determine the words.

b. The text line segmentation method remains the same, while for the word segmentation, a 2D Gaussian filter is used in the same way without eliminating the ascenders and descenders.

INMC method (Department of Electrical Engineering and Computer Science, Seoul National University, Korea in association with the Ajou University, Suwon, Korea): The text line segmentation algorithm is based on an EM framework considering the fitting errors of text lines and the distances between the detected text lines [27]. However, the state estimation was improved by performing oversegmentation at the initial stage. Moreover, the EM algorithm is also improved by developing additional steps based on dynamic programming. Concerning the word segmentation, the method of [28] is modified in order to deal with the irregularity in handwriting documents. A text line is segmented into words using the statistical information of the spacing in each text line, and a refinement is applied based on the local statistical information of word segments.

LRDE method (EPITA Research and Development Laboratory in Le Kremlin-Bicetre, France): Concerning text line segmentation, the interline spacing is first detected using a correlation measure of the projected histogram. The image is subsampled in both dimensions while turning it into a grayscale image. At a next step, an anisotropic Gaussian filtering is applied (mainly horizontal) whose kernel support depends on the interline spacing detected earlier. A simple merging procedure is applied on the region adjacency graph produced by the morphological watershed transform. Concerning word segmentation, a 2-means clustering allows setting a decision boundary between the horizontal distances of adjacent CCs. At a next step, dilation is performed with a horizontal structuring element and an attribute morphological closing followed by a morphological watershed transform produces the final word segmentation result.

MSHK method (Department of Management Sciences, City University of Hong Kong): The text line segmentation algorithm is based on CC analysis. The average width and height of CCs are estimated. The CCs of normal size, which are close to each other and almost at the same latitude, are grouped into short text lines. At a next step, these short text lines are merged according to their direction, latitude, as well as the intersections among them. Finally, the CCs with abnormal size are merged with the existing text lines by checking their neighborhood. Once the text lines are detected, the horizontal density of each text line is estimated and a closing operation is applied according to it. Finally, the average distance between adjacent CCs is calculated in order to merge adjacent CCs whose distances are smaller than this value.

NUS method (School of Computing at the National University of Singapore): The text line segmentation method is based on a seam carving algorithm. The accumulative energies are normalized by their distance to the current position using only the newest $W/2$ energies, where W is the width of the image. Seams with an energy value smaller than a threshold are removed, and the CCs which are intersected with a seam are marked with the same label. Each unlabeled stroke is merged with the nearest CC. Concerning word segmentation, the small strokes and other floating strokes, which are located above or below the main body of the text line, are removed. The gap between every pair of consecutive CCs is calculated using soft-margin SVM, and the second most dominant of these values is used as a threshold for word segmentation.

QATAR method (Qatar University):

a. First, the text of the document image is automatically detected using the features presented in [29]. Text line segmentation is performed by adaptively thresholding a double-smoothed version of the original image. The size of the thresholding window is chosen in such a way that it maximizes the number of vertical lines that intersect each CC at exactly two transition pixels. Some lines might be split into several CCs, which are subsequently merged using standard proximity rules trained separately for each script category. The word segmentation is performed by thresholding a smoothed version of a generalized chamfer distance in which the horizontal distance is slightly favored.

b. The second method is similar to the first one with the exception that it is trained on both the provided experimental data set and the Qatar University Writer Identification (QUWI) data set [30].

CVC method (Computer Vision Center, Universitat Autonoma de Barcelona in Spain) (*text line segmentation only*): The text line segmentation problem is formulated as finding the central path in the area between two consecutive text lines. This is solved as a graph traversal problem. A graph is constructed using the skeleton of the image. At a next step, a path-finding algorithm is used to find the best path to segment the text lines of the document.

IRISA method (IRISA Laboratory, University of Rennes 2, France) (*text line segmentation only*): The text line segmentation algorithm combines two levels of information: a blurred image as well as the CCs of the initial image. The blurred image is obtained by a recursive low-pass filter on columns, followed by a low-pass filter on rows in order to detect the significant holes of luminosity, which are grouped among the columns, depending on size and position criteria. Then, the presence of CCs is used to locally extend, if necessary, the pieces of text lines that have been found. Consequently, the body for each text line (position and thickness) is obtained. At a final step, each CC is associated with the nearest text line, after having re-segmented the CCs that belong to several text lines.

2.4 Recently Published Methods Using the Competition Data Sets

Several text line and word segmentation methods have been evaluated after the completion of a competition using the corresponding data set. A brief description of the RP segmentation methods, which achieved comparable results with the participating methods, is provided in the following section.

2.4.1 *Text Line Segmentation Methods*

Sanchez 2011 method: Sanchez *et al.* [31] compute the binary transition map of the document image, and then extract and refine the corresponding line regions through skeletonization. To improve the accuracy of text line segmentation, a new graph-based splitting method to separate the touching lines is applied. The performance of this method was measured using the ICDAR 2007 benchmarking data set.

Lemaitre 2011 method: Lemaitre *et al.* [32] combine several levels of resolution of the document image. The proposed text line segmentation technique is based on the cooperation among points of view which enables the localization of the text lines in a low-resolution image and on the association of the pixels at a higher level of resolution. Using this combination of levels, overlapping components can be detected and re-segmented. The performance of this method was measured using the ICDAR 2009 benchmarking data set.

Diem 2013 method: A bottom-up approach was proposed by Diem *et al.* [33], which utilizes profile boxes of words as a basic entity. Foreground elements are grouped into words using local projection profiles and these words are merged with respect to their minimal distance. At a next step, line rectangles are calculated using the principal component analysis for robust line orientation estimation. With a simple labeling strategy, the text line rectangles can be mapped to CCs in a post-processing step. The performance of this method was measured using the ICDAR 2009 and ICFHR 2010 benchmarking data sets.

Tang 2014 method: Tang *et al.* [34] propose a text line segmentation method based on matched filtering and top-down grouping for handwritten documents. It consists of three distinct steps. At first, the foreground pixel density of the document image is estimated and used to decide the size of the generated filter. This filter is created by convolving a band-shape filter and an isotropic Laplacian of Gaussian (LoG) filter. Then, the centers of the text lines are extracted by performing filtering, binarization, thinning, as well as a top-down grouping operation. Finally, the overlapping CCs which exist through multiple text lines are separated, and all the CCs are assigned to a text line using the nearest neighbor rule. The performance of this method was measured using the ICFHR 2010 benchmarking data set.

NCSR method: This work is an extension of the UoA-HT method submitted in the ICDAR 2007 competition [9] taking into account an improved methodology for the separation of vertically connected text lines (see Section 2.3.1). The performance of this method was measured using the ICDAR 2013 benchmarking data set.

2.4.2 Word Segmentation Methods

Sanchez 2011 method: Sanchez *et al.* in order to detect the words combine mathematical morphology with simple distance, position, and size heuristics for a meaningful grouping/splitting of the initially stated word hypotheses [31]. The performance of this method was measured using the ICDAR 2007 benchmarking data set.

Lemaitre 2011 method: Lemaitre *et al.* [32] propose a word segmentation method which is based on the cooperation among digital data and symbolic knowledge. The digital data are obtained from distances inside a Delaunay graph, which gives a precise distance between CCs, at the pixel level. Moreover, structural rules are introduced in order to take into account some generic knowledge about the organization of a text page. This cooperation among different types of information gives a stronger power of expression and ensures the global coherence of the recognition. The performance of this method was measured using the ICDAR 2009 benchmarking data set.

Ryu 2015 method: Ryu *et al.* [35] formulate the word segmentation problem as a binary quadratic assignment problem that considers pairwise correlations between the gaps as well as the likelihoods of individual gaps. All the parameters are calculated using the structured SVM framework in order to be independent of the writing styles and languages. The performance of this method was measured using the ICDAR 2009 and ICDAR 2013 benchmarking data sets.

NCSR method: This work is an extension of the UoA-HT method submitted in the ICDAR 2007 competition [9], which is based on an efficient distinction of interword and intraword gaps using the combination of two different distance metrics. The distance metrics comprise the Euclidean distance metric and the convex hull-based metric. The distinction of the two classes is considered as an unsupervised clustering problem, which makes use of the Gaussian mixture theory for modeling the two classes. The performance of this method was measured using the ICDAR 2013 benchmarking data set.

2.5 Benchmarking Data Sets

Performance evaluation using standard data sets is the only way to have a fair comparison of existing algorithms in document image analysis. Four handwriting segmentation competitions have been organized so far leading to the creation of four benchmarking data sets. All the data sets contain binarized handwritten document images along with associated ground truth for text line and word segmentation. The document images do not include any nontext elements (lines, drawings, etc.) and contain most of the challenging problems for handwritten document image segmentation. The ground truth includes raw data image files with zeros corresponding to the background and positive integer values, each corresponding to a segmentation region. Moreover, experimental data sets were provided to the participants for preparing their submissions, which consist of representative document image samples along with the corresponding ground truth. An overview of the benchmarking data sets is presented in Table 2.1 and a more detailed description of each data set follows.

2.5.1 *ICDAR 2007 Benchmarking Data Set*

The ICDAR 2007 benchmarking data set consists of 80 handwritten document images written in four Latin-based languages, which came from several writers that were asked to copy a given text as well as handwritten document images selected from the web (see Figure 2.1). The

Table 2.1. Overview of the benchmarking data sets.

Benchmarking data set	Number of documents	Number of text lines	Number of words	Languages	References
ICDAR 2007	80	1,771	13,311	English, French, German, Greek	[36]
ICDAR 2009	200	4,034	29,717	English, French, German, Greek	[37]
ICFHR 2010	100	1,629	15,130	English, French, German, Greek	[38]
ICDAR 2013	150	2,649	23,525	Indian, English, Greek	[39]

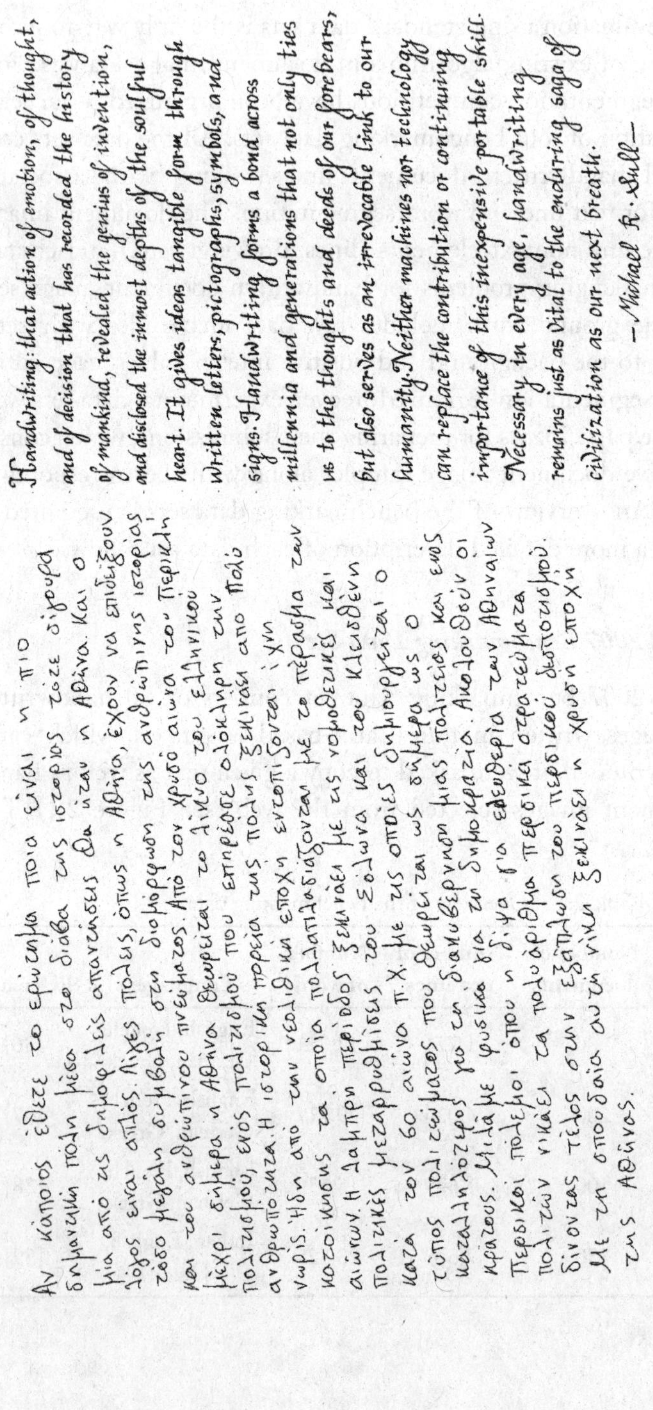

(a)

(b)

Figure 2.1. Document image samples part of the ICDAR 2007 benchmarking data set. (a) A handwritten document in the Greek language and (b) a handwritten document selected from the web in the English language.

numbers of text lines and words are 1,771 and 13,311, respectively. The experimental data set consists of 20 document image samples. The ICDAR 2007 data set is publicly available and can be found in [36].

2.5.2 *ICDAR 2009 Benchmarking Data Set*

The ICDAR 2009 benchmarking data set consists of 200 handwritten document images, and it was created with the help of several writers that were asked to copy 8 pages with each one corresponding to a different Latin-based language (see Figure 2.2). The number of text lines and words are 4,034 and 29,717, respectively. The ICDAR 2009 benchmarking data set is publicly available and can be found in [37]. The experimental data set of the ICDAR 2009 competition consists of the experimental and benchmarking data sets of the ICDAR 2007 competition (100 document images; see the previous section).

2.5.3 *ICFHR 2010 Benchmarking Data Set*

The ICFHR 2010 benchmarking data set is created in a similar way with the ICDAR 2009 data set, and it can be found in [38]. It consists of 100 handwritten document images (see Figure 2.3), and the number of text lines and words are 1,629 and 15,130, respectively. The experimental set of this competition corresponds to the benchmarking data set of the ICDAR 2009 competition described in the previous section.

2.5.4 *ICDAR 2013 Benchmarking Data Set*

A major difference of the ICDAR 2013 benchmarking data set from the previous data sets is that the languages involved have been extended by including an Indian language (Bangla, the second most popular language in India). This data set consists of 150 document images, and the numbers of text lines and words are 2,649 and 23,525, respectively. During the creation phase of the Latin part of the data set, several writers were asked to copy two samples of text in the English and Greek languages. For the Indian part, 50 document images with different content and size were considered. The ICDAR 2013 benchmarking data set is publicly

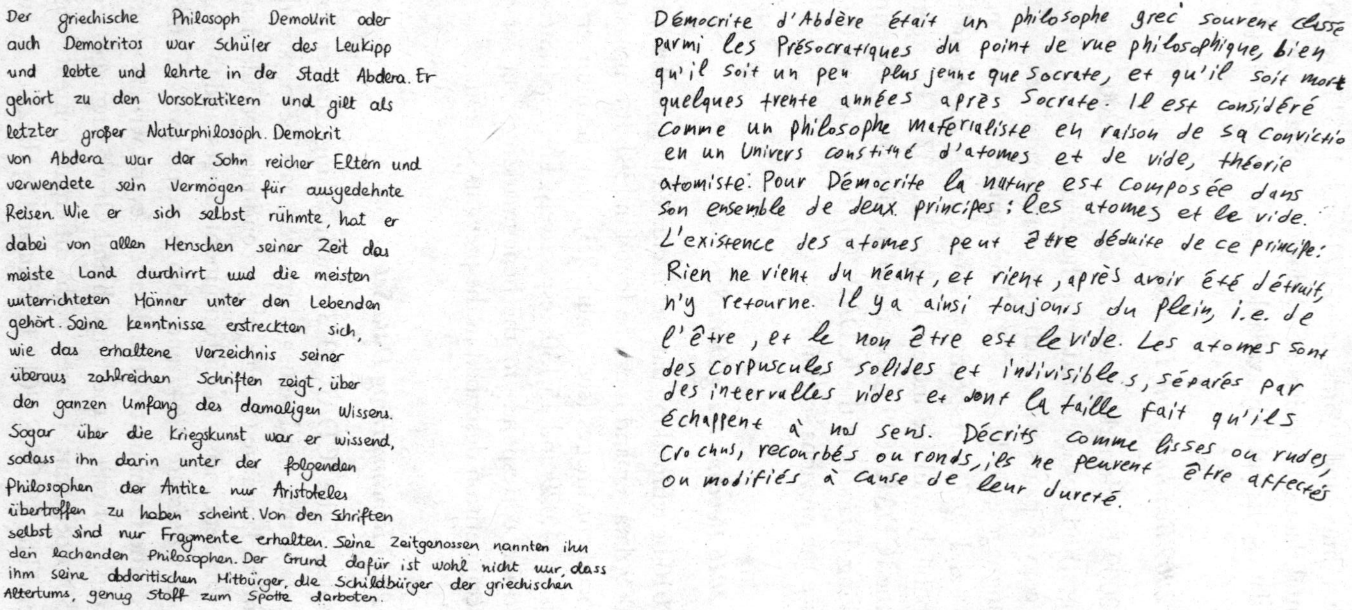

Der griechische Philosoph Demokrit oder auch Demokritos war Schüler des Leukipp und lebte und lehrte in der Stadt Abdera. Er gehört zu den Vorsokratikern und gilt als letzter großer Naturphilosoph. Demokrit von Abdera war der Sohn reicher Eltern und verwendete sein Vermögen für ausgedehnte Reisen. Wie er sich selbst rühmte, hat er dabei von allen Menschen seiner Zeit das meiste Land durchirrt und die meisten unterrichteten Männer unter den Lebenden gehört. Seine kenntnisse erstreckten sich, wie das erhaltene Verzeichnis seiner überaus zahlreichen Schriften zeigt, über den ganzen Umfang des damaligen Wissens. Sogar über die Kriegskunst war er wissend, sodass ihm darin unter der folgenden Philosophen der Antike nur Aristoteles übertroffen zu haben scheint. Von den Schriften selbst sind nur Fragmente erhalten. Seine Zeitgenossen nannten ihn den lachenden Philosophen. Der Grund dafür ist wohl nicht nur, dass ihm seine didaktischen Mitbürger, die Schildbürger der griechischen Altertums, genug Stoff zum Spotte darboten.

(a)

Démocrite d'Abdère était un philosophe grec souvent classé parmi les Présocratiques du point de vue philosophique, bien qu'il soit un peu plus jeune que Socrate, et qu'il soit mort quelques trente années après Socrate. Il est considéré comme un philosophe matérialiste en raison de sa conviction en un univers constitué d'atomes et de vide, théorie atomiste. Pour Démocrite la nature est composée dans son ensemble de deux princips : les atomes et le vide. L'existence des atomes peut être déduite de ce principe. Rien ne vient du néant, et rien, après avoir été détruit n'y retourne. Il y a ainsi toujours du plein, i.e. de l'être, et le non être est le vide. Les atomes sont des corpuscules solides et indivisibles, séparés par des intervalles vides et sont la taille fait qu'ils échappent à nos sens. Décrits comme lisses ou rudes, crochus, recourbés ou ronds, ils ne peuvent être affectés ou modifiés à cause de leur dureté.

(b)

Figure 2.2.   Document image samples part of the ICDAR 2009 benchmarking data set in (a) German and (b) French languages.

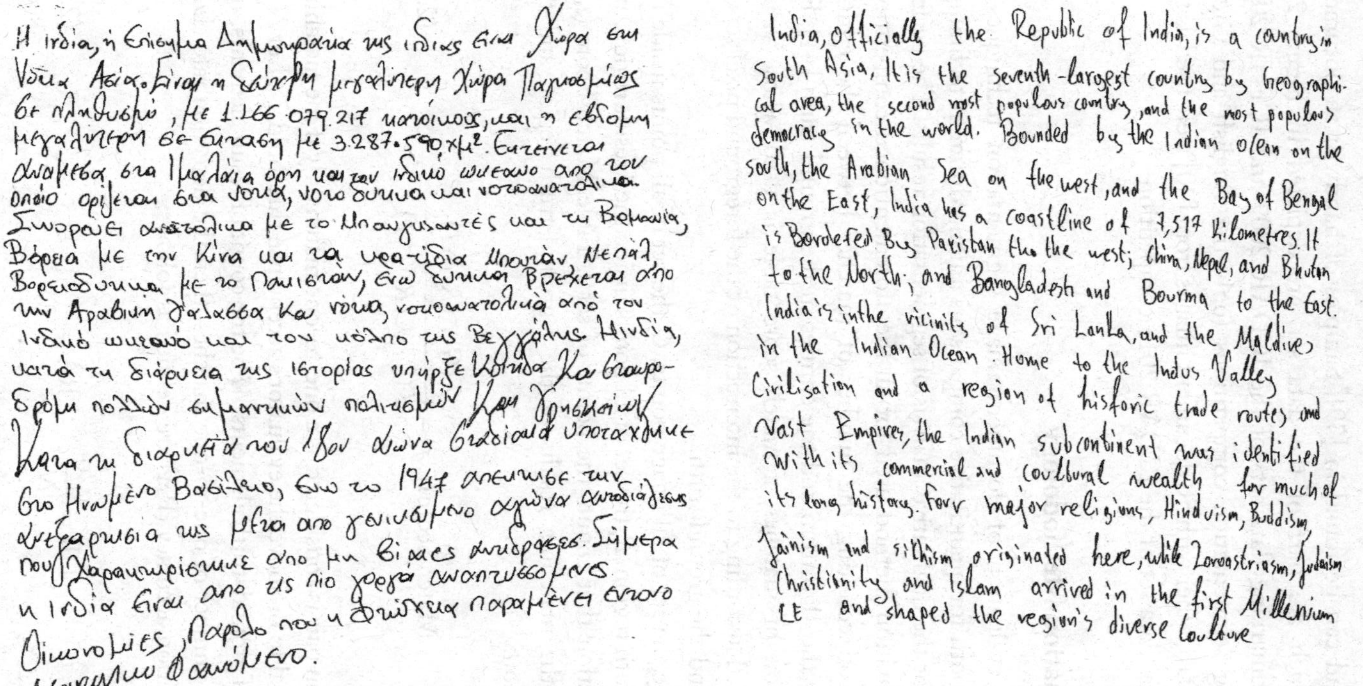

(a)

Η Ινδία, η Ενιαία Δημοκρατία της Ινδίας είναι μία χώρα στη Νότιο Ασία. Είναι η έβδομη μεγαλύτερη χώρα Παγκοσμίως σε έκταση. Με 1.166.079.217 κατοίκους, και η δεύτερη πιο πυκνοκατοικημένη δημοκρατία στον κόσμο. Εκτείνεται Διοικητικά σε Ηπειρωτικά όρη και σε νησιά αυτόνομα και τον Ινδικό ωκεανό, νότιο δυτικά και νοτιοανατολικά. Συνορεύει Δυτικά με το Πακιστάν και τα Ιμαλάϊα. Βόρεια με την Κίνα και τα νοτιότερα Ιμαλάϊα, Νεπάλ και Μπουτάν, με το Πακιστάν και Συνώνια Μπενγκόλ στα νότια με τον Αραβικό θάλασσα και νότια νοτιοανατολικά από του Ινδικό ωκεανό και τον νότιο της Βεγγάλης. Μικτία μετά τη Σύγγενεια της ιστορίας υπήρξε χώρα πολιτισμού. Εμπορικών...

(b)

India, officially the Republic of India, is a country in South Asia. It is the seventh-largest country by geographical area, the second most populous country, and the most populous democracy in the world. Bounded by the Indian Ocean on the south, the Arabian Sea on the west, and the Bay of Bengal on the East, India has a coastline of 7,517 kilometres. It is bordered by Pakistan to the the west; China, Nepal, and Bhutan to the North; and Bangladesh and Burma to the East. India is in the vicinity of Sri Lanka and the Maldives in the Indian Ocean. Home to the the Indus Valley Civilisation and a region of historic trade routes and vast Empires, the Indian subcontinent was identified with its commercial and cultural wealth for much of its long history. Four major religions, Hinduism, Buddhism, Jainism and Sikhism originated here, while Zoroastrianism, Judaism, Christianity and Islam arrived in the first Millennium CE and shaped the region's diverse culture.

Figure 2.3. Document image samples part of the ICFHR 2010 benchmarking data set in (a) Greek and (b) English languages.

available and can be found in [39]. Samples of handwritten document images, which are part of the data set, are depicted in Figure 2.4. Both benchmarking data sets of the ICDAR 2009 and ICFHR 2010 handwriting segmentation competitions (only the English and Greek documents) together with 50 document images from [40] were used as the experimental data set of the ICDAR 2013 competition.

2.6 Evaluation Methodology

Automatic evaluation of document image segmentation techniques is important both for quantitative comparisons among different techniques as well as for the qualitative analysis of segmentation results. The performance evaluation method used for all the aforementioned competitions was based on counting the number of matches between the entities detected by the algorithm and the entities in the ground truth [41]. For the detection of matches, a match score table is used whose values are calculated according to the intersection of the foreground pixel sets of the result and the ground truth.

Let I be the set of all image points, G_j the set of all points inside the j ground-truth region, R_i the set of all points inside the i result region, and $T(s)$ a function that counts the points of set s. Table Match Score (i, j) represents the matching results of the j ground-truth region and the i result region:

$$\text{Match Score}\,(i, j) = \frac{T(G_j \cap R_i \cap I)}{T((G_j \cup R_i) \cap I)} \qquad (2.1)$$

A region pair is considered as a one-to-one match only if the matching score is equal to or above the evaluator's acceptance threshold T_α. Let N be the count of ground-truth elements, M be the count of result elements, and o2o be the number of one-to-one matches, then the detection rate (DR) and recognition accuracy (RA) are defined as follows:

$$\text{DR} = \frac{o2o}{N}, \qquad \text{RA} = \frac{o2o}{M} \qquad (2.2)$$

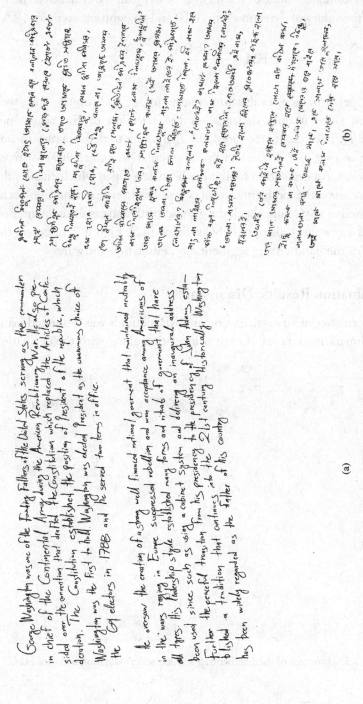

(a)

(b)

Figure 2.4.   Document image samples part of the ICDAR 2013 benchmarking data set in (a) English and (b) Indian languages.

A performance metric F-measure (FM) can be extracted if we combine the values of detection rate (DR) and recognition accuracy (RA):

$$FM = \frac{2 \cdot DR \cdot RA}{DR + RA} \tag{2.3}$$

The performance evaluation methodology is robust and well established since it only depends on the selection of the acceptance threshold T_a. The acceptance threshold T_a in order to define a one-to-one matching was set to 95% for text line segmentation and to 90% for word segmentation. An evaluation toolkit has been developed which enables the user to measure the performance of a handwritten segmentation technique as well as to visually check the ground truth and result segmentation files. This software is also publicly available [42]. Figure 2.5 depicts the interface of the handwriting segmentation evaluation software.

2.7 Evaluation Results: Discussion

The performance of all participating and RP methods was evaluated using the benchmarking data set of each competition along with the evaluation

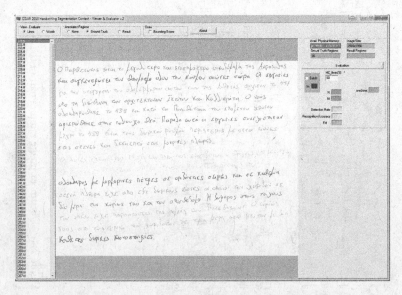

Figure 2.5.   Interface of the handwriting segmentation evaluation software [42].

methodology described in Section 2.6 in terms of the detection rate (DR), recognition accuracy (RA), and F-measure (FM). Detailed evaluation results are presented in Tables 2.2–2.5, while graphical representations of the evaluation results in terms of the F-measure are shown in Figures 2.6–2.9 for each competition, respectively.

As the ICDAR 2007 competition evaluation results indicate, the ILSP-LWSeg method outperforms all the other participating methods in text line and word segmentation tasks. However, the RP method Sanchez 2011 achieves higher F-measure concerning the text line segmentation task, whereas a significantly lower performance is observed for the word segmentation task. At this point, it is worth mentioning that the ICDAR 2007 competition evaluation protocol was slightly different from the one described in Section 2.6 since split and/or merged text lines/words (apart from the one-to-one matches) also contribute in the calculation of the DR and RA measures [1]. The evaluation results presented in this chapter (Table 2.2 and Figure 2.6) have been adapted according to the evaluation protocol described in Section 2.6 in order to be comparable

Table 2.2.   ICDAR 2007 competition: Detailed evaluation results.

Method		*N*	*M*	o2o	DR (%)	RA (%)	FM (%)
Participating							
BESUS	Text lines	1,771	1,904	1,494	84.36	78.47	81.31
	Words	13,311	19,091	9,114	68.47	47.74	56.26
DUTH-ARLSA	Text lines	1,771	1,894	1,214	68.55	64.10	66.25
	Words	13,311	16,220	9,100	68.36	56.10	61.63
ILSP-LWSeg	Text lines	1,771	1,773	1,713	96.73	96.62	96.67
	Words	13,311	13,027	11,732	88.14	90.06	89.09
PARC	Text lines	1,771	1,756	1,604	90.57	91.34	90.96
	Words	13,311	14,965	10,246	76.97	68.47	72.47
UoA-HT	Text lines	1,771	1,770	1,674	94.52	94.58	94.55
	Words	13,311	13,824	11,794	88.60	85.32	86.93
RP							
Sanchez 2011	Text lines	1,771	1,772	1,726	97.46	97.40	97.43
	Words	13,311	13,303	9,778	73.46	73.50	73.48

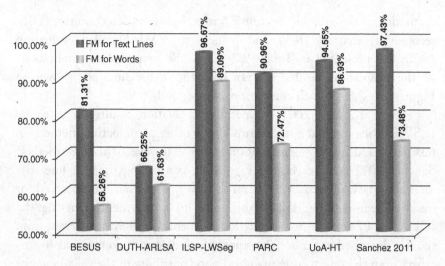

Figure 2.6.   ICDAR 2007 competition: Performance evaluation in terms of F-measure.

with the following competitions. The overall ranking of all participating methods remains unchanged.

Concerning the ICDAR 2009 competition evaluation results, the CUBS method achieved the best results with FM = 99.53% and the ILSP-LWSeg-09 method achieved the second best result with FM = 99.05% for the text line segmentation task. For the word segmentation task, the ILSP-LWSeg-09 method obtained the highest result with FM = 94.77% while on the other hand, the CUBS method achieved a significant lower result with FM = 86.96%. None of the RP methods achieved better results when compared with the participating methods.

The participating methods of the ICFHR 2010 competition, which obtained the highest results for the text line and word segmentation tasks are the same methods as in the ICDAR 2009 competition. However, the RP method Tang 2014 outperforms all the participating methods in the text line segmentation task with FM = 99.26%.

Concerning the ICDAR 2013 competition evaluation results, the INMC method achieved the highest result for the text line segmentation task and the CUBS method, the best participating method of the previous competitions, achieved the fourth best result. None of the RP methods achieves better results when compared with the participating methods. For the word segmentation task, the GOLESTAN — a method obtains the best result among the participating methods; however, the Ryu 2015 method achieves the highest result with FM = 91.02%.

Table 2.3. ICDAR 2009 competition: Detailed evaluation results.

Method		N	M	o2o	DR (%)	RA (%)	FM (%)
Participating							
CASIA-MSTSeg	Text lines	4,034	4,049	3,867	95.86	95.51	95.68
	Words	29,717	31,421	25,938	87.28	82.55	84.85
CMM	Text lines	4,034	4,044	3,975	98.54	98.29	98.42
	Words	29,717	31,197	27,078	91.12	86.80	88.91
CUBS	Text lines	4,034	4,036	4,016	99.55	99.50	99.53
	Words	29,717	31,533	26,631	89.62	84.45	86.96
ETS	Text lines	4,034	4,033	3,496	86.66	86.68	86.67
	Words	29,717	30,848	25,720	86.55	83.38	84.93
ILSP-LWSeg-09	Text lines	4,034	4,043	4,000	99.16	98.94	99.05
	Words	29,717	29,962	28,279	95.16	94.38	94.77
Jadavpur	Text lines	4,034	4,075	3,541	87.78	86.90	87.34
	Words	29,717	27,596	23,710	79.79	85.92	82.74
LRDE	Text lines	4,034	4,423	3,901	96.70	88.20	92.25
	Words	29,717	33,006	26,318	88.56	79.74	83.92
PAIS	Text lines	4,034	4,031	3,973	98.49	98.56	98.52
	Words	29,717	30,560	27,288	91.83	89.29	90.54
AegeanUniv	Text lines	4,034	4,054	3,130	77.59	77.21	77.40
PortoUniv	Text lines	4,034	4,028	3,811	94.47	94.61	94.54
PPSL	Text lines	4,034	4,084	3,792	94.00	92.85	93.42
REGIM	Text lines	4,034	4,563	1,629	40.38	35.70	37.90
RP							
Lemaitre 2011	Text lines	4,034	4,032	4,003	99.23	99.28	99.26
	Words	29,717	29,663	27,969	94.12	94.29	94.20
Diem 2013	Text lines	4,034	4,034	3,977	98.59	98.59	98.59
Ryu 2015	Words	29,717	29,489	28,008	94.25	94.98	94.61

Table 2.6 presents an overview of the evaluation results concerning the best performance achieved in the text line and word segmentation tasks along with the total number of the participating and RP methods, which was evaluated using the benchmarking data set of each competition.

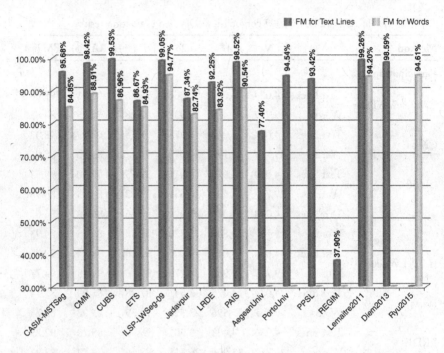

Figure 2.7.   ICDAR 2009 competition: Performance evaluation in terms of F-measure.

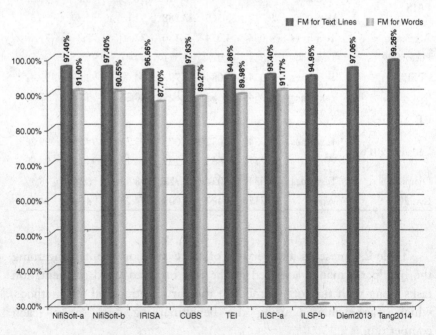

Figure 2.8.   ICFHR 2010 competition: Performance evaluation in terms of F-measure.

Table 2.4. ICFHR 2010 competition: Detailed evaluation results.

Method		N	M	o2o	DR (%)	RA (%)	FM (%)
Participating							
NifiSoft-a	Text lines	1,629	1,634	1,589	97.54	97.25	97.40
	Words	15,130	15,192	13,796	91.18	90.81	91.00
NifiSoft-b	Text lines	1,629	1,634	1,589	97.54	97.25	97.40
	Words	15,130	15,145	13,707	90.59	90.51	90.55
IRISA	Text lines	1,629	1,636	1,578	96.87	96.45	96.66
	Words	15,130	14,314	12,911	85.33	90.20	87.70
CUBS	Text lines	1,629	1,626	1,589	97.54	97.72	97.63
	Words	15,130	15,012	13,454	88.92	89.62	89.27
TEI	Text lines	1,629	1,637	1,549	95.09	94.62	94.86
	Words	15,130	14,667	13,406	88.61	91.40	89.98
ILSP-a	Text lines	1,629	1,656	1,567	96.19	94.63	95.40
	Words	15,130	14,796	13,642	90.17	92.20	91.17
ILSP-b	Text lines	1,629	1,655	1,559	95.70	94.20	94.95
RP							
Diem 2013	Text lines	1,629	1,633	1,583	97.18	96.94	97.06
Tang 2014	Text lines	1,629	1,629	1,617	99.26	99.26	99.26

After a careful analysis of the aforementioned evaluation results, we can draw several conclusions. Concerning the text line segmentation task, the winning methods perform very well achieving a score approximately at 99%, which indicates that there is a small potential for improvement. Only a few text lines are not detected correctly by the segmentation algorithms and mainly include touching text lines for which the separation of ascenders and descenders on adjacent text lines is a difficult problem (see Figure 2.10). On the other hand, word segmentation methods achieve lower scores around 91%, which implies that there exists a significant potential for improvement.

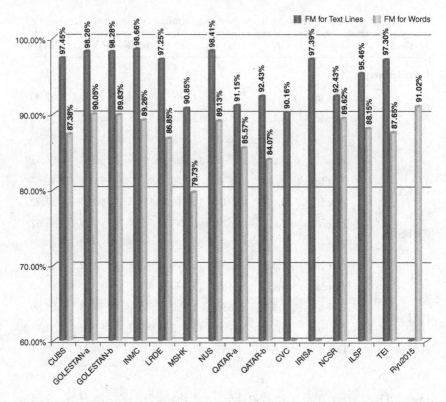

Figure 2.9.   ICDAR 2013 competition: Performance evaluation in terms of *F*-measure.

Another important point for discussion is that there is no significant deviation in the performance among the best two methods of each competition, both for the text line as well as for the word segmentation task. The performance deviation in terms of FM is approximately 1%, indicating that even though the methods follow different steps in order to solve the problem, the performance achieved is similar. However, it is worth pointing out that the ILSP segmentation method and its extensions, which have been tested on all competitions, are always ranked among the first positions for text line and word segmentation. Moreover, the CUBS method, which participated in the three last competitions, performs very well concerning text line segmentation task, but it achieves a lower performance on the word segmentation task. The aforementioned methods prove their generality and stability since their performance is similar in terms of all the benchmarking data sets.

Table 2.5.   ICDAR 2013 competition: Detailed evaluation results.

Method		N	M	o2o	DR (%)	RA (%)	FM (%)
Participating							
CUBS	Text lines	2,649	2,677	2,595	97.96	96.94	97.45
	Words	23,525	23,782	20,668	87.86	86.91	87.38
GOLESTAN-a	Text lines	2,649	2,646	2,602	98.23	98.34	98.28
	Words	23,525	23,322	21,093	89.66	90.44	90.05
GOLESTAN-b	Text lines	2,649	2,646	2,602	98.23	98.34	98.28
	Words	23,525	23,400	21,077	89.59	90.07	89.83
INMC	Text lines	2,649	2,650	2,614	98.68	98.64	98.66
	Words	23,525	22,957	20,745	88.18	90.36	89.26
LRDE	Text lines	2,649	2,632	2,568	96.94	97.57	97.25
	Words	23,525	23,473	20,408	86.75	86.94	86.85
MSHK	Text lines	2,649	2,696	2,428	91.66	90.06	90.85
	Words	23,525	21,281	17,863	75.93	83.94	79.73
NUS	Text lines	2,649	2,645	2,605	98.34	98.49	98.41
	Words	23,525	22,547	20,533	87.28	91.07	89.13
QATAR-a	Text lines	2,649	2,626	2,404	90.75	91.55	91.15
	Words	23,525	24,966	20,746	88.19	83.10	85.57
QATAR-b	Text lines	2,649	2,609	2,430	91.73	93.14	92.43
	Words	23,525	25,693	20,688	87.94	80.52	84.07
CVC	Text lines	2,649	2,715	2,418	91.28	89.06	90.16
IRISA	Text lines	2,649	2,674	2,592	97.85	96.93	97.39
RP							
NCSR	Text lines	2,649	2,646	2,447	92.37	92.48	92.43
	Words	23,525	22,834	20,774	88.31	90.98	89.62
ILSP	Text lines	2,649	2,685	2,546	96.11	94.82	95.46
	Words	23,525	23,409	20,686	87.93	88.37	88.15
TEI	Text lines	2,649	2,675	2,590	97.77	96.82	97.30
	Words	23,525	23,259	20,503	87.15	88.15	87.65
Ryu 2015	Words	23,525	23,255	21,290	90.50	91.55	91.02

Table 2.6. Overview of the evaluation results.

	Number of participating methods		Number of RP methods		Best performance achieved (FM)	
Competition	Text lines	Words	Text lines	Words	Text lines (%)	Words (%)
ICDAR 2007	5	5	1	1	97.43	89.09
ICDAR 2009	12	8	2	2	99.53	94.77
ICFHR 2010	6	6	2	0	99.26	91.17
ICDAR 2013	10	9	3	4	98.66	91.02

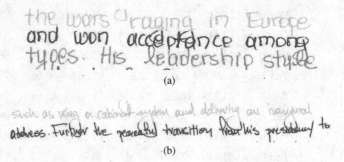

(a)

(b)

Figure 2.10. Examples of common text line segmentation errors in which the ascenders and descenders are hardly separated.

2.8 Conclusions

Four handwriting segmentation competitions have been organized in the context of the ICDAR and ICFHR conferences until 2013 in order to address the need for objective, comparative, and detailed evaluation of the handwriting segmentation techniques under realistic circumstances. In the framework of these competitions, four different benchmarking databases have been created, and a performance evaluation protocol has been established in order to have a fair comparison of segmentation algorithms as well as a qualitative analysis of segmentation results. In this chapter, the benchmarking data sets, the evaluation protocol, the participating methods, as well as detailed evaluation results have been presented. Moreover, several RP methods have been presented and evaluated using the benchmarking data sets. Future work should focus on the use of more complicated data sets with respect to the challenges encountered (e.g., small additions above a text line, strike-through text) as well as on the performance evaluation of segmentation methods that work on original document images (color or grayscale).

References

1. B. Gatos, A. Antonacopoulos, and N. Stamatopoulos, "ICDAR2007 handwriting segmentation contest," in *Proceedings of the 9th International Conference on Document Analysis and Recognition (ICDAR'2007)*, Parana, Brazil, pp. 1284–1288, September 23–26, 2007.
2. B. Gatos, N. Stamatopoulos, and G. Louloudis, "ICDAR2009 handwriting segmentation contest," in *Proceedings of the 10th International Conference on Document Analysis and Recognition (ICDAR'2009)*, Barcelona, Spain, pp. 1393–1397, July 26–29, 2009.
3. B. Gatos, N. Stamatopoulos, and G. Louloudis, "ICFHR2010 handwriting segmentation contest," in *Proceedings of the 12th International Conference on Frontiers in Handwriting Recognition (ICFHR'2010)*, Kolkata, India, pp. 737–742, November 16–18, 2010.
4. N. Stamatopoulos, G. Louloudis, B. Gatos, U. Pal, and A. Alaei, "ICDAR2013 Handwriting segmentation contest," in *Proceedings of the 12th International Conference on Document Analysis and Recognition (ICDAR'2013)*, Washington, DC, USA, pp. 1402–1406, August 25–28, 2013.
5. V. Papavassiliou, T. Stafylakis, V. Katsouros, and G. Carayiannis, "Handwritten document image segmentation into text lines and words," *Pattern Recognition*, vol. 43, no. 1, pp. 369–377, 2010.
6. Z. Shi and V. Govindaraju, "Line separation for complex document images using fuzzy runlength," in *Proceedings of the 1st International Workshop on Document Image Analysis for Libraries*, Palo Alto, CA, USA, pp. 306–312, 2004.
7. N. Nikolaou, M. Makridis, B. Gatos, N. Stamatopoulos, and N. Papamarkos, "Segmentation of historical machine-printed documents using adaptive run length smoothing and skeleton segmentation paths," *Image and Vision Computing*, vol. 28, no. 4, pp. 590–604, 2010.
8. M. Feldbach and K.D. Tonnies, "Line detection and segmentation in historical church registers," in *6th International Conference on Document Analysis and Recognition*, Seattle, WA, USA, pp. 743–747, September 13, 2001.
9. G. Louloudis, B. Gatos, I. Pratikakis, and C. Halatsis, "Text line and word segmentation of handwritten documents," *Pattern Recognition*, vol. 42, no. 12, pp. 3169–3183, 2009.

10. R. Saabni, A. Asi, and J. El-Sana, "Text line extraction for historical document images." *Pattern Recognition Letters*, vol. 35, no. 1, pp. 23–33, 2014.

11. H. Tseng and H.J. Lee, "Recognition-based handwritten Chinese character segmentation using a probabilistic Viterbi algorithm," *Pattern Recognition Letters*, vol. 20, no. 8, pp. 791–806, 1999.

12. G. Seni and E. Cohen, "External word segmentation of offline handwritten text lines," *Pattern Recognition*, vol. 27, no. 1, pp. 41–52, 1994.

13. G. Louloudis, G. Sfikas, N. Stamatopoulos, and B. Gatos, "Word segmentation using the Student's *t*-distribution," *12th IAPR International Workshop on Document Analysis System*, pp. 78–83, 2016.

14. A.K. Das, A. Gupta, and B. Chanda, "A fast algorithm for text line and word extraction from handwritten documents," *Image Processing and Communication*, vol. 3, no. 1–2, pp. 85–94, 2007.

15. M. Makridis, N. Nikolaou, and B. Gatos, "An efficient word segmentation technique for historical and degraded machine-printed documents," in *the 9th International Conference on Document Analysis and Recognition* (ICDAR'2007), Parana, Brazil, pp. 178–182, September 23–26, 2007.

16. T. Stafylakis, V. Papavassiliou, V. Katsouros, and G. Carayannis, "Robust text-line and word segmentation for handwritten document images," *International Conference on Acoustics, Speech and Signal Processing* (ICASSP'2008), Las Vegas, NV, USA, pp. 3393–3396, March 31–April 4, 2008.

17. G. Louloudis, C. Halatsis, B. Gatos, and I. Pratikakis, "A block-based Hough transform mapping for text line detection in handwritten documents," *10th International Workshop on Frontiers in Handwriting Recognition* (IWFHR'2006), pp. 515–520, 2006.

18. F. Yin and C.L. Liu, "Handwritten text line segmentation by clustering with distance metric learning," *11th International Conference on Frontiers in Handwriting Recognition*, pp. 229–234, 2008.

19. Z. Shi, S. Setlur, and V. Govindaraju, "Text extraction from gray scale historical document images using adaptive local connectivity map," *8th International Conference on Document Analysis and Recognition* (ICDAR'2005), pp. 794–798, 2005.

20. Z. Shi, S. Setlur, and V. Govindaraju, "A steerable directional local profile technique for extraction of handwritten Arabic text lines," *10th International Conference on Document Analysis and Recognition* (ICDAR'2009), pp. 176–180, 2009.

21. E. Kavallieratou, N. Fakotakis, and G. Kokkinakis, "An off-line unconstrained handwriting recognition system," *International Journal of Document Analysis and Recognition*, vol. 4, no. 4, pp. 226–242, 2002.

22. E. Kavallieratou, N. Dromazou, N. Fakotakis, and G. Kokkinakis, "An integrated system for handwritten document image processing," *International Journal of Pattern Recognition and Artificial Intelligence*, vol. 17, no. 4, pp. 617–636, 2003.

23. J.S. Cardoso, A. Capela, A. Rebelo, and C. Guedes, "A connected path approach for staff detection on a music score," *15th IEEE International Conference on Image Processing* (ICIP'2008), San Diego, CA, USA, pp. 1005–1008, October 12–15, 2008.

24. A. Lemaitre, J. Camillerapp, and B. Coüasnon, "Interest of perceptive vision for document structure analysis," *Human Vision and Electronic Imaging XV*, 752714, 2010.

25. A. Nicolaou and B. Gatos, "Handwritten text line segmentation by shredding text into its lines," *10th International Conference on Document Analysis and Recognition* (ICDAR'2009), Barcelona, Spain, pp. 626–630, July 26–29, 2009.

26. V. Papavassiliou, V. Katsouros, and G. Carayannis, "A morphological approach for text-line segmentation in handwritten documents," *Proceedings of the 12th International Conference on Frontiers in Handwriting Recognition* (ICFHR'2010), Kolkata, India, pp. 19–24, November 16–18, 2010.

27. H.I. Koo and N.I. Cho, "Text-line extraction in handwritten Chinese documents based on an energy minimization framework," *IEEE Transaction on Image Processing*, vol. 21, no. 3, pp. 1169–1175, 2012.

28. H.I. Koo and D.H. Kim, "Scene text detection via connected component clustering and non-text filtering," *IEEE Transaction on Image Processing*, vol. 21, no. 3, pp. 2296–2305, 2013.

29. A. Hassaïne, S. Al-Maadeed, and A. Bouridane, "A set of geometrical features for writer identification," *Neural Information Processing, Lecture Notes in Computer Science*, vol. 7667, pp. 584–591. Berlin, Heidelberg, Springer, 2012.

30. S. Al-Maadeed, W. Ayouby, A. Hassaine, and J. Aljaam, "QUWI: An Arabic and English handwriting dataset for offline writer identification," *13th International Conference on Frontiers in Handwriting Recognition* (ICFHR'2012), Bari, Italy, pp. 746–751, September 18–20, 2012.

31. A. Sanchez, C.A.B. Mello, P.D. Suarez, and A. Lopes, "Automatic line and word segmentation applied to densely line-skewed historical handwritten document images," *Integrated Computer-Aided Engineering*, vol. 18, no. 2, pp. 125–142, 2011.

32. A. Lemaitre, J. Camillerapp, and B. Coüasnon, "A perceptive method for handwritten text segmentation," *Document Recognition and Retrieval XVIII — Electronic Imaging, Proceedings of SPIE*, p. 7874 0C, San Francisco, USA, January 23–27, 2011.

33. M. Diem, F. Kleber, and R. Sablatnig, "Text line detection for heterogeneous documents," in *Proceedings of the 12th International Conference on Document Analysis and Recognition* (ICDAR'2013), Washington, DC, USA, pp. 743–747, August 25–28, 2013.

34. Y. Tang, X. Wu, and W. Bu, "Text line segmentation based on matched filtering and top-down grouping for handwritten documents," *11th IAPR International Workshop on Document Analysis System*, Tours, France, pp. 365–369, April 7–10, 2014.

35. J. Ryu, H.I. Koo, and N.I. Cho, "Word segmentation method for handwritten documents based on structured learning," *IEEE Signal Processing Letters*, vol. 22, no. 8, pp. 1161–1165, 2015.

36. ICDAR2007 benchmarking dataset: http://users.iit.demokritos.gr/~nstam/ICDAR2007HandSegmCont/.

37. ICDAR2009 benchmarking dataset: http://users.iit.demokritos.gr/~nstam/ICDAR2009HandSegmCont/.

38. ICFHR2010 benchmarking dataset: http://users.iit.demokritos.gr/~nstam/ICFHR2010HandSegmCont/.

39. ICDAR2013 benchmarking dataset: http://users.iit.demokritos.gr/~nstam/ICDAR2013HandSegmCont/Datasets/.

40. A. Alaei, U. Pal, and P. Nagabhushan, "Dataset and ground truth for handwritten text in four different scripts," *International Journal of Pattern Recognition and Artificial. Intelligence*, vol. 26, no. 4, p. 1253001, 2012.

41. I. Phillips and A. Chhabra, "Empirical performance evaluation of graphics recognition systems," *IEEE Transaction on Pattern Analysis and Machine Intelligence*, vol. 21, no. 9, pp. 849–870, 1999.

42. Handwriting Segmentation Evaluation Software: http://users.iit.demokritos.gr/~nstam/HandSegmEvalSoft/.

Part II
Digits and Mathematical Expressions

Chapter 3

Handwritten Digit
and Digit String Recognition

Markus Diem, Stefan Fiel, and Florian Kleber

3.1 Introduction

This chapter summarizes efforts made in benchmarking offline handwritten digit and digit string recognition methods. The recognition of handwriting is still considered an open research topic, since unconstrained handwriting has a high variability, which current methods cannot deal with. In this chapter, we introduce two competitions *ICDAR 2013 Competition on Handwritten Digit Recognition* (HDRC 2013; see [1]) and *ICFHR 2014 Competition on Handwritten Digit String Recognition in Challenging Datasets* (HDSRC 2014; see [2]). The competitions were held within the context of the *International Conference on Document Analysis and Recognition* (ICDAR) and *International Conference on Frontiers in Handwriting Recognition* (ICFHR). Both competitions deal with Arabic digits.

While digit recognition deals with the recognition of isolated handwritten digits, digit string recognition additionally tackles the problem of digit segmentation. Figure 3.1 shows samples of isolated digits to illustrate the high variability of handwritten digits, and an example of two-digit strings with partly connected digits. An additional challenge in real-world samples is innate noise present in document images, e.g., due to the layout or noisy strokes. Based on the results of the competitions, it is shown that

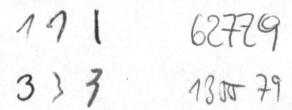

Figure 3.1.   Isolated digits from different writers showing a variation in writing style (left) and digit strings, which are partly connected (right).

the submitted methods have high accuracies for digit recognition (precision of 97.74%, precision of 99.33%, including the second guess), whereas digit string recognition methods achieve only a precision up to 80% or 90% with respect to the data set (real-world images vs. images with no background noise).

The following section describes existing data sets for digit and digit string recognition in detail. Afterwards, a general description of classification methods, which can be applied to this task, is given, followed by a description of approaches submitted to the two contests. Finally, a comparative performance analysis of the methods discussed is presented in combination with the data sets used. The chapter concludes with a discussion on the topic of digit and digit string recognition.

3.2 Digit and Digit String Data Sets

The recognition of handwritten digits has been studied for many years, and several benchmark data sets have been published, such as MNIST [3], USPS [4], Optidigits [5] and Semeion [5]. The presented competitions use the Computer Vision Lab Single Digit database (CVL HDdb) [1], the CVL Handwritten Digit String (HDS) data set [2], and the ORAND-CAR database [2]. In the following paragraphs, the data sets are described in detail with special focus on the competition data sets. All data sets deal with Arabic digits.

The USPS [4] database uses data from handwritten addresses (city names, state names, ZIP codes, alphanumeric characters) collected by a post office within a research project sponsored by the United States Postal Service (USPS). The digit data set is extracted from BR ZIP Codes for the training set (18,468 isolated digits), and from BS ZIP Codes for the test set (2,711 isolated digit images). All digits are binarized. For a detailed description about the distribution, see [4].

The MNIST (Mixed National Institute of Standards and Technology) database [3] provides a training set of handwritten digits of 60,000 samples and a test set of 10,000 samples. It is a subset of the NIST database, i.e., a combination of NIST Special Database 1 and Special Database 3, which contains digits written by high school students and employees of the United States Census Bureau. The images are binarized and size normalized to fit in a 20 × 20 pixel box [3].

The Semeion data set [5] provides binary images with a size of 16 × 16 pixel of handwritten digits. The data are collected from 80 persons and an overall of 1,539 handwritten digits are available. The data set was contributed to the Semeion Research Center of Sciences of Communication by Tactile Srl [5].

Optidigits [5] use handwritten digits from forms of 43 people (the digits of 30 people are used for the training set and 13 for the test set). The images are binarized and have a size of 32 × 32 pixel.

The NIST Special Database 19 [6] provides Handwriting Sample Forms (HSF) from 3,600 writers. Binary images at a resolution of 300 dpi are present in the database, as well as the original fields and separated digits. For a detailed description, see [6]. Figure 3.2 shows a part of the HSF and present digit strings with varying length.

Both CVL data sets (CVL HDdb and CVL HDS) have been collected mostly among students of the TU Wien (Vienna, Austria) and of an Austrian secondary school and consist of about 300 writers, female and male alike. The variability of writers allows us to get a high variability with respect to handwriting styles. The CVL HDS database is composed of 7,960 digit string images.

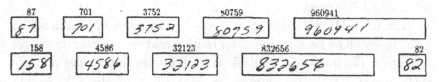

Figure 3.2. Part of a Handwriting Sample Form (HSF) of NIST SD19 (courtesy of [6]).

Figure 3.3. Samples of the HDdb evaluation set.

In order to create the single-digit data set (CVL HDdb), isolated (unconnected) digits were extracted from the CVL HDS. Figure 3.3 shows samples of the CVL HDdb, illustrating the writer variation of isolated digits.

The CVL HDdb data set provides digit samples in RGB. In the design process of the database, a uniform distribution of the occurrences of each digit was ensured. For the competition [1], the images are delivered in original size with a resolution of 300 dpi. Contrary to other data sets, the digits are not size normalized, since in real-world cases differences in a writers' handwriting include variation in size as well as writing style (see Figure 3.3). Additionally, also a size-normalized version is available; see [1]. The images for the training, validation, and evaluation set are randomly selected from a subset of writers, which are pairwise disjoint. The complete CVL single-digit data set consists of 10 classes (0–9) with 3,578 samples per class. For the HDR competition [1], 7,000 digits (700 digits per class) of 67 writers have been selected as a training set. A validation set of equal size has been published with a different set of 60 writers. The validation set may be used for parameter estimation and validation but not for supervised training. The evaluation set consists of 2,178 digits per class resulting in 21,780 samples of the remaining 176 writers.

The CVL HDS database uses 7,960 digit string images, from which 1,262 images have been proposed for training and the other 6,698 images for testing. The images are available as RGB images and not size normalized. Figure 3.4 shows an example digit string of the CVL HDS database.

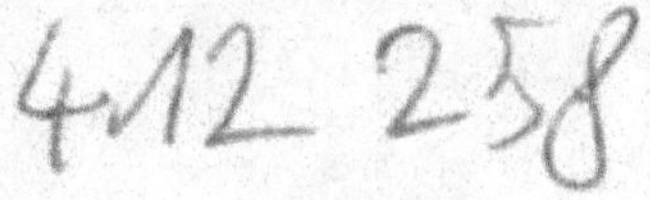

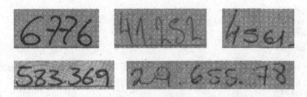

Figure 3.4.   Example digit string of the CVL HDS.

Figure 3.5.   Sample images from the ORAND-CAR database (ORAND-CAR-A).

The ORAND-CAR database contains digit strings from the Courtesy Amount Recognition (CAR) field of real bank checks containing innate noise and variability. Figure 3.5 shows sample images of the ORAND-CAR database.

The CAR images are composed of a combination of special numeric symbols representing a monetary value. The ORAND-CAR images come from two different sources, which give the images different characteristics. These characteristics are mainly related to the image quality, kind of noise, and handwriting style. Therefore, considering the two different sources, the ORAND-CAR database is split into two subsets: ORAND-CAR-A that comes from a Uruguayan bank and ORAND-CAR-B that comes from a Chilean bank. The ORAND-CAR-A database consists of 2,009 images for training and 3,784 images for testing and the ORAND-CAR-B database consists of 3,000 images for training and 2,936 images for testing. As can be noticed, real CAR images bring a variety of noise like background patterns, check layout, or user strokes. In addition, the natural variability of the handwritten text represents another challenge that must be dealt with.

The distribution of string lengths in the databases used for the digit string competition is shown in Figure 3.6. This property is important to track differences between the performance metrics which are introduced in Section 3.5. It is illustrated that the CVL database has on average the longest strings (6.1 digits), while the ORAND-CAR-A contains mostly short strings (4.5 digits).

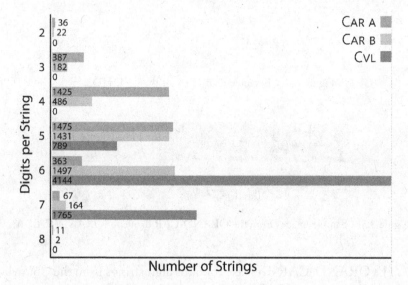

Number of Strings

Figure 3.6. Distribution of string lengths with respect to the ORAND-CAR-A, ORAND-CAR-B, and CVL HDS data set.

3.3 General Approaches for Digit and Digit String Recognition

The first step for digit recognition is the normalization of the image to reduce the intraclass variability. This process involves the mapping of the image to an image plane with fixed dimensions. Liu *et al.* investigate 10 different normalization functions [7], as shown in Figure 3.7. Five approaches use a linear normalization by multiplying the original image with a coefficient and different aspect ratios (F0–F5), a nonlinear normalization using the line density histogram (F6), and three different aspect ratios with a moment normalization (F7–F9). The normalization of the slant can also be done using second-order moments. After this preprocessing step, the modified digit images are used for classification.

LeCun *et al.* introduce a baseline for digit recognition by using a k-nearest neighbor (kNN) classifier with an Euclidean distance measure between input images and achieve an error rate of 5.0% on the test set of the MNIST database with $k = 3$ [3]. On the deslanted data, the error rate decreases to 2.4%. Belongie *et al.* propose a new descriptor for shape, called shape context, and using a nearest-neighbor classifier, they achieve an error rate of 0.63% [8].

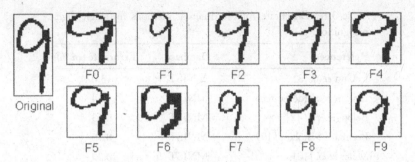

Figure 3.7. Normalized binary images of the 10 normalization functions investigated by Liu *et al.* [7].

Decoste and Schölkopf use a support vector machine (SVM) with a polynomial kernel of degree 9 for classifying digits. When training on an enlarged data set by applying a translation to the center point and also deslanted digits, the error rate is reduced to 0.56%. A neural network with one hidden layer consisting of 100 neurons is applied to the MNIST data set by Meier *et al.* with an error rate of 0.39% [10].

Convolutional neural networks (CNNs) are also proposed to solve the problem of digit recognition. LeCun *et al.* propose the LeNet-5 [3], which has also the capability to learn the features used for classification by itself. The LeNet-5 consists of three convolutional layers and two sub-sampling layers, followed by two fully connected layer, where the last layer is responsible for the final classification. With this Net, an error rate of 0.7% is achieved. This approach was extended by Cireşan *et al.* by using 35 different deep neural networks [11]. They normalized the width of the digits from 10 to 20 with a step size of two, and, for each normalization, five networks are trained. The output of all the networks is then averaged to get the final output resulting in an error rate of 0.23% on the MNIST data set. This method achieves currently the best performance on the MNIST data set. The results of the methods presented are summarized in Table 3.1.

When dealing with digit strings, two different approaches can be found in the literature. The first approaches try to avoid segmentation by directly classifying touching digits, whereas the second approaches apply segmentation as preprocessing step and then perform a single-digit classification. A method for the segmentation-free recognition of digit strings

Table 3.1.   Error rates of the different methods for single-digit recognition.

References	Database	Error rate (in %)
LeCun et al. [3]	MNIST	5.0
LeCun et al. (deslanted)	MNIST	2.4
Belongie et al. [8]	MNIST	0.63
Bernhard Schölkopf [9]	MNIST	0.56
Meier et al. [10]	MNIST	0.39
Cireşan et al. [11]	MNIST	0.23

is proposed by Cireşan [12]. Two CNNs are used to recognize CCs, which have been preprocessed by connecting small components to larger ones in their neighborhood according to certain criteria. One CNN is used for the classification of single digits, and another is used for recognizing two partially overlapping digits. Three or more touching digits cannot be recognized. The decision which of the two outputs is taken as a result is based on the maximum score of the CNNs and the differences of scores. On strings of NIST SD 19 data set with three digits, a recognition rate of 93.77% is achieved.

A comparative study of segmentation procedures of digit strings is presented by Ribas et al. in [13]. According to them, the segmentation algorithms can be divided into two classes. First, the segmentation-recognition methods, which submit a single sequence hypothesis of digits to the recognizer. Second, the recognition-based segmentation algorithms determine a list of hypotheses which are given to the recognizer for assessment. A method belonging to the first class is proposed by Pal et al. [14]. The image is divided into isolated and touching digits, and then the touching ones are further segmented by analyzing "water reservoirs," which represents the "large scale created by the touching" [14]. On a data set with 2,250 connected numerals, an accuracy of 94.8% is achieved.

Sadria et al. propose a recognition-based segmentation method for the recognition of handwritten numeral strings [15]. They use a genetic algorithm for building segmentation hypothesis and then use the recognition scores to rank them. This method has a recognition rate of 96.42% on part of the NIST SD 19 data set, which contains only three- and six-digit

Table 3.2.   Results of the methods presented for digit string recognition.

References	Database	Error rate (in %)
Cireşan [12]	1476 strings of NIST SD 19 with length of 3	6.23
Sadria *et al.* [15]	2,947 strings of NIST SD 19 with length of 3 and 6	3.58
Wu *et al.* [16]	2,947 strings of NIST SD 19 with length of 3 and 6	2.68

strings. Wu *et al.* propose to use a geometric context model for numeral string recognition. On a part of the NIST SD 19 data set, they achieve an error rate of 2.68%. The error rates of the methods presented are shown in Table 3.2.

3.4 Approaches Submitted to the Competitions

This section summarizes the approaches submitted to the competitions. For the digit-recognition competition [1], seven research groups submitted nine methods, while for the digit string recognition competition, five research groups submitted six methods. Subsequently, a brief description of the approaches is given (for a detailed description, see [1–2]). Table 3.3 summarizes the participating methods of both contests.

3.4.1 *Methods Submitted to the ICDAR 2013 Competition on Handwritten Digit Recognition*

The method Salzburg II positions the size-normalized digit (20×20 pixel) within a 28×28 pixel image based on the center of mass and converts it to grayscale. A neural network based on [17] is used. Finally, a one partially connected Finite Impulse Response Multilayer Perceptron (FIR MLP) with four layers is used. Compared to Salzburg II, Salzburg I uses an ensemble of four FIR MLPs (see [1]).

Orand uses binarized images and calculates an ensemble of three features: stroke orientation based on the histogram of oriented gradients (HOG), relation between foreground and background based on concavities,

Table 3.3.   Participating methods of the digit and digit string recognition competition.

Method	Affiliation/Company	Authors
	ICDAR 2013 Competition on Handwritten Digit Recognition (HDRC 2013)	
François Rabelais	Université François Rabelais, Laboratoire d'Informatique, France	O. Razafindramanana, F. Rayar, G. Venturini
Hannover	Hochschule Hannover, Germany	K.-H. Steinke, M. Gehrke
Jadavpur	Jadavpur University, CMATER, India	N. Das, A. Roy, R. Sarkar, S. Basu, M. Kundu, M. Nasipuri
Orand	ORAND S.A., Chile	J.M. Saavedra, J.M. Barrios
Paris Sud	University of Paris Sud, Linear Accelerator Laboratory and Computer Science Laboratory & CNRS, France	F. Dubard, B. Kégl
Salzburg I	University of Salzburg, Institute of Computer Sciences, Austria	C. Codrescu, C.L. Badea
Salzburg II	University of Salzburg, Institute of Computer Sciences, Austria	C. Codrescu, C.L. Badea
Tébessa I	University of Tébessa, Lamis/University of Sciences and Technology Houari Boumediene, LCPTS, Algeria	A. Gattal/Y. Chibani
Tébessa II	University of Tébessa, Lamis/University of Sciences and Technology Houari Boumediene, LCPTS, Algeria	A. Gattal, C. Djeddi/Y. Chibani

ICFHR 2014 Competition on Handwritten Digit String Recognition in Challenging Data sets (HDSRC 2014)		
Beijing	National Laboratory of Pattern Recognition (NLPR) Institute of Automation of Chinese Academy of Sciences, Beijing, China	Yi-Chao Wu, Fei Yin, Chang Zhong, Chen-Lin Liu
Pernambuco	Universidade de Pernambuco, Santo Amaro, Brasil	Byron Leite and Cleber Zanchettin
Shanghai	ECNU-SRI Joint Lab for Pattern Analysis and Intelligent Systems, Shanghai Research Institute of China Post, Shanghai, China	Shijing Lu and Yue Lu
Singapore	Institute for Infocom, Research Singapore/School of Computing, National University of Singapore, Singapore	Su Bolan, Lu Shijiang/Zhang Xi, Tan Chew Lim
Tébessa I	University of Tébessa, Algeria/Speech Communication and Signal Processing Laboratory, Faculty of Electronics and Computer Sciences and Technology Houari Boumedienne, Bab-Ezzouar, Algiers, Algeria	A. Gattal/Y. Chibani
Tébessa II	University of Tébessa, Algeria/Speech Communication and Signal Processing Laboratory, Faculty of Electronics and Computer Sciences and Technology Houari Boumedienne, Bab-Ezzouar, Algiers, Algeria	A. Gattal, C. Djeddi/Y. Chibani

and the contour based on horizontal projection profiles. Afterward a multiclass SVM using a radial basis function kernel (RBF) classifies digits. Jadavpur applies an SVM with a fuzzy-entropy-based feature selection (convex-hull-based and quad-tree-based longest run). In contrast, Paris Sud uses AdaBoost.MH with Hamming trees over Haar filters as a base classifier.

Also, an SVM with an RBF kernel for the classification task is applied by Francois Rabelais. This method determines the bounding box of the binarized digit image and scales the image to 128×128 pixel. Then, a k-means clustering is used to reduce the number of (digit) pixels to 10% and a Delaunay triangulation is built. Based on a multilevel static uniform zoning, the average number of input elements in the cell and the average in the neighborhood for each cell grid, and the centers of gravity of the triangles, and the black pixels are determined.

As preprocessing, Hannover also uses a binarization, normalization, and slope correction. The feature vector is composed of the normalized central moments, the number of foreground pixels for each row, and column and the "lengths of 12 probes in different directions from different positions" [1]. The features are classified with a kNN.

Both Tébessa I and Tébessa II use a multiclass SVM with a one-against-all approach. Tébessa I utilizes structural features and Tébessa II exploits multiscale run-length features (horizontal, vertical, left diagonal, and right diagonal).

3.4.2   *Methods Submitted to the ICFHR 2014 Competition on Handwritten Digit String Recognition*

Pernambuco uses a combination of classifiers on preprocessed images (noise removal). In detail, a kNN is combined with an SVM approach, and a MDRNN is combined with SVM methods.

A preprocessed image (binarized, noise removal, split components with a large width/height ratio) is utilized by Beijing. Candidate patterns "are classified using a polynomial classifier with gradient direction histogram feature. Via confidence transformation, the character classifier and binary class-dependent geometric model are combined together to evaluate the segmentation path" [14].

Singapore uses sequential features based on HOG and classifies it with a recurrent neural network (without segmentation).

A segmentation is performed by Shanghai, and local directional features are used for classification. As a classifier, SVM, SOM, and BP networks are applied.

Tébessa I and Tébessa II use a segmentation based on an oriented sliding windows. If a digit image could not be recognized, the "algorithm based on oriented sliding windows is applied" [2]. Tébessa II uses the same methodology, but with a specific set of angles for the oriented sliding window.

3.5 Competition Results

The methods submitted to both competitions were evaluated in terms of precision. In order to get more accurate results, a confusion matrix was created for the performance evaluation of single-digit approaches. This measure allowed us to draw conclusions as to which digit was most likely to be confused with another. For the digit string competition, the Levenshtein distance (LD) was computed in addition to the precision of the first, second, and third guesses. While the precision considers a sample as true positive only if all the digits in a string are correct, the LD finds how many digits are misclassified in a sample. By these means, we could assert how often an approach failed and if it failed, how many digits were wrong. We will introduce the error metrics together with the results subsequently.

3.5.1 *ICDAR 2013 Competition on Handwritten Digit-Recognition Results*

For the evaluation of methods for digit recognition, precision, recall, and F-score are used. The precision p is defined by

$$p = \frac{t_p}{t_p + f_p}$$

with t_p being the sum of true positives and f_p the sum of false positives. A true positive is an element, where the class label c_i of class i equals the assigned class label a_i. In contrast, a false positive is defined by $c_i \neq a_i$. For the precision p, including the second guess, t_p is defined as the sum of all elements whose first or second prediction equals the class label.

In addition to the precision calculated on each sample, a confusion matrix is created for each digit class. This allows for retrieving precision, recall and F-score. For these error measures, true positives t_{pi}, false positives f_{pi}, and false negatives f_{ni} of a given class i are defined by

$$t_{pi} \dots \left\langle a_i, c_j \right\rangle$$

$$f_{pi} \dots \left\langle a_i, c_{j \neq i} \right\rangle$$

$$f_{ni} \dots \left\langle a_{j \neq i}, c_i \right\rangle$$

where $i, j \in 0, \dots, n$ and $n = 9$ to represent all digit classes. To illustrate the definitions, a confusion matrix with corresponding labels is shown in Table 3.4.

Finally, the F-score F_i, the recall r_i, and precision p_i are defined as follows:

$$p_i = \frac{t_{p_i}}{t_{p_i} + f_{p_i}}$$

$$r_i = \frac{t_{p_i}}{t_{p_i} + f_{n_i}}$$

$$F_i = \frac{t_{p_i}}{2t_{p_i} + f_{p_i} + f_{n_i}}$$

All approaches submitted to HDRC are compared and ranked upon their precision. The test is conducted on the evaluation set which consists of 21,780 isolated handwritten digits. Figure 3.8 visualizes the precision of each method. The second bar, lighter, indicates the precision including a second guess. Therefore, methods provide a second-class label. If either of the labels is correct, then the sample is seen as true positive. The results indicate that Salzburg II has the best performance with the precisions of $p = 97.74\%, 99.33\%$, including the second guess. In total, six methods have

Table 3.4. Confusion matrix with $n = 9$ to cover all digit classes; a_i are the predictions of class i, and c_i are the true class labels.

	a_0	a_1	...	a_i	...	a_n
c_0				f_p		
c_1				f_p		
...				...		
c_i	f_n	f_n	...	t_p	...	f_n
...				...		
c_n				f_p		

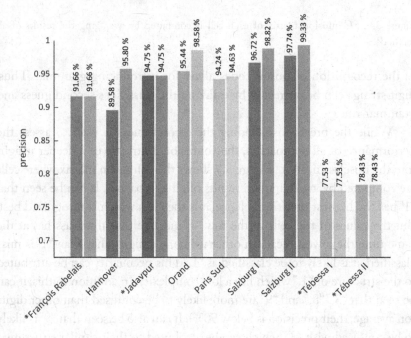

Figure 3.8. Precision of all approaches, including the second guess (light bars). Approaches marked with * did not provide a second guess.

a precision $p > 90\%$, out of which three methods correctly recognize more than 95% of the handwritten digits.

While methods like Paris Sud do not improve much if the second guess is considered, the Hannover method improves by 6.22%. The second guess is relevant if full recognition systems are considered. Scenarios such

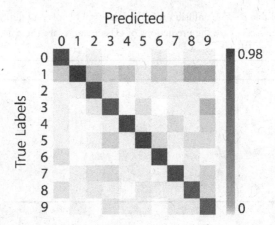

Figure 3.9. Confusion matrix of each cell is computed by averaging the results of all methods.

as the recognition of postal codes allow for introducing grammar. Thus, digit strings can be corrected by utilizing the classifier's second guess and grammar rules.

While the precision including the second guess is used to assess the performance of all approaches, the confusion matrix gives a deeper insight into the misclassification. Figure 3.9 shows the confusion matrix where cells are computed by averaging the results of all approaches. It can be seen that "1" has the highest precision. Hence, it is the class which is recognized best. But the values of the cells in the row "1" indicate that this class has at the same time the lowest recall. In other words, if a digit other than "1" is misclassified, it is likely to be classified as "1." This peculiarity can be attributed to the structure of "1," which has a low complexity. In addition to this, it can be seen that "3," "8," and "9" are more likely to be confused than other digits (on average, their precision is below 90%). It can also be seen that "9" is likely to be confused with "3," which can be attributed to their similar structure.

3.5.2 *ICFHR 2014 Competition on Handwritten Digit String Recognition Results*

While at the HDRC approaches were evaluated only on the CVL database, which contains clean sample images, the HDSRC uses three data sets to assess the performance of different methods. Again, the CVL string database is used for benchmarking the approaches if clean data is considered. In addition to this, two real-world data sets (CAR-A and the CAR-B) are used for evaluation. They show the performance if the background clutter and noise are present.

For the evaluation of digit string recognition methods, a hard metric and a soft metric are defined. In the case of the hard metric, the precision (recognition rate) is measured, i.e., the number of correctly recognized digit strings divided by the total number of strings. The best three guesses are evaluated (TOP-3). The soft metric evaluates how close a resulting answer is to a target amount. The proposed soft metric is based on the LD, which is also known as the edit distance. In particular, we use the Normalized LD (NLD) to avoid any bias with respect to the string length.

Let a_T be a target string (GT) and a_R be the corresponding recognized string; then the NLD metric is computed by

$$NLD(a_T, a_R) = \frac{LD(a_T, a_R)}{|a_T|}$$

where $|a_T|$ is the length of the string a_T and LD is the Levenshtein distance. Only the best response (TOP-1) is evaluated. The average normalized LD (ANLD) is defined by

$$ANLD = \frac{\sum_{i=1}^{T} NLD(a_T^i, a_R^i)}{T}$$

where T is the number of test digit strings. The ANLD is an inverse performance metric, i.e., a low value indicates high performance, while a high value indicates low performance.

Figure 3.10 shows the precision of all participating methods on the three data sets. The dark bars represent the performance considering only the first guess (only if all digits of a string are correct, the sample is counted as true positive). Lighter bars represent the performance, including the second and third guesses. Even though the CVL data set contains clean digit strings without background noise, solely two participants (*Tébessa* and *Beijing*) achieve better performance on this data set. *Singapore* (−1.9%) and *Pernambuco* (−16.8%) achieve their worst performance on the

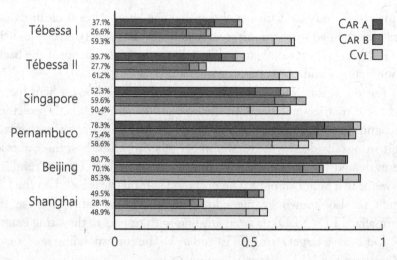

Figure 3.10.   Precision of all participants on the three databases. The light bars represent the second guess and third guess, respectively.

CVL data set if the first guess is considered. The former method achieves its best result on the ORAND-CAR-B data set which allows for drawing the conclusion that the approach is best at dealing with the background clutter and noise.

While Figure 3.10 allows for comparing different digit string methods on different data set, the overall performance of digit string recognition compared to single-digit recognition is also striking. While the participating methods of HDRC achieved a performance between 77.5% and 97.7%, the performance of digit string recognition is much lower (26.6–85.3%). This can be attributed to the fact that the segmentation of connected digits is an issue, on the one hand. But, on the other hand, the lower performance also relies on simple statistics. While for single digits, each classification result is considered when computing the precision, the hard criterion of the digit string recognition evaluation demands all digits of a given string to be correct. Hence, if a method correctly classifies four out of five digits, the string is still considered as false positive.

The soft criterion, in contrast, accounts for all errors made. Figure 3.11 shows the ANLD, again on all databases and participating methods. Remember that a small NLD indicates a low number of errors.

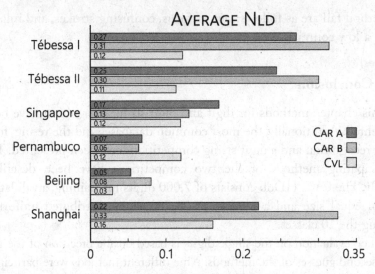

Figure 3.11.   Average NLD for all participating methods.

Figure 3.12.   Samples of failures for the two best performing methods on all data sets.

If the results of the ANLD are compared with those presented in Figure 3.10, it can be seen that *Shanghai* (28.1%) has a better performance than *Tébessa II* (27.7%) on the ORAND-CAR-B data set. However, the error of the ANLD is larger for Shanghai (0.33 vs. 0.3). This indicates that *Tébessa II* classifies more digits strings wrong but with fewer errors.

It was previously mentioned that *Singapore* achieves the worst performance on the CVL database. However, considering the ANLD, its error is lower (0.12) compared to the ORAND-CAR databases. This divergence results from two circumstances. First, *Singapore* has few errors per string and second, the average string length of the CVL database is larger (6.1) than that of ORAND-CAR-B (5.2) and ORAND-CAR-A (4.5).

Figure 3.12 shows a set of sample images from all databases for which the two best performing methods failed. Some factors that make a method fail are as follows: out of focus, confusing strokes, and images with a low contrast.

3.6 Conclusions

In this chapter, methods for digit and digit string recognition have been presented. Additionally, the most common databases and the results for a digit recognition and a digit string competition have been presented. The participating methods of the two competitions have been described briefly. The CVL HDdb consists of 7,000 digits for training, a validation set of equal size and a test set of 21,780 digits distributed uniformly among the 10 classes.

The evaluation on the single digits is based on the precision of the first and second guesses of the methods. Nine different methods were participating in this competition, and the best performance was achieved by *Salzburg II* with 97.74% using the first guess and 99.33% using the second guess.

The evaluation of the digit string competition is based on the precision of the recognized strings considering the top three guesses. This means that a recognition is only counted as correct if the complete string is recognized. The second evaluation metric is the NLD which measures the distance between the result string of the method and the ground truth. Six different methods have been submitted to this competition, and the best results were achieved by *Bejing* with a 78.7% recognition rate on the first guess on all three data sets used. Regarding the second and third guesses, the performance increases to 84.7% and 85.6%, respectively.

Considering the performance evaluation of the HDRC and results reported on the MNIST data set, one can conclude that nowadays classifiers are strong enough to correctly classify handwritten digits written on a clean background. However, the recognition of digit strings with connected digits and background clutter has not been solved as yet. Current results in handwritten text recognition show that approaches which are using deep learning outperform traditional methods [18]. Using a short-term memory, the system is not only able to learn the recognition of the characters but also the connection between multiple characters, e.g., which character often follows another. For the digit string recognition, this information cannot be exploited since the probability of subsequent digits is the same for all digits. However, the system can be able to learn how to segment two overlapping characters and thus improving the recognition rate. It can be expected that deep learning methods can be used for digit string recognition and that good results will be achieved.

The confusion matrix showed that the misclassification is not equally distributed among digits. Hence, all approaches likely confuse digits with "1."

References

1. M. Diem, S. Fiel, A. Garz, M. Keglevic, F. Kleber, and R. Sablatnig, "ICDAR 2013 competition on handwritten digit recognition (HDRC 2013)," in *Proceedings of the 12th International Conference on Document Analysis and Recognition (ICDAR'2013)*, Washington, DC, USA, pp. 1422–1427, August 25–28, 2013.
2. M. Diem, S. Fiel, F. Kleber, R. Sablatnig, J.M. Saavedra, D. Contreras, J.M. Barrios, and L.S. Oliveira, "ICFHR 2014 Competition on Handwritten Digit String Recognition in Challenging Datasets (HDSRC 2014)," in *International Conference on Frontiers in Handwriting Recognition*, Heraklion, Greece, pp. 779–784, September 1–4, 2014.
3. Y. LeCun, L. Bottou, Y. Bengio, and P. Haffner, "Gradient-based learning applied to document recognition," *Proceedings of the IEEE*, vol. 86, no. 11, pp. 2278–2324, 1998.
4. J. Hull, "A database for handwritten text recognition research," *IEEE Transactions on Pattern Analysis and Machine Intelligence*, vol. 16, no. 5, pp. 550–554, 1994.
5. M. Lichman, "UCI Machine Learning Repository," University of California, Irvine, School of Information and Computer Sciences, 2013. [Online]. Available: http://archive.ics.uci.edu/ml/datasets.html. [Accessed 1 10 2015].
6. P. J. Grother, "NIST Special Database 19," Visual Image Processing Group, Advanced Systems Division, National Institute of Standards and Technology, Gaithersburg, 1995.
7. C.-L. Liu, K. Nakashima, H. Sako, and H. Fujisawa, "Handwritten digit recognition: Investigation of normalization and feature extraction techniques," *Pattern Recognition*, vol. 37, no. 2, pp. 265–279, 2004.
8. S. Belongie, J. Malik, and J. Puzicha, "Shape matching and object recognition using shape contexts," *IEEE Transactions on Pattern Analysis and Machine Intelligence*, vol. 24, no. 4, pp. 509–522, 2002.

9. Bernhard Schölkopf, "Training invariant support vector machines," *Machine Learning,* vol. 46, no. 1, pp. 161–190, 2002.

10. U. Meier, D. Cireşan, L. Gambardella, and J. Schmidhuber, "Better digit recognition with a committee of simple Neural Nets," in *2011 International Conference on Document Analysis and Recognition (ICDAR),* Beijing, pp. 1250–1254, 2011.

11. D. Cireşan, U. Meier, and J. Schmidhuber, "Multi-column deep neural networks for image classification," in *Computer Vision and Pattern Recognition,* Providence, RI, USA, pp. 3642–3649, June 16–21, 2012.

12. D. Cireşan, "Avoiding segmentation in multi-digit numeral string recognition by combining single and two-digit classifiers trained without negative examples," in *10th International Symposium on Symbolic and Numeric Algorithms for Scientific Computing, 2008 (SYNASC '08),* Timisoara, pp. 225–230, 2008.

13. F.C. Ribas, L.S. Oliveira, A.S. Britto Jr., and R. Sabourin, "Handwritten digit segmentation: A comparative study," *International Journal on Document Analysis and Recognition,* vol. 16, no. 2, pp. 127–137, 2013.

14. U. Pal, A. Belaid, and C. Choisy, "Touching numeral segmentation using water reservoir concept," *Pattern Recognition Letters,* vol. 24, no. 1–3, pp. 261–272, 2003.

15. J. Sadria, C.Y. Suena, and T.D. Buib, "A genetic framework using contextual knowledge for segmentation and recognition of handwritten numeral strings," *Pattern Recognition,* vol. 40, no. 3, pp. 898–919, 2007.

16. Y.-C. Wu, F. Yin, and C.-L. Liu, "Evaluation of geometric context models for handwritten numeral string recognition," in *14th International Conference on Frontiers in Handwriting Recognition (ICFHR'2017),* Heraklion, pp. 193–198, 2014.

17. C. Codrescu, "Temporal processing applied to speech recognition," in *4th International Conference on Intelligent Systems Design and Applications,* Budapest, Hungary, pp. 151–156, 2004.

18. J.A. Sánchez, V. Romero, A.H. Toselli, and E. Vidal, "ICFHR 2016 competition on handwritten text recognition on the READ dataset," in *15th International Conference on Frontiers in Handwriting Recognition (ICFHR),* Shenzen, pp. 630–635, 2016.

Chapter 4

Handwritten Mathematical Expressions

Harold Mouchère, Christian Viard-Gaudin,
Richard Zanibi, and Utpal Garain

4.1 Introduction

Handwritten entry of mathematical expressions (MEs) is a challenging task that has been an active research area over the last decade [1–4]. Research in this field began in the late 1960s, and since then a number of research labs around the world have worked on the problem. The relatively small community of math recognition researchers along with the absence of benchmark data sets, standard encodings, and evaluation tools-limited progress on this problem for years. In this chapter, we summarize the Competition on Recognition of On-line Handwritten Mathematical Expressions (CROHME), which began as part of the *International Conference on Document Analysis and Recognition* (ICDAR) in 2011 [5]. The main goal of this competition was to facilitate meaningful comparisons of systems and make it easier for newcomers to work on handwritten math recognition.

Handwriting-based math entry systems promise to provide an elegant alternative to traditional mouse and menu-based input. However, difficulties encountered in handwritten text recognition are exacerbated with MEs. Unlike text, which is composed of symbols on a writing line, MEs contain a much larger set of symbols arranged on *multiple* writing lines. These writing lines are also organized hierarchically using spatial relationships (e.g., subscript/superscript, above/below, and inside for square roots). Figure 4.1 illustrates, in a limited way, some of the diversity of MEs.

The 2D layout of formulae complicates the search for a valid interpretation. This search involves a number of difficult, interdependent pattern recognition tasks: the segmentation and classification of symbols, and the parsing of symbols to identify the expression structure. An important subtask is the use of language models to remove invalid formulae from the space of possible interpretations: this increases the likelihood of producing a correct interpretation while reducing the amount of search required. For example, in Figure 4.1(e), the comma between the "x" and "y" should be treated as adjacent to the "x," even though, spatially, it is located primarily in the subscript region of the "x." In Figure 4.1(d), "x_0" might be interpreted as "x0" if we do not require integers after a variable name to be subscripted.

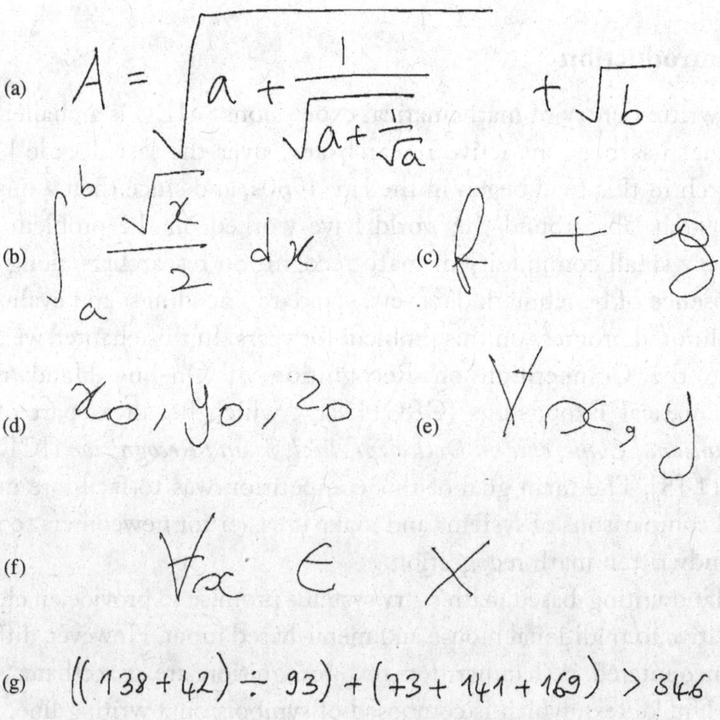

Figure 4.1.   Example formulae from CROHME.

This chapter details the main outcomes for the five CROHME competitions held annually between 2011 and 2016; these include advancing the available data, tools, evaluation models, and algorithms for math written online, e.g., using a tablet computer.

4.2 Description of Data Set

The most recent version of the CROHME data set was created in 2016 [9]. It contains all training and test expressions used in the five competitions between 2011 and 2016. This package is available on the International Association for Pattern Recognition (IAPR)'S TC-11 data set website. In the remainder of this section, we describe these data sets. First, we present the expression grammars that define the space of input formulae for each competition. Next, we provide a statistical analysis of the data set, in terms of symbol frequencies, expression complexity, etc. Finally, we present the file formats.

4.2.1 *Corpus Definition*

Each year, the formulae that may be included in the training and test sets are constrained by a LaTeX expression grammar. This grammar, which is updated from year to year, is defined by a handmade context-free grammar. Table 4.1 summarizes these grammar definitions, and how the sets of

Table 4.1.   Summary of expression grammars.

Years of usage	List of symbols	Grammar
2011/2012	36 symbols abcdeiknxyz0123456789φπθ+ − ± sin cos ≠ = ≤ > ( ) √	Gram-I (38 rules)
2011/2012	56 symbols (20 new) ABCFj αβγ ∞ ÷ × Σ log tan ... ≥→ lim ∫ !	Gram-II (60 rules)
2012/2013	75 symbols (19 new) { } [ ]XY<tfgmrp/, .∃ ∀ ∈	Gram-III (95 rules)
2013/2014/2016	101 symbols (26 new) EGHILMNPRSTVhloqsuvw |′σΔλμ	Gram-IV (155 rules)
2014/2016	101 symbols (same) and matrix structures	Gram-IV-matrix (168 rules)

symbols and grammar rules evolved. The handwritten expressions presented in Figure 4.1 are consistent with the more general grammar named Gram-IV.

Grammars and tasks. Over the years, progressively more complex ME languages were permitted, making the recognition task progressively more complex. Indeed, mathematical recognition can be done in various contexts, from a simple calculator with a limited vocabulary on a small device to a complex application supporting the recognition of a large vocabulary of symbols with different layouts. For the first competition (2011), two difficulty levels were defined. Gram-I with 36 symbols contains expressions primarily on a single writing line, preventing nested subexpressions in fraction arguments and sub/superscripts. Gram-II introduces new "large" operator symbols such as sum, integral, and limit that may have subexpressions above, below, or in scripted position, and the constraint upon nested subexpressions is removed.

In the 2012 and 2013 competitions, the main differences are in the larger symbol sets. Gram-III uses 75 symbols, adding set operations and complex bracketing (to define sets or ranges). Gram-IV is even more general, with 101 symbols and adding the nth root. In 2014, matrix expressions were added to Gram-IV for an experimental data set. The grammars are "backward-compatible," in that each accepts all expressions from the previous competitions, e.g., expressions in Gram-I are also accepted by Gram-II, Gram-III, Gram-IV, and Gram-IV-matrices.

The grammars were made available to participants in each competition, so that they can study and predict the types of expressions used for training and testing. Most participants used these grammars to design language models for their systems (see Section 4.5).

Handwritten formulae. For each competition, once the grammar(s) for tasks were defined, the selection of formulae to include and collection of handwritten samples were carried out. To create training data, in 2011 and 2012, the organizers primarily used existing data sets from different laboratories: CIEL [10] and HAMEX [11] (University of Nantes), MfrDB [12] (Czech Technical University), ExpressMatch [13] (University of Sao Paulo), and data sets from KAIST and CVPR/ISI; and in 2013

MathBrush [14] (University of Waterloo). In addition to these training expressions, for each competition, new test expressions were collected for evaluating and ranking systems. These initial data sets suffered from a lack of diversity and realism. Indeed, in these collections, some expressions are written several times (e.g., CIEL and ExpressMatch) or the source expressions are randomly generated (MathBrush). To circumvent this problem, in CROHME 2013 and CROHME 2014, test expressions were collected from Wikipedia pages to obtain more realistic test expressions and in CROHME 2016 from arXiv paper using data prepared for KDD cup [15].

An important restriction on the handwritten formulae is that each stroke belongs to exactly one symbol. Function names (e.g., "sin") are treated as single symbols — strokes may connect letters within the function name, but cannot connect the function name to neighboring symbols. This constraint is often valid: for math, linking two symbols without lifting the pen is rare. This may not be true in other domains such as chemical formulae or sketches. This constraint simplifies recognition, as the smallest input primitives (strokes) are guaranteed to oversegment the symbols in an expression. However, a symbol may still be written using several strokes that are not adjacent in time, such as when a dot is added to an "+" after drawing other symbols in a formula.

4.2.2 *Statistical Analysis of ME Data Set*

Acquiring and labeling handwritten MEs is a time-consuming and tedious process. Each year the organizers provided new samples for the training and testing sets. Table 4.2 shows the number of expressions used in each competition. Each training set includes the training data from previous years; thus, 296 expressions from Part I task are included in more than 8,000 training expressions for Part IV. However, each year a new testing data set was created. As can be seen, the progressive control of the global process allowed us to significantly increase the size of the data sets.

Table 4.3 presents statistics extracted from the training set for Part IV. The symbol frequency follows a realistic distribution: symbols such as "+," "−," "1," "2," and "×" are very frequent, whereas set operators and some Greek characters are infrequent. In practice, these frequencies depend upon the mathematical domain that formulae are sampled from. Statistics

Table 4.2.   Number of handwritten MEs in data sets. Each task corresponds to a grammar in Table 4.1, e.g., Gram-I is the grammar for Part I recognition task.

Year	Task	Training	Testing
2011	Part I	296	181
	Part II	921	348
2012	Part III	1,341	486
2013	Part IV	8,836	671
2014	Part IV	8,836	986
	Part IV matrix	362	175
2016	Part IV	8,836	1,147
	Part IV matrix	362	250

summarizing the complexity of expressions are also provided using a number of measures: the number of symbols per expression, the number of writing lines (baselines), and the maximum baseline depth. For example, expression (b) in Figure 4.1 has nine symbols, six baselines (three baselines with the fraction, two more with integral bounds, and one nested expression in the root), and a maximum depth of 3 (from the main baseline, to the fraction numerator, and then inside the square root). We can see in Table 4.3 that simple expressions represent about one-third of the data set: less than five symbols using one baseline. Nevertheless, the data set contains many complex expressions: 45% have more than 15 symbols, 34% have more than 4 baselines, and 23% have more than 3 levels of nested subexpressions.

The testing sets defined in 2013, 2014, and 2016 have similar symbol frequency distributions.

4.2.3 File Formats

Two main file formats have been used for the CROHME competitions: InkML and label graphs (LGs). From the beginning, ink traces with ground truth for the segmentation of strokes into symbols and symbol layout were provided in the InkML format. Each expression is stored in one InkML file. This XML language is defined by the W3C (http://www.w3.org/TR/InkML/) and can easily be extended.

Table 4.3. Symbol and structure statistics from the training set Part IV.

Highly frequent symbols	"–" (9.2%), "1" (7.2%), "2" (7.2%), "+" (6.3%), "×" (5.8%), "(" (4.6%)
Infrequent symbols (< 0.1%)	σ (52) μ (46) Δ (35) λ (27) ∈ (14) ∀(8) ∃(4)
Number of symbols per expressions	≤ 5: 35%; ≤ 10: 25% ≤ 15: 23%; ≤ 20: 10% > 20: 7%
Number of subexpressions with different baselines	1: 33%; 2: 16%; 3: 16% 4: 10%; 5: 9% >5: 15%
Maximum depth in nested subexpressions	1: 33%; 2: 45%; 3: 16% > 3: 7%

A CROHME InkML file contains: (1) ink traces: X and Y coordinates of each point sampled nearly equally in time, grouped into strokes with XML identifiers, (2) information about the sample and the writer: unique identifier of the expression (IUD), writer identifier, writer age, gender, and handedness, if available, and finally (3) ground truth. The ground truth contains the following:

- LaTeX string: often a rendering of this string was shown to the writer when the formula was written.
- MathML (http://www.w3.org/Math/) representation of the expression using the Presentation encoding, representing the layout of symbols (with their XML identifiers) on baselines, and not their mathematical semantics.
- Segmentation of strokes into groups with a symbol label and XML identifier; each segment (symbol) is linked to its corresponding MathML symbol by the symbol's identifier.

This format contains all the necessary information needed for training a system. Ground-truth information is removed from test files provided to participants.

The second format was LGs in comma-separated variable (CSV) files, introduced for the 2013 competition [7]. A handwritten expression can be represented by a labeled graph, where nodes are strokes and edges represent relationships between strokes and symbols. Figure 4.2 provides an example of how LGs are defined.

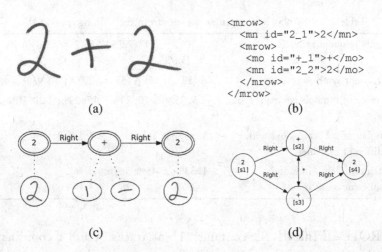

```
<mrow>
    <mn id="2_1">2</mn>
    <mrow>
        <mo id="+_1">+</mo>
        <mn id="2_2">2</mo>
    </mrow>
</mrow>
```

(a)   (b)

(c)   (d)

Figure 4.2.   (a) A simple handwritten expression with four strokes, (b) its representation of the symbol layout using MathML, (c) the corresponding symbol layout, and (d) the stroke label graph.

Figure 4.2(a) displays the ink traces as written by the user. The ground-truth information defining the ME "2+2" with its layout is represented in MathML in Figure 4.2(b). The <mrow> tag represents that the contained children are on the same baseline (row). The <mn> and <mo> tags define numbers and operators. An additional section in the InkML file contains the symbol segmentation information, which is not shown in Figure 4.2. Each group of strokes belonging to a symbol is assigned the same label, comprised of the symbol class, "_" and an index to distinguish multiple occurrences of a symbol (e.g., "2_1" and "2_2" in Figure 4.2(b)).

From the MathML tree, we can create a symbol relation tree (SRT). Six relations are defined: Right, Above, Below, Sup, Sub, and Inside. In Figure 4.2(c), we can see the two "Right" relationships between the three symbols (shown as nodes with double circles), defined by <mrow> tags in Figure 4.2(b). Each symbol is associated with its corresponding strokes (shown by the dotted edges in Figure 4.2(c)). From this SRT, the layout graph of strokes can be constructed using the same spatial relation edges plus segmentation edges as in Figure 4.2(d). The segmentation edges were labeled by "*" in 2013. In the 2014 and 2016 competitions, segmentation edges are labeled with the label of the corresponding symbol. Nodes

```
N, s1, 2, 1.0
N, s2, +, 1.0
N, s3, +, 1.0
N, s4, 2, 1.0
E, s1,s2, Right, 1.0
E, s1,s3, Right, 1.0
E, s2,s3, *, 1.0
E, s3,s2, *, 1.0
E, s2,s4, Right, 1.0
E, s3,s4, Right, 1.0
```

Figure 4.3. LG file for the expression "2 + 2" of Figure 1.2.

(strokes) from the same symbol are fully connected (i.e., form a clique), and share the same label. This allows several levels of segmentation in the same graph, with multiple labels on edges and nodes. This feature was used to define the matrix recognition task (the structural levels defined were: symbol, cell, row, column, and matrix).

The LG file format for LGs was designed to be as simple as possible, human readable, and easily used in any programming language. As shown in Figure 4.3, the graph is defined by a list of nodes and edges in a CSV text file. Nodes are defined using stroke identifiers (matching stroke identifiers in the InkML file), and a label. Edges are defined using the node identifiers they connect and a spatial relation or segmentation label. The last value of each line indicates a confidence value for the given label (symbol or relation). For the ground-truth files, these values are always 1.

Evaluation is performed by comparing the respective LGs for the ground-truth and each system output, as described in the next section. Consequently, participants are asked to output LG files. To this end, we provide a tool to convert the InkML files (from ground truth or output) to the LG format (the crohme2lg tool).

4.3 Evaluation Methodology

Prior to CROHME, it was common to evaluate math recognizer performance using the percentage of LaTeX formula strings matching the ground truth. This *expression rate* provides a simple global performance metric, and for CROHME, the expression rate has been used to rank participating systems. However, comparing LaTeX strings is not straightforward (e.g., two different strings can have the same rendering), and so in CROHME, the expression rate was first computed using canonicalized Presentation MathML (in 2011 and 2012), and then LGs.

However, it is also useful to analyze partially correct results — for example, a very large expression may be correct in all but the identity of a single symbol or spatial relationship. Previous attempts to quantify partially correct recognition in LaTeX have been made. The Evaluation of Mathematical Expression Recognition Systems (EMERS) [16] metric is a tree edit distance using an Euler string representation for MathML trees. Symbol errors are weighted based on their distance from the main writing line (baseline) of the expression. The Image-Based Mathematical Expression Global Error (IMEGE) metric [17] is an image-based comparison of LaTeX strings, using the number of matching pixels in a rendered LaTeX string with the corresponding ground-truth LaTeX rendering. For CROHME, we instead used LGs to compute errors directly at the stroke level, removing any uncertainty about which relationships and symbols in an expression are incorrect, or how.

In the remainder of this section, we focus on the metrics and associated tools used in the last CROHME.

4.3.1 *Stroke-level Evaluation with Label Graphs*

As explained in the previous section and illustrated in Figure 4.2, the LG for a handwritten expression is a directed labeled graph, with nodes representing strokes, and edges representing relationships between strokes and symbols. The label of a node (stroke) is the label of the symbol it belongs to. An edge label represents one of three relationships between two strokes:

1. **Stroke merge.** The two strokes belong to the same symbol; thus, the edge label is the symbol label (matching the node/stroke labels). (Note: for when the edge label "*" is used, then the two strokes are identified as being merged directly).
2. **Symbol relationship.** Each stroke belongs to a separate symbol, and these symbols are in a relationship; thus, the edge label corresponds to one of six spatial relationships (Above, Below, Right, Superscript, Subscript, Inside).
3. **Unrelated strokes.** The two strokes have no relationship, in which case the default label "_" (underscore) is used.

A symbol with n strokes generates a clique, where all nodes and edges have the same label [$n(n-1)$ edges + n nodes = n^2 labels]. Two symbols with n and m strokes generate $n \times m$ edges with the corresponding spatial relation label. If stroke (node) identifiers are preserved, the output of a recognition system in an LG can be directly compared to the ground truth. The number of disagreeing nodes' and edges' label is simply the label Hamming distance between the two graphs. For an expression with n strokes, the Hamming distance is between 0 (perfect recognition) and n^2 (all node and edge labels are incorrect).

In [18], we define distances for different classes of error: ΔC for stroke (node) label disagreements, ΔS for segmentation conflicts (i.e., one graph indicating a stroke merge, and the other a symbol relationship), and ΔR for spatial relation conflicts. The total number of errors is $\Delta B = \Delta C + \Delta S + \Delta R$. As the number of edges and nodes is not the same, we also defined a normalized measure ΔE. The evaluation tool from the LgEval package provided for the competition generates the total number of node and edge errors globally for the full data set, as well as for each individual expression. The tools also provide confusion matrices for node and edge labels. These matrices allow error analysis. They can also be used to help detect bugs and weaknesses of a recognition system.

4.3.2 *Symbol and Expression-level Evaluation*

The symbol segmentation in an LG is defined by cliques of nodes (strokes) and edges sharing a label. However, the evaluation tool looks at the connected components using node labels. This is more efficient than looking for cliques, and is equivalent if the LG is well defined. Using stroke identifiers allows groups of strokes in the ground truth and a recognized expression to be compared directly. Furthermore, it is possible to compute precision and recall for symbol segmentation, and also for symbol segmentation and class labels. Using correctly detected symbols, evaluating spatial relation recognition between symbols is also possible.

The evaluation tool stores these metrics in a summary text file containing:

- **Segmentation (for symbols, and related symbol pairs).** Recall and precision for symbols in the recognized expressions, along with recall and precision for the detection of symbols that share (any) spatial relationship,

- **Segmentation + labels.** Recall and precision for correctly segmented and recognized symbols, and for correctly segmented and related symbols (taking relationship labels into account),
- **Recognition rates for valid detections.** Symbol recognition rate for correctly segmented symbols, and relationship recognition rate for correctly segmented symbol relationships.

By knowing whether each symbol and relation is correct in an expression, it is possible to extract targeted metrics at the expression level: the provided evaluation tools compute 1) the number of expressions where all objects (symbols) are correctly detected, or detected and recognized, 2) the number of expressions where all relations are correctly detected, or detected and recognized, and 3) where all symbols and relations are correctly detected, or detected and recognized. The strictest case (Case 3) corresponds to two expression rates: first, the percentage of formulae with the correct *structure* (i.e., identical LG structure, ignoring labels), and second, the standard expression recognition rate where we require both the LG structure and labels to match the ground truth.

4.3.3 Bigram Error Analysis

Both statistical error analyses and the compilation of specific errors provide helpful information for understanding and improving recognition system behavior. The previous metrics focus upon isolated decisions for symbol or spatial relationship recognition. Nevertheless, as decisions take context into account (through features or language models), having the context for errors available is important. To characterize this context for errors, we extract small subexpressions and check whether they match the ground truth. Three problems were addressed to achieve this: which subexpressions to extract, how to compare subexpressions with ground truth, and finally how to aggregate individual results to make them readable and useful.

For simplicity, all subexpressions of a fixed size are extracted from the SRT recursively starting from isolated symbols, neighboring symbols along labeled edges are added incrementally to the current subgraph set; at each iteration for subexpressions with $n - 1$ symbols, subexpressions with n symbols are generated. Subexpressions are identified uniquely by the set of strokes they contain, but the same subexpression may appear several times at different locations in a formula. As our aim is to detect which small structures are misrecognized, a set of subgraphs are generated from ground-truth expressions and not from recognized expressions.

Each generated subexpression from the ground-truth graph is compared at the stroke level to the corresponding subgraph in the recognized expression. We do this by comparing the corresponding sub-LG using the node and edge labels. Stroke identifiers allow us to efficiently compare sub-LGs if all stroke labels are the same. We use a sparse representation that compares only the existing edges in both graphs. Whenever two small LGs disagree on one or more labels, a triplet is added to a list of errors. This triplet contains the symbol-level sub-SRT from the ground truth, the stroke-level sub-LG from the ground truth, and the stroke-level sub-LG from the recognition output with errors.

For recognition system developers, after debugging, knowing if one specific occurrence of a small set of strokes is properly recognized is too specific; more global information such as "is the layout of these symbols generally well recognized?" will be more useful. The error triplets from the comparison step are aggregated by discarding stroke identifiers, and constructing a histogram of structure confusion errors, counting the number of times each triplet appears for each target subgraph. Unlike a standard confusion matrix where the space of confusion is defined in advance, in computing this structure confusion histogram, we need to compare existing error triplet labels and counts to find a matching bin, or add a new histogram entry; otherwise, we would have a confusion matrix where rows and columns correspond to a very large set of possible subgraphs, with very few nonempty entries.

Error triplets are compared using the three corresponding subgraph entries, looking only at labels of nodes and edges (ignoring stroke identifiers so that we can compile results across expressions). This classical graph matching problem is nondeterministic polynomial (NP) complete. However, as the compared graphs are small, it is not an obstacle. To organize the histogram for analysis, the structure confusion histogram is organized in three levels: triplets sharing the same ground-truth sub-SRT are grouped together, and within this group, those sharing the same ground-truth sub-LG are also grouped. As the number of symbols in the subgraphs of the first level is smaller than the number of strokes in the two other levels, this hierarchy improves the efficiency and clarity of the structure.

For ease of use, the default subgraph size is two nodes. The result is generated in an HTML file readable with standard web browsers. Figure 4.4 shows a small part of this file generated on outputs for the 2014 test set from the system *Nan*. The page of results follows the three levels of the histogram: first the target object-level structure is shown ("x+" in the example of Figure 4.4); then all stroke-level structures are listed (with two, three, four, or five strokes in the example); finally, specific errors are listed, and shaded circles highlight the labeling errors.

4.4 Overview of Participant Strategies

Recognition of handwritten MEs is a complex task involving multiple interacting pattern recognition tasks. To make this task tractable, a formulae language model needs to be defined. Expression grammars were provided for CROHME (see Section 4.2.1), but participants used many variations, including restrictions upon the maximum number of strokes per symbol, whether delayed strokes are permitted; the composition of complex symbols with simple ones, and different expression grammars (e.g., introducing additional constraints to ignore unlikely interpretations). In addition to the creation of a language model definition, the classical steps needed for document analysis systems are used: preprocessing, segmentation, classification, and parsing.

The preprocessing steps used for online handwriting are primarily scale normalization and point resampling operations. CROHME data have been collected with different devices with heterogeneous resolutions; therefore, preprocessing is very important for accurate performance.

Segmentation involves grouping strokes into symbols. To reduce the number of segmentations considered, participants use continuity constraints. Symbols drawn with multiple strokes have a temporal and/or a spatial continuity: the strokes are close in time or space. Once the space

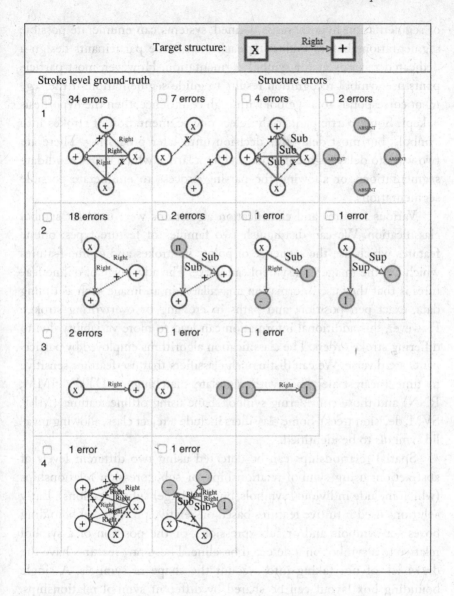

Figure 4.4. Structure confusion histogram for Target "x+." These results are represented in an HTML file, computed using the *Nan* outputs for the 2014 test set Part IV. The first column shows the different stroke-level ground-truth graphs and total number of mis-recognitions, numbered: 1 (four strokes), 2 (three strokes), 3 (two strokes), and 4 (five strokes). The remaining columns in each row contain specific errors and their counts for each ground truth stroke pattern. Many confusions are omitted for space.

of segmentation hypotheses is defined, systems can enumerate possible segmentations before evaluating each one. Some participants design a dedicated recognizer for symbol segmentation. However, most participants use symbol recognition results to guide segmentation: if the segment corresponds to a symbol with high confidence, then the hypothesis is kept. Some participants only select one segmentation of strokes into symbols, but most delay this decision until later processing. There are two ways to delay segmentation: first, in a lattice which stores candidate segmentations, or allowing the parsing process to enumerate possible segmentations.

Various features and classification algorithms were used for symbol classification. We can distinguish two families of feature types: online features which use the sequence of points in strokes and offline features which use the image of a symbol candidate. The advantage of online features is that they use information unavailable in an image such as timing data, exact pen position, and paths in crossing or overwriting strokes. However, this additional information can lead to more variability due to differing stroke orders. The classification algorithms employed by participants are diverse. We can distinguish classifiers that use features sensitive to time (nearest neighbor with template matching or DTW, HMM, RNN) and those considering symbol shape using offline features (MLP, SVM, decision trees). Some classifiers include a reject class, allowing invalid symbols to be identified.

Spatial relationships can be detected using two different levels of abstraction: using symbol relationships, or subexpression relationships (which include individual symbols, but also larger subexpressions). Early solutions used intuitive features based on relative positions of bounding boxes for symbols and/or subexpressions, or the position of a symbol relative to a symbol on a detected baseline. These raw features have the drawback of not taking into account the shape of symbols. A single bounding box layout can be shared by different symbol relationships. A promising solution defines layout features as shape contexts which provide visual information absent in bounding box-based features. From a given layout feature, it is possible to recognize spatial relations with a classifier. Several hypotheses of spatial relations can be kept for the parsing step.

Most participants define the formula recognition problem as a global optimization, requiring the minimization of a cost or maximization of a joint probability for symbols and relationships. Formula rank scores are defined by a combination of symbol, relationship, and production rule confidences. These scores are used to guide the parsing process and select final interpretations.

Participants using a Context Free Grammar-based (CFG) language model employ the Cocke–Yonger–Kasami (CYK) parsing algorithm. To initialize the CYK table, symbol recognition hypotheses from the previous step may be used directly. Other participants initialize the dynamic programming table with individual strokes, and then fill the first lines with the corresponding symbols. The search space between these initialization strategies can be similar, particularly when the temporal stroke order is preserved. Probabilistic graph grammars have also been used, using a parsing algorithm similar to CYK. In this case, grammar rules are defined using graphs, making grammars more intuitive to define and read, but more computationally expensive to parse. Aside from these bottom-up strategies, top-down approaches can be defined, e.g., using Unger's algorithm. Some participants instead use baseline approaches which first detect horizontal alignments of symbols on the main baseline, and then add vertical relationships with remaining symbols. These greedy algorithms are less accurate than the CFG-based approaches, particularly as they impose few constraints on legal layouts (e.g., allowing digits to have digits as subscripts).

4.5 Description of Approaches Submitted to Competition

In this section, we summarize techniques that have been used in CROHME 2014. Results from these systems are discussed in the next section. For brevity, the identifiers shown in Table 4.4 are used to identify participants.

4.5.1 *Val: Universitat Politècnica de València*

The system parses expressions using a 2D stochastic CFG. The parser first computes several hypotheses for symbol segmentation and recognition at

Table 4.4.   List of participating systems for CROHME 2014.

System	Affiliation	References
Val	Universitat Politècnica de València	[19, 23]
Sap	University of São Paulo	[13, 20]
Mys	MyScript	
Ria	Rochester Institute of Technology, DRPL	[21–23]
Rib	Rochester Institute of Technology, CIS	[23–25]
Tok	Tokyo University of Agriculture and Technology	[26]
Nan	University of Nantes, IRCCyN	[27, 28]

the stroke level using several stochastic sources (symbol classifier, segmentation model, and duration model). Symbol classification is performed by a combination of online and offline features with a BLSTM-RNN classifier. Then, the parser builds new hypotheses by combining subexpressions using a spatial relationship classifier (a Gaussian mixture model with geometric features). Finally, the most likely derivation tree represents the recognized ME. Symbol recognition, segmentation, and the structural analysis decisions are integrated by taking the expression grammar and contextual information into account at each step in parsing.

4.5.2 Sap: University of São Paulo

Recognition is divided into three steps. First, each stroke is combined with its three nearest-neighbor strokes to generate the symbol hypotheses. A symbol classifier with a reject option labels each hypothesis as a specific symbol label nonsymbol. Second, using the symbol hypotheses, several stroke partitions are generated and a baseline structure tree is built for each partition. A cost that combines the symbol hypotheses and relation costs is assigned to each baseline tree. In the final step, the LaTeX code for each baseline tree is extracted and a parser evaluates its validity. The legal expression with the lowest cost is selected for the output.

4.5.3 Mys: MyScript

The recognition engine analyses the spatial relationships between all the parts of the equation, in conformity with the rules laid down in its grammar, to determine the segmentation of all its parts. Each rule is associated with a specific spatial relationship. A symbol expert estimates the probabilities for all the parts in the suggested segmentation. This expert is based on different sets of features: a combination of online and offline information. A statistical language model uses context information between different symbols depending on their spatial relationships in the equation. Statistics have been estimated on hundreds of thousands of equations. A global discriminant training scheme on the equation level with automatic learning of all classifier parameters and meta-parameters of the recognizer is employed. The recognizer has been trained on samples that have been collected from writers in several countries.

4.5.4 *Ria: Rochester Institute of Technology, DRPL*

The segmenter considers strokes in time series, using AdaBoost with confidence-weighted predictions to determine whether to merge each pair of strokes. The symbol classifier is an SVM with a Gaussian kernel trained for probabilistic classification using a combination of online and offline features. The parser is a modified version of a minimum-spanning-tree-based parsing algorithm. It recursively groups vertical structures, extracts the dominant operator in each group, and then detects symbols on the main baseline and on baselines in superscripted and subscripted regions. Spatial relationships are classified using bounding box geometry and shape context features for regions around symbol pairs.

4.5.5 *Rib: Rochester Institute of Technology, CIS*

Given an expression with n strokes, the segmentation method considers merging or splitting the $n - 1$ stroke pairs in time order. For each pair, 405 features are measured and then reduced to 100 dimensions using PCA. An SVM with a radial basis function kernel is trained to take the segmentation decision. Then the classification of these symbols is done using online and offline features. The first parsing stage detects "strong" geometric relationships (above, below, and inside) searching for symbols that horizontally overlap horizontal lines. The expression is then split into several subexpressions (numerator and denominator of a fraction, base of a square root, and remaining symbols). In each subexpression, the "weak" geometric relationships (right, superscript, and subscript) are detected using a polar histogram layout descriptor in 15 (distance) × 20 (angle) resolution for each two adjacent symbols. After PCA reduction, an SVM classifier is employed to classify relationships.

4.5.6 *Tok: Tokyo University of Agriculture and Technology*

After a normalization preprocessing, the symbol classifier extracts a 512D feature vector based on Normalization-Cooperated Gradient Feature (NCGF). The feature vector is reduced to 300 dimensions by FLDA and classified by a Generalized Learning Vector Quantization classifier. For classifying invalid symbols more accurately, patterns are clustered into 64 clusters by using the LBG algorithm. Structural relations are learnt from training patterns by using two SVM models based on bounding box features. In structure analysis, the stroke order is maintained to reduce the complexity of the parsing.

4.5.7 *Nan: University of Nantes, IRCCyN*

This system considers the recognition problem into a search for the best possible interpretation of a sequence of input strokes. The symbol classifier is a classical MLP, which has the capability to reject invalid segmentation hypotheses. The originality of this system stems from the global learning schema, which allows training a symbol classifier directly from complete handwritten MEs to consider the invalid symbol segments in the training. Furthermore, contextual modeling based on structural analysis of the expression is employed, where the models are learnt directly from expressions using a global learning scheme.

4.6 Detailed Results from CROHME 2014

The CROHME 2014 [8] competition involved three related tasks. The first one was isolated symbol recognition, using symbols extracted from the full expressions. As explained in the previous section, several systems are able to detect incorrect segmentations, thus we added a 'junk' (reject) class. To produce both under- and over-segmented symbols, we randomly selected sequences of one to four strokes written in time-order that do not correspond to valid symbols. Thus the systems have to recognize symbols and to reject wrong segmentations. We will not give detailed results here, but instead share some interesting observations. The 3 best systems use classical classification algorithms (SVM, MLP and RNN) but all use both online and offline features which capture dynamic and static information. Trying to detect the incorrect segmentation samples decreases recognition rates (from [91.24, 91.04, 88.66] to [84.14, 85.54, 83.61] in %). This task clearly illustrates that recognizing MEs is not a simple task, even if we consider only isolated symbols.

The second competition task was the main one: full ME recognition. In the remainder of the section we will focus on its detailed results. A top-down approach is used to present the results, following the three levels of evaluation: full expression recognition, object detection and recognition, and stroke-level metrics. In Section 4.3.3, we illustrate one use for structure confusion histograms.

The third task was a frontier challenge for recognition of matrix structures with embedded expressions and expressions using several small matrices. The available data sets were small and only two systems participated. This first proposal required definition of a new data format (the LGs with multiple levels of structure, described earlier), and a new evaluation protocol. What we find from the results is that this task is very challenging: the expression rates for two systems were 31.15% and 53.28%.

4.6.1 *Evaluation at Expression, Object and Stroke Levels*

Table 4.5 presents expression recognition rates for the seven participants using the 986 expressions for the Part IV test set of CROHME 2014. The complete recognition rates are in a wide range up to 62.68% of expressions. To be considered correct, all labels of the LG graph should be correct (stroke labels and relation labels). The next columns show how many expressions are correct if one, two, or three label errors are tolerated. Accepting three errors makes recognition rates increase by about 12%. This shows not only that a significant portion of misrecognized expressions have only a small error (which could be easily corrected by the user in an adapted graphical user interface) but also that most of expressions

Table 4.5. Correct expression recognition rates for the Part IV test set of CROHME 2014.

System	Correct (%)	<= 1 error	<= 2 errors	<= 3 errors
Val	37.22	44.22	47.26	50.20
Sap	15.01	22.31	26.57	27.69
Mys	62.68	72.31	75.15	76.88
Ria	18.97	28.19	32.35	33.37
Rib	18.97	26.37	30.83	32.96
Tok	25.66	33.16	35.90	37.32
Nan	26.06	33.87	38.54	39.96

have more complex problems which cannot be analyzed at this expression-level evaluation.

Table 4.6 shows object (symbol and related symbol pair) detection and recognition results. We can distinguish three subproblems: segmentation of objects, recognition of these objects, and relations between these objects. The first two columns present the recall and precision rates for object segmentation. The recall rate represents how many objects are correctly detected among ground-truth objects, while the precision represents the percentage of correct segmentations among objects in the recognition output.

Most participants detect more than 83% of the symbols (up to 98.42%), suggesting that the segmentation problem is far from been solved. In the remaining columns, symbols should be well segmented and recognized to be considered as correct. In this case, all recall rates decrease by 5–10% to 78.4% on average. If we compare these results to the isolated symbol recognition task, we notice that for some systems, their accuracy is higher or lower, illustrating the link between recognition tasks. Further, we see that differences between systems observed at the expression level are attenuated at the object level. One point, which distinguished participant systems, is the relation detection in the last columns of Table 4.6. To be correct, a relation should connect two correctly segmented symbols with a correct relation label in the SRT.

Table 4.7 uses Hamming distances to count individual errors at the stroke level. It allows a more detailed analysis, e.g., we can see how

Table 4.6. Object recognition-level evaluation for the Part IV test set of CROHME 2014.

System	Segments (%)		Seg + class (%)		Tree rels. (%)	
	Rec.	Prec.	Rec.	Prec.	Rec.	Prec.
Val	93.31	90.72	86.59	84.18	84.23	81.96
Sap	76.63	80.28	66.97	70.16	60.31	63.74
Mys	98.42	98.13	93.91	93.63	94.26	94.01
Ria	85.52	86.09	76.64	77.15	70.78	71.51
Rib	88.23	84.20	78.45	74.87	61.38	72.70
Tok	83.05	85.36	69.72	71.66	66.83	74.81
Nan	89.43	86.13	76.53	73.71	71.77	71.65

Table 4.7. Stroke and stroke to stroke-level evaluation for the Part IV test set of CROHME 2014.

System	Label	Hamming distances			μ error (%)	
	Strokes	Pairs	Seg	Rel	ΔBn	ΔE
Val	2,026	7,174	2,540	4,634	6.23	11.98
Sap	4,523	17,449	7,772	9,677	14.42	25.77
Mys	845	2,489	836	1,653	2.21	4.56
Ria	3,406	12,768	5,328	5,328	9.98	19.17
Rib	2,742	13,477	4,386	9,091	10.26	18.24
Tok	4,039	13,325	5,670	7,655	10.05	19.43
Nan	3,558	11,795	4,388	7,407	9.38	17.66

missegmented symbols are recognized. For example, Ria has fewer stroke label errors than Nan, even if the Seg + Class rates are comparable. It means that Ria has more partially correct symbols than the Nan system: correct recognitions with incorrect segmentation. As recognition tasks interact, a small improvement in symbol segmentation can improve relation recognition and vice versa. The last columns of Table 4.7 show metrics merging these three levels: the average percentage of mislabeled node and edge labels per expression (ΔBn) along with a variation designed to weight segmentation, classification, and relation decisions more equally (ΔE). The latter allows us to group the systems in three groups: the winner Mys with an average error of 4.56%, the second place Val with 11.98%, and the rest of participants with about 20% of decisions which are incorrect.

4.6.2 *Bigram Error Analysis*

The results shown previously allow us to compare participant systems at different levels or globally, but do not suggest specifically how to improve the results. A common way is to perform an error analysis and focus upon more frequent errors. Compiling and counting errors in different situations manually is inefficient and impractical, but error summaries such as confusion matrices can be useful (as provided for symbols and relations in the tools for the competition). However, this stroke-level point of view is insufficient for understanding symbol-level relations and parsing problems. Here we show how bigram error analysis can help in this task. Table 4.8 compares the most frequent bigrams of symbols misrecognized by each participating systems. Each system can see its weaknesses and try

Table 4.8. Symbol bigram error counts (CROHME 2014). Errors are shown for each system, and globally for all systems (All). Lines are sorted by the first column (All). The top three errors in each column are shown in bold.

Bigram	All	Mys	Nan	Ria	Rib	Sap	Tok	Val
1	358	5	27	**60**	**91**	**108**	**52**	15
$x +$	285	11	**55**	41	41	56	**55**	**26**
$(x$	224	5	**32**	**44**	32	52	**50**	9
$+ 1$	224	7	**34**	29	44	**67**	38	5
$= -$	209	6	20	34	49	**60**	22	18
$= 1$	180	0	17	33	**52**	46	26	5
00	160	0	31	**53**	31	20	17	5
$- =$	157	0	17	21	**55**	39	15	7
$x \times$	145	**24**	22	20	24	22	10	**23**
$\times x$	141	**23**	20	19	24	22	10	**23**
$f ($	136	4	30	21	18	21	19	**23**
Σ^n	114	**17**	17	17	12	17	17	17

to find an adapted solution with a specific purpose, but here we will compare them together.

It is interesting to note that while systems have different behaviors, they share some common challenges. The two subexpressions $x +$ and $\frac{1}{-}$ are the most frequent errors, maybe because these four symbols are the most frequent ones (see Table 4.3). Furthermore, $x +$, $x \times$, and $\times x$ are very frequent. This is because these bigrams involve several ambiguities: they are written with multiple strokes, so there is difficulty in segmentation; these symbols can also easily be confused in a valid subexpression (if $xx -$, is recognized instead of $x \times$, either may be a valid expression). All participants share these two errors. The $- =$ and $= -$ subexpressions are difficult to recognize because horizontal lines can be merged to define an extended fraction bar. For example, $= -$ can be recognized as $\equiv$. Note that the horizontal bar can be a fraction bar or a minus sign. It is surprising that the most frequent bigrams all have a left–right spatial relationship. The only vertical relationship is $\frac{1}{-}$, and several errors are possible; for instances, merging of the symbol in a + sign or in a digit 1 written with a horizontal stroke at the base.

4.7 Conclusions and Recommendations

The detailed results presented in the previous section were related to the CROHME 2014 edition; updated results can be found in the most recent CROHME 2016 [9]. Even if these new results are slightly better in accuracy (but computed on a new test set), the following conclusion is still relevant.

The CROHME 2014 detailed results show two important things. First, the CROHME community has proposed effective solutions to solve a part of the problem: on average, over all participants, 78% of the symbols and 29% of expressions are recognized correctly. The second point is that this problem is still challenging. Therefore, having efficient tools to analyze complex elements like math expressions is important. They can highlight specific problems which can be hidden in the mass of information. Error analysis shows that symbol segmentation and recognition are still difficult in the context of complex expressions. Our bigram error analysis indicates that spatial relationship recognition needs further improvement, even in linear expressions. It is important that the community continues to share the tools, data sets, and parts of their systems in order to fully capitalize upon previous efforts.

To conclude, exciting perspectives for this field of research can be suggested. One of the most promising is to incorporate statistical language models in a deeper way. Using basic n-gram, or more elaborated skip-gram, models defined either at the symbol or at the subexpression level are appealing. Such models have proved to be very effective for improving text recognition performance. The adaptation to formulae is not straightforward, because of the multiple writing lines (2D layout) which is not present in regular text. Extending this concept, it may be tempting to get rid of the use of formal CFGs to guide the interpretation stage, and to instead consider more semantic approaches, so that mathematical concepts could be revealed. Following this idea, it would be interesting to look in the direction of continuous bag of words for computing vector representations of subexpressions.

References

1. K. Chan and D. Yeung, "Mathematical expression recognition: A survey," *International Journal on Document Analysis and Recognition*, vol. 3, no. 1, pp. 3–15, 2000.
2. U. Garain and B. Chaudhuri, "OCR of printed mathematical expressions," pp. 235–259. Berlin, Springer, 2007.
3. E. Tapia and R. Rojas, "A survey on recognition of on-line handwritten mathematical notation," *Technical Report B-07-01*, Free University of Berlin, January 2007.
4. R. Zanibbi and D. Blostein, "Recognition and retrieval of mathematical expressions," *International Journal of Document Analysis and Recognition*, vol. 15, no. 4, pp. 331–357, 2012.
5. H. Mouchère, C. Viard-Gaudin, D.H. Kim, J.H. Kim, and U. Garain, "CROHME 2011: Competition on recognition of online handwritten mathematical expressions," in *Proceedings of International Conference on Document Analysis and Recognition*, Beijing, China, September 18–21, 2011.
6. H. Mouchère, C. Viard-Gaudin, D.H. Kim, J.H. Kim, and U. Garain, "ICFHR 2012: Competition on recognition of on-line mathematical expressions (CROHME 2012)," in *International Conference on Frontiers in Handwriting Recognition* (ICFHR), (Bari, Italy), 2012.

7. H. Mouchère, C. Viard-Gaudin, R. Zanibbi, U. Garain, D.H. Kim, and J.H. Kim, "ICDAR 2013 CROHME: 3rd international competition on recognition of online handwritten mathematical expressions," in *International Conference on Document Analysis and Recognition (ICDAR'2013)*, Washington, DC, USA, August 2013.

8. H. Mouchère, C. Viard-Gaudin, R. Zanibbi, and U. Garain, "ICFHR 2014: Competition on recognition of on-line mathematical expressions (CROHME 2014)," in *International Conference on Frontiers in Handwriting Recognition (ICFHR'2014)*, Creta, Greece, September 1–4, 2014.

9. H. Mouchère, C. Viard-Gaudin, R. Zanibbi, and U. Garain, "ICFHR 2016: Competition on recognition of on-line mathematical expressions (CROHME 2016)," in *International Conference on Frontiers in Handwriting Recognition (ICFHR'2016)*, Shenzhen, China, October 23–26, 2016.

10. A.-M. Awal, H. Mouchère, and C. Viard-Gaudin, "Towards handwritten mathematical expression recognition," in *10th International Conference on Document Analysis and Recognition (ICDAR'2009)*, Barcelona, Spain, pp. 1046–1050, July 26–29, 2009.

11. S. Quiniou, H. Mouchère, S. Saldarriaga, C. Viard-Gaudin, E. Morin, S. Petitrenaud, and S. Medjkoune, "Hamex: A handwritten and audio dataset of mathematical expressions," in *11th International Conference on Document Analysis and Recognition (ICDAR'2011)*, Beijing, China, pp. 452–456, September 2011.

12. J. Stria, M. Bresler, D. Průsa, and V. Hlavc, "MfrDB: Database of annotated on-line mathematical formulae," in *International Conference on Frontiers in Handwriting Recognition (ICFHR'2012)*, Bari, Italy, pp. 542–547, September 18–20, 2012.

13. F.D.J. Aguilar and N.S. Hirata, "ExpressMatch: A system for creating ground-truthed datasets of online mathematical expressions," in *10th IAPR International Workshop on Document Analysis Systems*, Gold Cost, QLD, Australia, pp. 155–159, 2012.

14. S. MacLean, G. Labahn, E. Lank, M. Marzouk, and D. Tausky, "Grammar-based techniques for creating ground-truthed sketch corpora," *International Journal on Document Analysis and Recognition*, vol. 14, no. 1, pp. 65–74, 2011.

15. J. Gehrke, P. Ginsparg, and J. Kleinberg, "Overview of the 2003 KDD cup," *ACM SIGKDD Explorations Newsletter*, vol. 5, no. 2, pp. 149–151, 2003.

16. K. Sain, A. Dasgupta, and U. Garain, "Emers: A tree matching-based performance evaluation of mathematical expression recognition systems," *International Journal on Document Analysis and Recognition*, vol. 14, no. 1, pp. 75–85, 2011.

17. F. Àlvaro, J.-A. Sànchez, and J.-M. Benedì, "An image-based measure for evaluation of mathematical expression recognition," in J. Sanches, L. Micò, and J. Cardoso, Eds. *Pattern Recognition and Image Analysis, Lecture Notes in Computer Science*, vol. 7887, pp. 682–690. Berlin, Heidelberg, Springer, 2013.

18. R. Zanibbi, A. Pillay, H. Mouchère, C. Viard-Gaudin, and D. Blostein, "Stroke-based performance metrics for handwritten mathematical expressions," in *Proceedings of the 11th International Conference on Document Analysis and Recognition (ICDAR'2011)*, Beijing, China, pp. 334–338, September 18–21, 2011.

19. F. Àlvaro, J.-A. Sànchez, and J.-M. Benedì, "Recognition of online handwritten mathematical expressions using 2D stochastic context-free grammars and hidden Markov models," *Pattern Recognition Letters*, vol. 35, pp. 56–67, 2014.

20. F. Julca-Aguilar, N. Hirata, C. Viard-Gaudin, H. Mouchère, and S. Medjkoune, "Mathematical symbol hypothesis recognition with rejection option," in *Proceedings of the 14th International Conference on Frontiers in Handwriting Recognition (ICFHR'2014)*, Crete, Greece, pp. 500–504, September 1–4, 2014.

21. K. Davila, S. Ludi, and R. Zanibbi, "Using off-line features and synthetic data for on-line handwritten math symbol recognition," in *Proceedings of the 14th International Conference on Frontiers in Handwriting Recognition (ICFHR'2014)*, Crete, Greece, pp. 323–328, September 1–4, 2014.

22. R. Zanibbi, D. Blostein, and J.R. Cordy, "Recognizing mathematical expressions using tree transformation," *IEEE Transactions on Pattern Analysis and Machine Intelligence*, vol. 24, no. 11, pp. 1455–1467, 2002.

23. F. Àlvaro and R. Zanibbi, "A shape-based layout descriptor for classifying spatial relationships in handwritten math," in *ACM Symposium Document Engineering, Florence, Italy*, pp. 123–126, 2013.

24. L. Hu and R. Zanibbi, "Segmenting handwritten math symbols using AdaBoost and multi-scale shape context features," in *Proceedings International Conference Document Analysis and Recognition*, Washington, DC, USA, pp. 1180–1184, August 25–28, 2013.

25. A. Schlapbach, M. Liwicki and H. Bunke, "Feature selection for HMM and BLSTM based handwriting recognition of whiteboard notes," *International Journal on Pattern Recognition and Artificial Intelligence*, vol. 23, no. 5, pp. 907–923, 2009.

26. D. Le, T. Van Phan, and M. Nakagawa, "A system for recognizing online handwritten mathematical expressions and improvement of structure analysis," *in 11th IAPR Workshop on Document Analysis Systems*, Tours, France, April 7–10, 2014.

27. A.-M. Awal, H. Mouchère, and C. Viard-Gaudin, "Improving online hand-written mathematical expressions recognition with contextual modeling," in *Proceedings of the 12th International Conference on Frontiers in Handwriting Recognition (ICFHR'2010)*, Kolkata, India, pp. 427–432, November 16–18, 2010.

28. A.-M. Awal, H. Mouchère, and C. Viard-Gaudin, "A global learning approach for an online handwritten mathematical expression recognition system," *Pattern Recognition Letters*, vol. 35, no. 1, pp. 68–77, 2014.

Part III
Writer Identification and Signature Verification

Chapter 5
Writer Identification

Georgios Louloudis, Nikolaos Stamatopoulos, and
Basilis Gatos

5.1 Introduction

Writer identification is a behavioral handwriting-based recognition problem, which proceeds by matching unknown handwritings against a database of samples with known authorship. From the document image analysis scope, writer identification can be defined as the retrieval of handwritten samples of the same writer from a database using a handwritten sample as a graphical query. The large number of recent publications as well as the organization of several competitions [1–3] proves that writer identification is a very active and promising area of research.

The identification of the writer of a handwritten document has a wide variety of applications. For example, the analysis of handwritten documents has great bearing on the criminal justice systems. As stated by Srihari *et al.* [4], "Numerous cases over the years have dealt with evidence provided by handwritten documents such as wills and ransom notes." Other application areas include security, financial activity, forensic analysis, and access control.

The main challenges of a writer identification system as described by Schomaker *et al.* [5] include the variability and variation of handwritten patterns even among documents of the same writer, the limited amount of image data and the presence of noise patterns. Another challenge concerns the large number of classes (writers) among which the final decision should be taken.

In this chapter, we summarize the results of the writer identification competition series for Latin documents presented in the ICDAR and ICFHR conferences until 2013, including the benchmarking datasets, the evaluation protocol, participating methods together with several recently published methods, which made use of the benchmarking datasets and finally, we draw some comments and conclusions.

5.2 General Approaches

A wide variety of writer identification techniques have been reported in the literature. Writer identification methods can be classified according to three different aspects: (i) the input method of the writing, (ii) the input data that is used by the methods in order to decide the identity of the writer, and (iii) whether the system is trained or not on a specific set of writers.

Based on the input method of the writing, writer identification methods can be classified into **online** and **offline**. Online refers to methods dealing with the identification of the writer of a message as it is written using a digitizer or an instrumental stylus that captures information about the pen tip, its position, velocity, or acceleration as a function of time [9]. For the case of offline writer identification methods, data is digitized after the writing process is over [10]. In this case, the identification of the writer is more complex than the former case, due to the loss of temporal information such as the writing sequence and the velocity. To this end, the online writer identification task is considered to be less difficult than the offline writer identification task.

The second taxonomy is based on the data requirements of the method that is used in order to decide the identity of the writer. Following this taxonomy, writer identification methods can be divided into **text dependent** and **text independent**. Text dependent writer identification methods require a specific text sample to be written [4] (i.e., the same text for all writers), whereas text independent writer identification systems can work on any given text [11]. The major drawback of text dependent methods is the restriction on the generality of these methods due to their limitation on specific textual content, which is not always reproducible from one writer to another. On the other hand, even though text independent methods have a wider applicability due to the independence of the textual content used as input, they cannot obtain the accuracy of text dependent methods.

The last categorization on writer identification methods is based on the existence or not of a supervised method that is trained on a specific set of writers. Using this taxonomy, the methods can be categorized as either **training based** or **training free**. For the training based methods, a labeled dataset of all the writers is necessary beforehand in order to train a classifier or to create a model per writer [12]. For the case of training free methods, a database of documents with the known writer identity is also necessary. However, these methods tend to compare the query with all documents in the dataset using a similarity measure in order to produce a ranked list of the documents included in the database [13]. Although training based methods perform better than training free methods, their major disadvantage is the lack of adaptation in the database of documents written by new writers.

All writer identification competitions presented by the authors in the ICDAR and ICFHR conferences measure the performance of methods that are offline, text independent, and belong to the training free category with respect to the aforementioned taxonomies.

5.3 Methods Participating to the Competitions

A brief description of the submitted methods to the writer identification competitions are provided in the following sections.

5.3.1 *Participating Methods to the ICDAR 2011 Competition*

Seven research groups submitted their methods to the competition. One of these research groups submitted two different methods making the total number of participating methods equal to eight.

ECNU method (East China Normal University, China): The submitted method uses contour-directional features (CDFs), which encode orientation and curvature information in a local grid around every edge pixel to give an intrinsic characteristic of the individual handwriting style. The improved weighted Chi-square metric is applied to measure the similarity of two handwriting documents.

QUQA-a method (Qatar University, Qatar and Northumbria University, UK): The submitted method uses the edge-based directional probability distribution features [14] and the grapheme features [15]. These features have previously been applied for Arabic writer identification and for signature verification, and have shown interesting results. The classification step is performed using a logistic regression classifier applied on the whole document directly.

QUQA-b method: It is the second method submitted by the group. The difference with respect to QUQA-a method is that the classification step is performed using a logistic regression classifier applied to the document after decomposing it into four blocks.

TSINGHUA method (Tsinghua University, China): The method adopts a grid microstructure feature approach (GMSF), which processes handwritten texts in multiline. A set of microstructures are calculated using a moving grid window. The probability distribution of the microstructures forms the GMSF, which describes the writing style. A method using variance weighted Chi-square distance is implemented for writer similarity measurement. For more details, the reader should see [16].

GWU method (George Washington University, USA and Qatar University, Qatar): The submitted method combines nine image features which are part of the image features provided by the ICDAR 2011 — Arabic Writer Identification Contest [17]. In order to compare two feature vectors, a modification of the Mahalanobis metric was used which produces a zero value for two unrelated documents and a value approximating infinity for a perfect match.

CS-UMD method (University of Maryland, USA): K-adjacent segment (KAS) features are used in a bag-of-features (BOF) framework to model a user's handwriting. A BOF model is used to compare the writers from two documents by converting the KAS features extracted from a document into a histogram of code words.

Once a codebook is constructed, the original document is represented by a histogram of KAS "code words" present in the document. This histogram is normalized to sum up to one so that the histogram is invariant to the size of the input. The two histograms are compared using their Euclidean distance [18].

TEBESSA method (Tebessa University and Badji Mokhtar University, Algeria): The probability distribution of black and white run-lengths in four directions (horizontal, vertical, left diagonal, and right diagonal) has been used. The histogram of run-lengths is normalized and interpreted as a probability distribution. The method considers horizontal and right-diagonal white run-lengths extracted from the original image as well as horizontal, vertical, left-diagonal, and right-diagonal black run-lengths extracted from the image after applying Sobel edge detection to generate a binary image in which only the edge pixels are "on." To compare two documents, the Manhattan distance metric is used. For more details, see [19].

MCS-NUST method (National University of Sciences and Technology, Pakistan): The method is based on a set of features that capture orientation and curvature information in writing at different levels of observation. These features are computed starting from image contours represented by chain codes as well as by a set of polygons. A total of 14 features are extracted including histograms of chain code and their first and second-order differentials, histograms of chain-code pairs and triplets, histograms of the curvature index, and weighted and nonweighted histograms of slope and curvature of line segments, approximating the contours. The distance between two documents is defined as the average of distances between all corresponding features.

5.3.2 *Participating Methods to the ICFHR 2012 Competition*

Four research groups submitted their methods to the competition. One of these research groups submitted three different methods, while another one submitted two making the total number of participating methods equal to 7. A brief description of these methods is provided in this section.

TEBESSA-a method (Tebessa University, Badji Mokhtar University, Algeria and Rouen University, France): The submitted method is based on the edge-hinge features, which estimate the joint distribution of edge angles in a writer's handwriting. They are constructed by performing an edge detection using a Sobel kernel on the input images and, subsequently, measuring the angles of both edge segments that emanate from each edge pixel. To compare two documents, the Manhattan distance metric is used.

TEBESSA-b method: This approach is based on multiscale run-length features [11, 19], which are determined on the binary image taking into consideration both the black pixels corresponding to the ink trace and the white pixels corresponding to the background. The probability distribution of black and white run-lengths has been used. There are four scanning methods: horizontal, vertical, left-diagonal, and right-diagonal. The run-length features are calculated using the gray-level run-length matrices, and the histogram of run-lengths is normalized and interpreted as a probability distribution. The method considers horizontal, vertical, left-diagonal, and right-diagonal white run-lengths as well as horizontal, vertical, left-diagonal, and right-diagonal black run-lengths extracted from the original image. To compare two documents, the Manhattan distance metric is used.

TEBESSA-c method: The method is based on the combination of both types of features used by the previous two methods: multiscale edge-hinge and multiscale run-length features [19]. The Manhattan distance metric is also used to compare two documents.

QATAR-a method (Qatar University, Qatar): The submitted method combines hundreds of geometrical features that were made available in [20] using a logistic regression classifier. Those features are based on the number of holes, moments, projections, distributions, position of the center of gravity, number of branches in the skeleton, Fourier descriptors, tortuosities, directions, curvatures, and chain codes.

QATAR-b method: Submitted by the same group as the previous method. It uses the most discriminant of the features cited earlier.

TSINGHUA method (Tsinghua University, China): The method was described in Section 5.3.1. It should be mentioned that this method was the winner of the ICDAR 2011 Writer Identification Contest [1].

HANNOVER method (Hochschule Hannover, Germany): The submitted method is a statistical approach. The handwriting is seen as a texture with a steady structure of line elements all over the image. For the description of such a texture, a suitable set of primitive elements has to be found whose frequency of occurrence is suited to distinguishing different writers to the greatest possible extent. The line segments of which the writing is composed can be taken as primitive elements of a handwriting specimen. Straight line segments may be obtained by the run-lengths of pixel chains. The number and length of pixel chains are determined in eight different directions, and, for each direction, a frequency distribution is made. The features obtained by this shift-invariant transformation are nearly text independent as long as there is enough text at hand (about 3–5 handwriting lines). The feature vector furnishes information about the sloping position, size, regularity, and roundness of the handwriting. The submitted method can be imagined as a shredder, which is fed with eight rotated documents. The feature vectors obtained by the described method have a very high dimension. As neighbored components of the vector are strongly correlated, they are added to a certain degree so that only eight features in each direction remain. The final feature vector used has 64 components.

5.3.3 *Participating Methods to the ICDAR 2013 Competition*

Six research groups submitted their methods to the competition. Several groups submitted multiple methods making the total number of participating methods equal to 12. A brief description of these methods along with information of the participating groups is provided in this section.

CS-UMD-a method (University of Maryland, USA): This approach splices words into "character-like" segments using seam cuts. These segments are described using gradients taken from their contour to form a feature vector. At a next step, features are clustered to find a representative character set. The feature vector sets taken from the cluster centers from two images are compared to determine similarity. More details on the submitted method can be found in [21].

CS-UMD-b method: This approach is similar to the previously described approach [21]. The main difference is related to the way of splitting words. In this method, the splitting is accomplished using vertical cuts instead of making use of seam cuts.

CS-UMD-c method: See method CS-UMD, which is described in Section 5.3.1.

CVL-IPK method (Vienna University of Technology, Austria): It is based on [22]. The method uses scale-invariant feature transform (SIFT) features and the Fisher vector. The calculated features of a training set are clustered using a Gaussian mixture model (GMM) to build a vocabulary which is the basis to calculate the Fisher vector of each image. As a final step, the method uses the cosine distance to calculate the writer similarity between two document images.

HANNOVER-a method (Hochschule Hannover, Germany): This method is an extension of the HANNOVER method described in Section 5.3.2. The main differences correspond to (i) the consideration of primitive elements from the background in the neighborhood of the handwriting and (ii) the size of the final feature vector, which in this case contains 128 features. To compare two document images in terms of writer similarity, the city block distance is used. The interested reader should see [23].

HANNOVER-b method: Since the feature vector obtained by the aforementioned method has a very high dimension (128 features), a dimensionality reduction of the feature vector is considered in this approach. As neighboring components of the feature vector are strongly correlated, they are added to a certain degree so that only eight features in each direction remain. The final feature vector used has 64 components. The Mahalanobis distance between two feature vectors is used in order to compare two document images.

HIT-ICG method (Harbin Institute of Technology, China): This method adopts two feature sets based on SIFT for writer identification. The first feature set (SDS) is extracted by using the SIFT descriptors (SDs) and a codebook constructed from training SDs by self-organizing maps (SOMs). The second feature set is a scale and orientation histogram (SOH) generated by using the scales and orientations of SIFT key points. The Chi-square distance is implemented for writer similarity measurement. A direct feature combination by simple distance-weighted sum is calculated for the final decision.

QATAR-a method (Qatar University, Qatar): The method combines the geometrical features described in [24] through a logistic regression classifier. Those features are based on tortuosities, directions, curvatures, chain codes, and edge-based directional features.

QATAR-b method: This method uses the most discriminant features among those described earlier after training them on both the provided experimental dataset of the competition and on the QUWI dataset [25].

TEBESSA-a method (Tebessa and Annaba University, Algeria, Rouen University, France, Bahria University, Pakistan): See the TEBESSA-b method, which is described in Section 5.3.2.

TEBESSA-b method: See the TEBESSA-a method, which is described in Section 5.3.2.

TEBESSA-c method: This method is based on the combination of both types of features used by the previous two methods (multiscale edge-hinge features and multiscale run-length features [26]). The Manhattan distance metric is used to compare two document images.

5.4 Recently Published Methods Using the Competition Datasets

Several recently published writer identification methods used the benchmarking datasets of the writer identification competitions in order to measure their performance against other state-of-the-art methods. The following sections provide a brief description of each of these methods grouped according to the benchmarking dataset that was used.

5.4.1 *Methods Using the ICDAR 2011 Benchmarking Dataset*

CVL-IPK method: Fiel and Sablatnig [22] make use of textural features for writer identification. First, local features are computed on the normalized image using the SIFT. In addition, a vocabulary is created by clustering features using a GMM. At a next step, the Fisher kernels are applied on the visual vocabulary, which is then used to calculate a feature vector for each document image. The produced vector is used in order to determine the similarity between two handwriting documents.

Daniels 2013 method: Daniels and Baird [27] investigate the use of highly discriminating features for writer identification on offline handwritten text lines and passages. Five different categories of features are tested: slant and slant energy, skew, pixel distribution, curvature, and entropy.

Wu 2014 method: Wu *et al.* [28] propose a method which is composed of three stages, namely training, enrollment, and identification. For all stages, a segmentation of the handwriting image into word regions (WRs) is applied. SDs of WRs together with scale and orientation information (SOs) are calculated. In the training stage, an SD codebook is constructed. Concerning the enrollment stage, the SDs of the input handwriting are adopted in order to form an SD signature (SDS) using the SD codebook, and the SOs are utilized for generating an SOH. Finally, in the identification stage, the SDS and SOH of the input handwriting (query) are matched with the enrolled ones for identification.

Fiel 2015 method: Fiel and Sablatnig [29] propose a method, which uses CNNs for the generation of a feature vector for each writer, which is then compared with the precalculated vectors stored in the database. The feature vectors correspond to the output of the neurons of the second last fully connected layer since the last layer of the CNN, which basically performs the labeling of the input data, is not taken into account. These vectors are used for the distance measurement of different document images in order to describe the similarity of the handwriting.

5.4.2 *Methods Using the ICFHR 2012 Benchmarking Dataset*

Jain 2013 method: Jain and Doermann [21] present a new method for writer identification, which emulates the approach taken by forensic document examiners. It combines a novel feature, which uses contour gradients to capture local shape and curvature, with character segmentation to create a pseudo-alphabet for a given handwriting sample. A distance metric is then defined between elements of these alphabets, which captures character similarity between two handwriting samples.

Wu 2014 method: This method is described in Section 5.4.1.

Xiong 2015 method: Xiong *et al.* [30] propose a method which uses a combination of an SD together with a CDF and comprises two stages. The first stage concerns the creation of a codebook of local texture patterns by clustering a set of SDs extracted from the images. Using this codebook, the occurrence histograms are calculated in order to determine the similarities between different images. For each image, a candidate list of reference images is obtained. At the second stage, a refinement of the candidate list is performed using the CDF together with the SD.

5.4.3 *Methods Using the ICDAR 2013 Benchmarking Dataset*

Jain 2014 method: In this work, the authors make use of three different types of features: features produced from segmentation-free methods such as SIFT or SURF that extract features from interest points; edge-base features extracted from character contours; and features from allograph methods that aim to capture a character's shape and style. The Fisher vector is used for feature pooling, and a linear combination of the Fisher vector distances is then used to combine the features. A more detailed description can be found in [31].

Christlein 2014 method: Christlein *et al.* [32] propose a writer identification method, which uses GMM supervectors to encode the feature distribution of individual writers. Each supervector originates from an individual GMM, which has been adapted from a background model via a maximum-a-posteriori step followed by mixing the new statistics with the background model.

Fiel 2015 method: This method is described in Section 5.4.1.

Nicolaou 2015 method: The authors make use of Sparse Radial Sampling Local Binary Patterns (SRS-LBP), a variant of Local Binary Patters (LBP) for text-as-texture classification. The main contribution of the method concerns the introduction of sparse radial sampling of the circular patterns used for the LBP construction. They show that using a single local descriptor (SRS-LBP), a low-dimensional feature representation can be achieved which yields state-of-the-art performance. The interested reader should see [33].

Xiong 2015 method: This method is described in Section 5.4.2.

Christlein 2015 method: Christlein *et al.* [34] propose an allograph-based method for offline writer identification. The method uses contour-Zernike moments as local descriptors, which are encoded using vectors of locally aggregated descriptors (VLADs) and eventually compared using the cosine distance.

5.5 Benchmarking Datasets

It is imperative to use standard datasets in order to measure the accuracy of several writer identification methods. To this end, three different competitions were organized from 2011 until 2013 with the aim to record recent advances in the field of writer identification for Latin documents. For each of these competitions, a new benchmarking dataset was created differing mainly on the number of writers that contributed to the creation of the dataset as well as the amount of text that was required to be written by the authors. An overview of the benchmarking datasets is presented in Table 5.1 and a more detailed description is provided in the following sections.

5.5.1 Benchmarking Dataset of the ICDAR 2011 Competition

The ICDAR 2011 benchmarking dataset was created with the help of 26 writers who were asked to copy eight pages that contain text in four

Table 5.1. Overview of the benchmarking datasets.

Benchmarking dataset	No. of documents	No. of writers	No. of docs per writer	Languages	Public link
ICDAR 2011	208	26	8	English, French, German, Greek	[6]
ICFHR 2012	400	100	4	English, Greek	[7]
ICDAR 2013	1,000	250	4	English, Greek	[8]

languages (English, French, German, and Greek). All images were binary and did not include any nontext elements (lines, drawings, etc.; see Figure 5.1) The benchmarking data is publicly available and can be found at [6].

5.5.2 Benchmarking Dataset of the ICFHR 2012 Competition

The ICFHR 2012 benchmarking dataset was created with the help of 100 writers who were asked to copy four parts of text in two languages (two in English and two in Greek; see Figure 5.2). These parts of text were the same for all writers. Among all documents, only the Greek documents were written in the native language of the writer. We should also note that the number of text lines that were produced by the writers ranged between 3 and 6. The benchmarking dataset is publicly available and can be found in [7].

5.5.3 Benchmarking Dataset of the ICDAR 2013 Competition

The ICDAR 2013 benchmarking dataset was created with the help of 250 writers who were asked to copy four parts of text in two languages (two in English and two in Greek; see Figure 5.3). The total number of document images of the benchmarking dataset was 1,000. The benchmarking data-set is publicly available and can be found in [8]. Among all documents, only the Greek documents were written in the native language of the writer. It should be noted that the number of text lines that were produced by the writers ranged between 2 and 6.

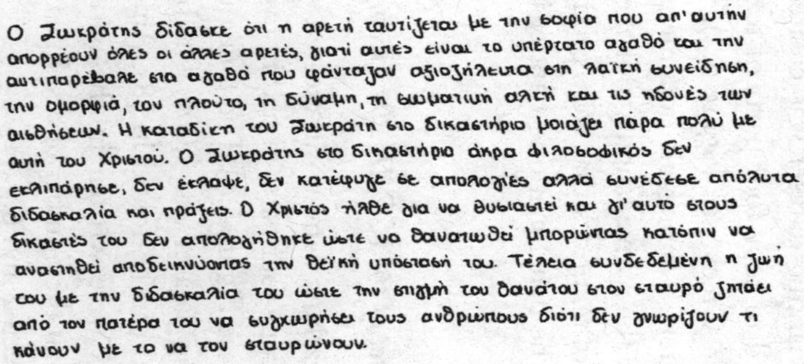

Ο Σωκράτης δίδαξε ότι η αρετή ταυτίζεται με την σοφία που απ' αυτή απορρέουν όλες οι άλλες αρετές, διότι αυτές είναι το υπέρτατο αγαθό και την αντιπαραβάλε στα αγαθά που φαίνεται αξιοζήλευτα επι λατίν ευνείδησιν, την σωματική, του πλούτο, τη πλάστα, τη δύναμη, τη σωματική αρετή και τα ηδονές των αισθήσεων. Η καταβική του Σωκράτη στο δικαστήριο μοιάζει παρα πολύ με αυτή του Χριστού. Ο Σωκράτης στο δικαστήριο άφρα διλογδικός δεν εξελίχθηκε, δεν εσκαψε, δεν καταψυφ' σε απολογίες αλλά συνέδεσε απόλυτα διδασκαλία και πράξεν. Ο Χριστός ήλθε για να θυσιαστεί και δι' αυτό στους δικαστές του δεν απολογήθηκε ώστε να θανατωθεί μπορούσας καταπίν να ανασταβεί αποδεινύοντας την θεϊκή υπόσταση του. Τέλεια ευνδεδεμένη η ζωή σου με την διδασκαλία του ώστε την στιγμή του θανάτου στου σταυρό ήματοι από τον πατέρα του να ευχχωριες τους ανθρώπους διότι δεν χωριζουν τι κάνουν με το να του σταυρώνουν.

(a)

Democritus was an Ancient Greek philosopher born in Abdera in the north of Greece. He was the most prolific, and ultimately the most influential, of the philosophers; His atomic theory may be regarded as the culmination of early Greek thought. His exact contributions are difficult to disentangle from his mentor Leucippus, as they are often mentioned together in texts. Their hypothesis on atoms is remarkably similar to modern science, and avoided many of the errors found in their contemporaries. Largely ignored in Athens, Democritus was nevertheless well-known to his fellow northern-born philosopher Aristotle. Plato is said to have disliked him so much that he wished all his books to be burned. Many consider Democritus to be the father of modern science. Democritus followed in the tradition of Leucippus, who seems to have come from Miletus, and he carried on the scientific rationalist philosophy associated with that city.

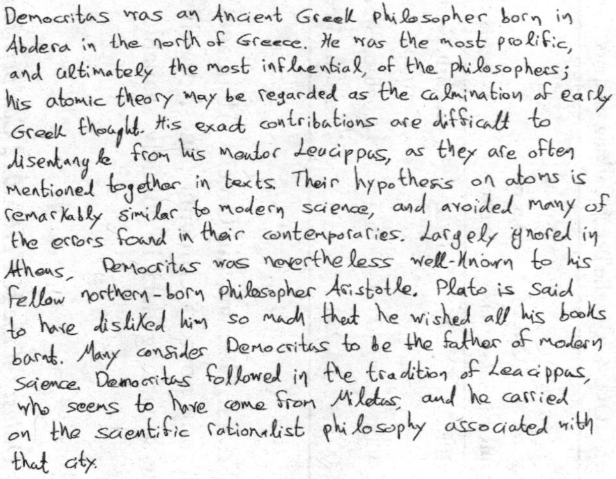

(b)

Figure 5.1.   Image samples from the ICDAR 2011 benchmarking dataset written in (a) Greek and (b) English languages.

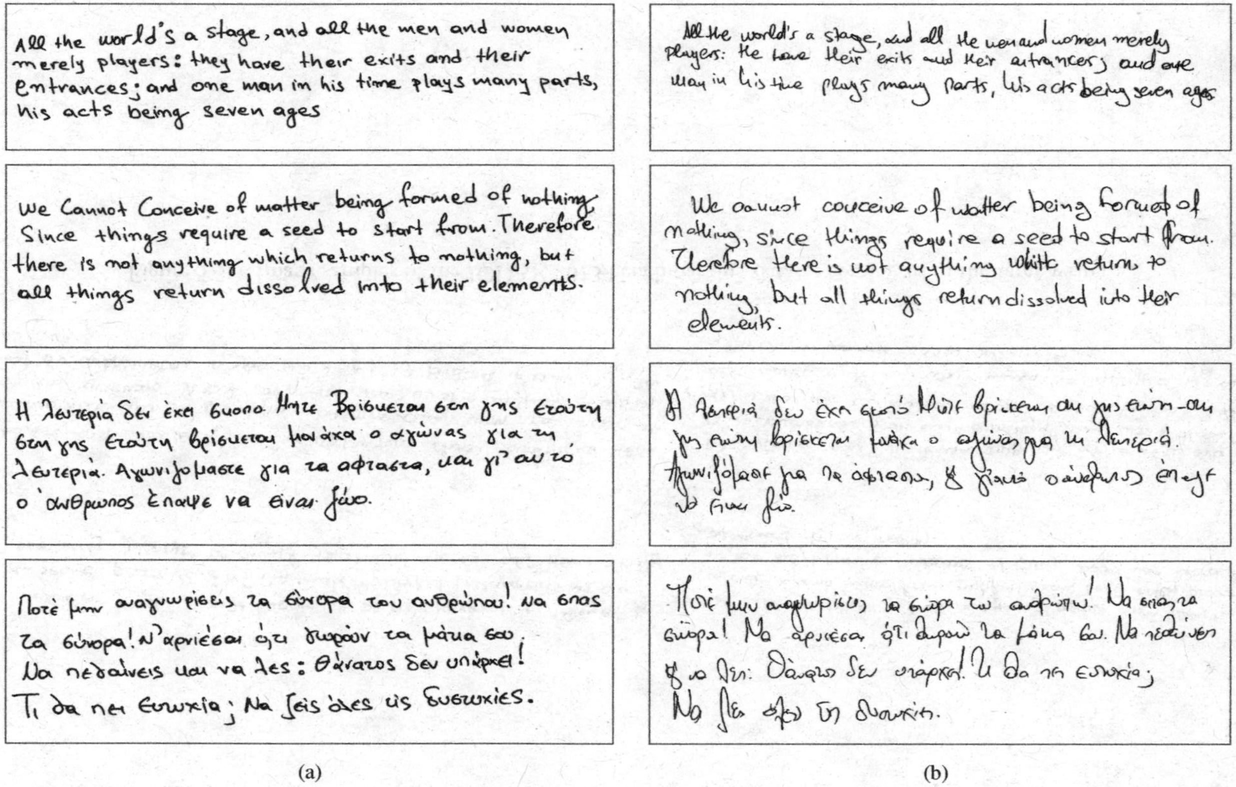

(b)

(a)

Figure 5.2. Image samples of the ICFHR 2012 benchmarking dataset from two different writers (a), (b) in English and Greek languages.

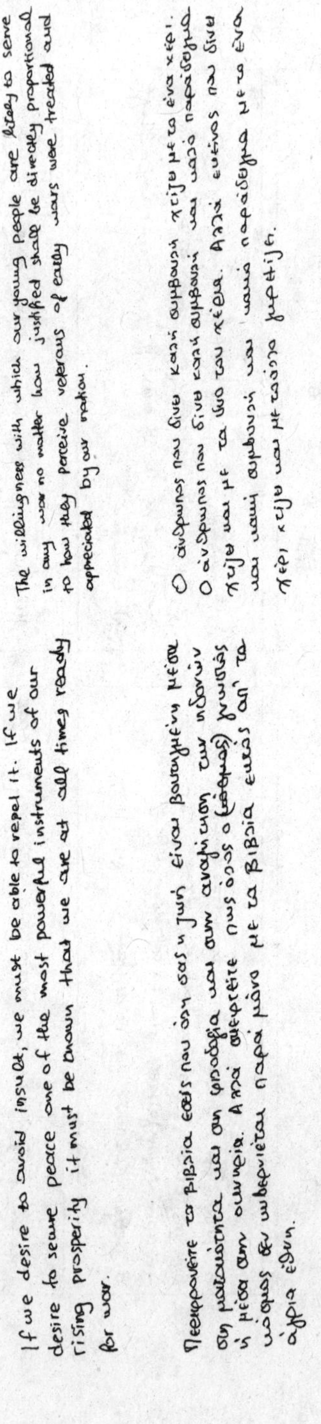

Figure 5.3.   Image samples of the ICDAR 2013 benchmarking dataset coming from the same writer.

5.6 Evaluation Methodology

In order to measure the accuracy of a writer identification method, we use the **soft TOP-N** and **hard TOP-N** criteria. For every document image of a benchmarking dataset, we calculate the distance to all other document images of the dataset. Then, we sort the results from the most similar to the less similar document image.

For the soft TOP-N criterion, we consider a correct hit when **at least one** document image of the same writer is included in the N most similar document images. Concerning the hard TOP-N criterion, we consider a correct hit when **all N** most similar document images are written by the same writer. For all document images of a benchmarking dataset, we count the correct hits. The ratio of the total number of correct hits to the total number of the document images in the benchmarking dataset corresponds to the TOP-N accuracy. The values of N used for the soft criterion are 1, 2, 5, and 10. The values of N used for the hard criterion are not fixed and are related to the total number of documents that were written by a single writer.

5.7 Evaluation Results

The performance of all participating methods was evaluated using the benchmarking dataset of each competition in terms of the soft TOP-N and the hard TOP-N criterion (see Section 5.6). In the following sections, we present the results of each competition together with the different scenarios that were applied.

5.7.1 *ICDAR 2011 Evaluation Results*

Two different scenarios were applied for the evaluation of the performance of the participating methods as well as for recently published methods described in Section 5.4.1. According to the first scenario (S1), the whole images of the benchmarking dataset were used. In the second scenario (S2), the images of the benchmarking dataset were cropped, preserving only the first two text lines with the aim to check the efficiency of the submitted methods when decreasing the amount of available information.

For both scenarios, we calculated the performance using the entire dataset as well as using each language independently. Tables 5.2 and 5.3 summarize the results with respect to the soft criterion for the entire dataset (A) as well as for each language independently ((E)nglish, (GR)eek, (F)rench, (GE)rman) on S1 and S2 scenarios, respectively. The best performance for each column is highlighted in bold. Indicative results for the hard criterion with respect to S1 and S2 scenarios are shown in Tables 5.4 and 5.5, respectively. The best overall performance among the methods participating to the competition, taking into account both scenarios, was achieved by the TSINGHUA method. Figure 5.4 presents experimental results using the soft and hard criteria on the entire dataset for scenario S1, whereas Figure 5.5 shows the same information for scenario S2 (the winning method is marked with a * symbol). It should be noted that the methods participating to the competition appear on the left side of the figures, whereas recently published methods which made use of the dataset appear on the right side of the graphs.

The results of the competition indicate that there is a significant degradation in the performance of all participating methods from S1 to S2 scenario. It is evident from Table 5.2 that the recently published methods achieve comparable results with the best participating methods to the competition. Additionally, Table 5.3 shows that the recently published methods perform better than the participating methods on S2 scenario. When considering the hard criterion (Tables 5.4 and 5.5), it is clear that the Wu 2014 recently published method outperforms all methods and the majority of recently published methods perform better than the participating methods to the competition.

5.7.2 ICFHR 2012 Evaluation Results

In order to evaluate the performance of the participating methods described in Section 5.3.2 as well as the recently published methods presented in Section 5.4.2, we used the soft TOP-N and hard TOP-N criteria (Section 5.6). The soft TOP-N was measured on the entire dataset (A), on the English subset of document images (E), and on the Greek subset of document images (GR). Table 5.6 summarizes the results for the soft

Table 5.2.   ICDAR 2011 — Evaluation results for the soft criterion on scenario S1 for (A)ll, (GR)eek, (E)nglish, (F)rench, and (GE)rman documents.

Method	TOP-1					TOP-2					TOP-5					TOP-10				
	A	GR	E	F	GE	A	GR	E	F	GE	A	GR	E	F	GE	A	GR	E	F	GE
ECNU	84.6	19.2	15.4	23.1	46.2	86.5	19.2	15.4	23.1	46.2	88.0	19.2	15.4	23.1	46.2	88.9	21.2	17.3	26.9	46.2
QUQA-a	90.9	76.9	78.9	94.2	86.5	94.2	86.5	84.6	96.2	90.4	98.1	96.2	96.2	96.2	98.1	99.0	98.1	96.2	100.0	100.0
QUQA-b	98.1	90.4	100.0	98.1	100.0	98.6	90.4	100.0	98.1	100.0	99.5	92.3	100.0	100.0	100.0	100.0	94.2	100.0	100.0	100.0
TSINGHUA	99.5	92.3	96.2	96.2	100.0	99.5	94.2	96.2	98.1	100.0	100.0	98.1	98.1	100.0	100.0	100.0	100.0	100.0	100.0	100.0
GWU	93.8	80.8	84.6	96.2	92.3	96.2	86.5	88.5	96.2	94.2	98.1	90.4	96.2	100.0	94.2	99.0	94.2	98.1	100.0	100.0
CS-UMD	99.5	96.2	98.1	100.0	100.0	99.5	96.2	100.0	100.0	100.0	99.5	96.2	100.0	100.0	100.0	99.5	96.2	100.0	100.0	100.0
TEBESSA	98.6	84.6	96.2	92.3	94.2	100.0	88.5	96.2	94.2	98.1	100.0	90.4	98.1	100.0	100.0	100.0	94.2	100.0	100.0	100.0
MCS-NUST	99.0	94.2	96.2	100.0	100.0	99.5	94.2	96.2	100.0	100.0	99.5	96.2	98.1	100.0	100.0	99.5	96.2	100.0	100.0	100.0
CVL-IPK	99.5	—	—	—	—	100.0	—	—	—	—	100.0	—	—	—	—	100.0	—	—	—	—
Daniels *et al.* [27]	97.1	90.4	94.2	94.2	100.0	99.5	94.2	98.1	98.1	100.0	100.0	100.0	100.0	100.0	100.0	100.0	100.0	100.0	100.0	100.0
Wu *et al.* [28]	99.5	96.2	100.0	100.0	100.0	—	—	—	—	—	100.0	100.0	100.0	100.0	100.0	100.0	100.0	100.0	100.0	100.0
Fiel and Sablatnig [29]	99.5	—	—	—	—	100.0	—	—	—	—	100.0	—	—	—	—	100.0	—	—	—	—

Table 5.3. ICDAR 2011 — Evaluation results for the soft criterion on scenario S2 for (A)ll, (GR)eek, (E)nglish, (F)rench, and (GE)rman documents.

Method	TOP-1					TOP-2					TOP-5					TOP-10				
	A	GR	E	F	GE	A	GR	E	F	GE	A	GR	E	F	GE	A	GR	E	F	GE
ECNU	65.9	11.5	13.5	21.2	46.2	71.6	15.4	15.4	21.2	46.2	81.7	19.2	15.4	23.1	46.2	86.5	23.1	19.2	26.9	46.2
QUQA-a	74.0	44.2	55.8	71.2	51.9	81.7	51.9	67.3	78.9	67.3	91.8	73.1	75.0	86.5	88.5	96.2	90.4	82.7	94.2	92.3
QUQA-b	67.3	34.6	63.5	44.2	48.1	79.8	55.8	69.2	63.5	67.3	91.8	76.9	90.4	84.6	84.6	94.7	80.8	96.2	92.3	88.5
TSINGHUA	90.9	51.9	76.9	84.6	80.8	93.8	**71.2**	**90.4**	**90.4**	**90.4**	98.6	**98.1**	96.2	96.2	96.2	99.5	98.1	100.0	100.0	96.2
GWU	74.0	42.3	50.0	69.2	57.7	81.7	46.2	57.7	76.9	69.2	91.4	65.4	69.2	88.5	86.5	95.2	76.9	82.7	92.3	92.3
CS-UMD	66.8	40.4	44.2	73.1	59.6	75.5	44.2	50.0	80.8	67.3	83.7	67.3	69.2	90.4	84.6	89.9	76.9	82.7	96.2	90.4
TEBESSA	87.5	42.3	69.2	71.2	63.5	92.8	63.5	84.6	75.0	78.9	97.6	80.8	88.5	88.5	90.4	99.5	92.3	100.0	98.1	94.2
MCS-NUST	82.2	55.8	67.3	78.9	65.4	91.8	69.2	80.8	88.5	82.7	96.6	84.6	88.5	94.2	92.3	97.6	94.2	92.3	98.1	96.2
CVL-IPK	91.3	–	–	–	–	94.2	–	–	–	–	97.6	–	–	–	–	99.5	–	–	–	–
Daniels et al. [27]	–	–	–	–	–	–	–	–	–	–	–	–	–	–	–	–	–	–	–	–
Wu et al. [28]	**95.2**	**80.8**	**88.5**	**98.1**	92.3	–	–	–	–	–	**99.5**	96.2	**98.1**	100.0	100.0	100.0	100.0	100.0	100.0	100.0
Fiel and Sablatnig [29]	94.7	–	–	–	–	97.6	–	–	–	–	98.1	–	–	–	–	99.5	–	–	–	–

Table 5.4. ICDAR 2011 — Evaluation results for the hard criterion on scenario S1.

Method	TOP-2	TOP-5	TOP-7
ECNU	51.0	2.9	0.0
QUQA-a	76.4	42.3	20.2
QUQA-b	92.3	77.4	41.4
TSINGHUA	95.2	84.1	41.4
GWU	80.3	44.2	20.2
CS-UMD	91.8	77.9	22.1
TEBESSA	97.1	81.3	50.0
MCS-NUST	93.3	78.9	38.9
CVL-IPK	96.2	89.9	55.3
Daniels *et al.* [27]	92.8	69.2	31.3
Wu *et al.* [28]	**98.6**	**91.4**	**63.9**
Fiel and Sablatnig [29]	**98.6**	87.0	52.4

Table 5.5. ICDAR 2011 — Evaluation results for the hard criterion on scenario S2.

Method	TOP-2	TOP-5	TOP-7
ECNU	39.4	2.9	0.0
QUQA-a	52.4	15.9	3.4
QUQA-b	47.6	22.6	6.3
TSINGHUA	79.8	48.6	12.5
GWU	51.4	20.2	6.3
CS-UMD	51.9	22.1	3.4
TEBESSA	76.0	34.1	14.4
MCS-NUST	71.6	35.6	11.1
CVL-IPK	81.3	47.1	15.4
Daniels *et al.* [27]	—	—	—
Wu *et al.* [28]	**88.5**	**63.0**	**31.3**
Fiel and Sablatnig [29]	84.6	53.8	10.1

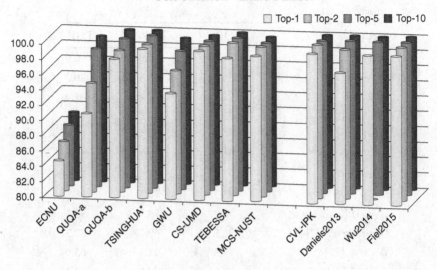

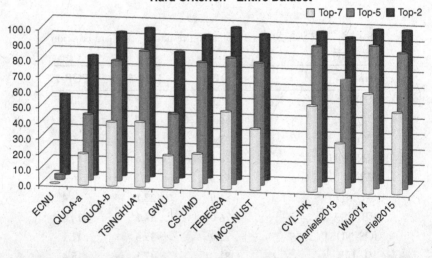

Figure 5.4.   ICDAR 2011 — Experimental results for the soft and hard criteria (S1 scenario) on the entire dataset.

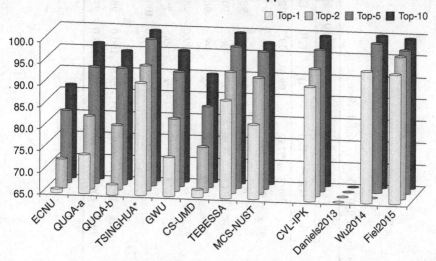

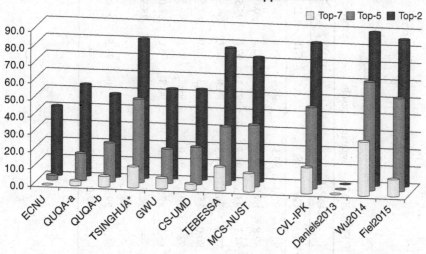

Figure 5.5.   ICDAR 2011 — Experimental results for the soft and hard criteria (S2 scenario) on the entire dataset.

Table 5.6.   ICFHR 2012 — Evaluation results using the soft criterion for (A)ll, (GR)eek, (E)nglish, documents.

Method	TOP-1			TOP-2			TOP-5			TOP-10		
	A	GR	E	A	GR	E	A	GR	E	A	GR	E
TEBESSA-a	92.3	92.0	89.5	96.5	95.0	96.0	98.8	98.5	97.0	99.0	99.0	98.5
TEBESSA-b	89.8	85.5	83.0	94.3	93.5	90.0	97.8	95.5	96.0	98.8	99.0	97.0
TEBESSA-c	94.5	93.5	91.5	97.3	97.0	95.5	99.3	99.5	97.5	99.3	99.5	98.0
QATAR-a	70.3	76.0	53.5	80.8	86.0	66.5	91.8	94.5	85.0	95.3	96.5	90.0
QATAR-b	80.0	85.5	72.5	87.3	90.0	82.5	95.0	96.0	92.5	98.0	98.5	96.5
TSINGHUA	92.8	90.0	94.0	95.8	94.0	94.5	97.8	98.5	95.5	98.3	99.0	98.0
HANNOVER	85.5	87.5	82.0	90.3	93.0	88.0	95.3	98.5	91.5	97.3	99.5	95.0
Jain and Doermann [21]	—	96.5	98.0	—	99.0	98.5	—	—	—	—	100.0	100.0
Wu et al.[28]	98.0	99.0	95.5	99.0	99.5	96.0	99.5	100.0	98.0	99.8	100.0	98.5
Xiong et al. [30]	96.8	97.0	94.0	—	—	—	99.3	100.0	97.0	99.3	100.0	97.5

Table 5.7. ICFHR 2012 — Evaluation results using the hard criterion.

Method	TOP-2	TOP-3
TEBESSA-a	57.5	38.0
TEBESSA-b	57.5	29.3
TEBESSA-c	65.0	37.8
QATAR-a	32.3	11.3
QATAR-b	34.0	15.3
TSINGHUA	51.5	27.3
HANNOVER	41.5	22.8
Jain and Doermann [21]	—	—
Wu *et al.* [28]	65.3	38.0
Xiong *et al.* [30]	**67.8**	**39.8**

criterion, whereas Table 5.7 presents the corresponding results using the hard criterion. A graphical representation of the soft and the hard criteria on the entire dataset is shown in Figure 5.6. The best overall performance among the methods participating to the competition was achieved by the TEBESSA-c method (marked with a * symbol on Figure 5.6).

Several remarks can be made for the methods participating to the competition after a careful analysis of the experimental results. The winning method (TEBESSA-c) outperforms all other participating methods to the competition in most cases. Another remark is that none of the participating methodologies achieves 100% accuracy even for the TOP-10 criterion. This is because we have document images of different writers with very similar writing styles. The accuracy of the hard TOP-3 criterion is very low (<40%). We can thus claim that participating methods are far from succeeding to cluster all documents provided by the same writer at the top of the ranking list.

Concerning the recently published methods, it is clear that all perform better than the methods participating to the competition, with the Wu 2014 method performing better than all other techniques in most cases for the soft TOP-N criterion and the Xiong 2015 achieving the best performance in all categories of the hard criterion.

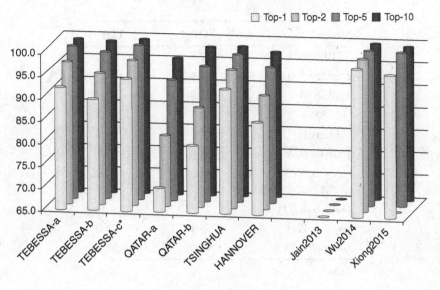

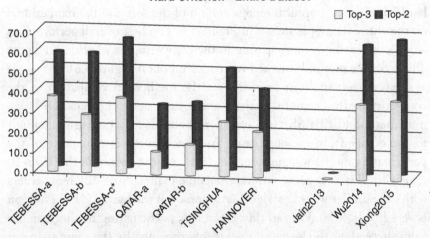

Figure 5.6.   ICFHR 2012 — Experimental results for the soft and hard criteria on the entire dataset.

5.7.3 ICDAR 2013 Evaluation Results

The performance of the competition participants as well as the recently published methods presented in Section 5.4.3 was also measured in terms of the soft and hard TOP-N criteria. Table 5.8 summarizes the

Table 5.8. ICDAR 2013 — Evaluation results using the soft criterion for (A)ll, (GR)eek, and (E)nglish, documents.

Method	TOP-1			TOP-2			TOP-5			TOP-10		
	A	GR	E	A	GR	E	A	GR	E	A	GR	E
CS-UMD-a	95.1	95.6	94.6	97.7	98.2	97.0	98.6	98.6	98.4	99.1	99.2	98.8
CS-UMD-b	95.0	95.2	94.4	97.2	97.6	96.6	98.6	98.8	98.4	99.2	99.0	99.0
CS-UMD-c	85.5	86.0	86.4	90.9	90.6	90.4	95.0	94.6	93.2	96.8	96.4	96.0
CVL-IPK	90.9	88.4	91.4	93.6	92.0	94.2	97.0	96.8	95.8	98.0	97.8	97.2
HANNOVER-a	86.9	86.4	84.6	91.9	91.2	88.6	95.4	95.2	92.0	97.0	97.4	94.0
HANNOVER-b	91.5	90.2	85.6	94.2	92.8	90.6	97.0	95.6	93.6	98.0	97.4	95.6
HIT-ICG	94.8	93.8	92.2	96.7	96.4	94.6	98.0	97.2	96.4	98.3	97.8	96.8
QATAR-a	54.8	58.8	50.0	67.3	66.6	64.2	80.8	79.6	78.0	88.3	85.8	85.4
QATAR-b	78.4	78.8	75.8	85.8	84.6	84.6	91.5	91.2	90.4	95.1	94.4	93.6
TEBESSA-a	90.3	91.0	86.0	94.4	94.0	91.6	96.7	96.8	94.4	98.3	97.8	96.0
TEBESSA-b	90.1	87.2	88.2	93.4	92.0	90.8	97.0	96.4	94.6	97.9	97.8	96.2
TEBESSA-c	93.4	92.6	91.2	96.1	96.0	93.4	97.8	98.0	96.2	98.5	98.4	96.6
Jain and Doermann [21]	—	99.2	97.4	—	99.6	97.8	—	99.8	98.6	—	99.8	98.8
Christlein et al. [32]	97.1	—	—	—	—	—	—	—	—	—	—	—
Fiel and Sablatnig [29]	88.5	—	—	92.2	—	—	96.0	—	—	98.3	—	—
Nicolaou et al. [33]	98.5	98.4	97.2	99.1	99.2	97.4	99.5	99.4	98.2	99.6	99.8	99.0
Xiong et al. [30]	96.2	96.2	94.0	—	—	—	98.6	98.4	96.4	99.0	99.0	97.2
Christlein et al. [34]	99.4	—	—	—	—	—	—	—	—	—	—	—

Table 5.9. ICDAR 2013 — Evaluation results using the hard criterion.

Method	TOP-2	TOP-3
CS-UMD-a	19.6	7.1
CS-UMD-b	20.2	8.4
CS-UMD-c	21.2	5.7
CVL-IPK	44.8	24.5
HANNOVER-a	50.0	26.1
HANNOVER-b	54.3	27.3
HIT-ICG	63.2	36.5
QATAR-a	11.8	3.9
QATAR-b	34.6	16.5
TEBESSA-a	58.2	33.2
TEBESSA-b	55.5	29.5
TEBESSA-c	62.6	36.5
Jain and Doermann [21]	—	—
Christlein *et al.* [32]	42.8	23.8
Fiel and Sablatnig [29]	40.5	15.8
Nicolaou *et al.* [33]	63.8	38.3
Xiong *et al.* [30]	63.5	35.0
Christlein *et al.* [34]	**81.0**	**61.8**

results for the soft criterion, whereas Table 5.9 presents the corresponding results using the hard criterion. A graphical representation of the soft and the hard criteria on the entire dataset is shown in Figure 5.7. The best overall performance among the methods participating to the competition was achieved by the CS-UMD-a method (marked with a * symbol in Figure 5.7).

General remarks, for the participating methods to the competition, can be made after analyzing the experimental results. A first remark is that the winning method (CS-UMD-a) outperforms all other methods on the TOP-1, TOP-2 cases of the soft criterion. However, this method performs poorly on the two cases of the hard criterion. Also, none of the participating methods manages to achieve 100% accuracy on any criterion. In fact, the highest accuracy achieved is 99.2% for the soft TOP-10

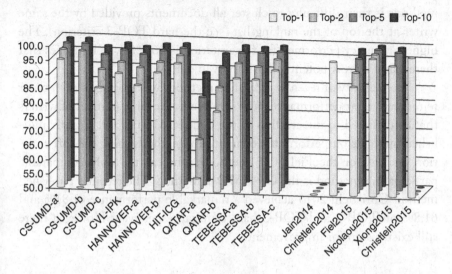

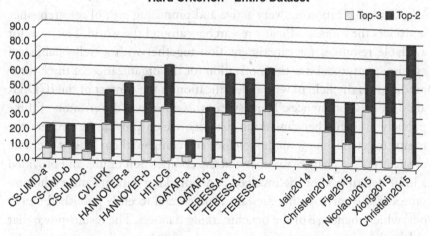

Figure 5.7. ICDAR 2013 — Experimental results for the soft and hard criteria on the entire dataset.

criterion when using the entire dataset. This behavior can be justified due to the large number of different writers included in the benchmarking dataset as well as to the similarity of the writing styles among different writers. The HIT-ICG method outpefrorms all other methods in all cases of the hard criterion. It seems that the main drawback of all submitted methods is their difficulty to cluster all documents provided by the same writer at the top of the ranking list (see the hard TOP-3 criterion). The highest accuracy performed for this criterion is 36.5%, which implies that there exists a great potential for improvement.

The majority of recently published methods used this dataset in order to measure their performance, probably due to the large number of writers that contributed to the creation of the dataset. Most of the recently published methods outperform the competition methods using the soft criterion (except for the Fiel 2015 method), whereas the only comparable participating method is the CS-UMD-a method. The recently published method Christlein 2015 achieved a remarkable performance of 81% and 61.8% on TOP-2 and TOP-3 hard criteria, respectively. However, there still exists room for improvement.

5.8 Conclusions

Writer identification is a very active and promising area of research since it attracts the interest of many researchers around the world. The need for available resources for experimentation together with a well-established evaluation protocol was the motivation for the organization of three competitions on the field of writer identification in the context of the ICDAR and ICFHR conferences. The result of this effort was the creation of three publicly available benchmarking datasets, which provide researchers the means to establish new methodologies and compare them against the state of the art. This chapter summarized the competition results and provided a brief description of the involved benchmarking datasets and evaluation protocol, the participating methods, and several recently published methods, which made use of the benchmarking datasets. The results prove that although an enormous effort has been made toward the solution of the problem, there is still potential for improvement. The main difficulty of all methods concerns their inability to cluster all documents of the same writer among the TOP-N choices (hard TOP-N criterion). Future work should focus on the use of larger datasets (with respect to the number of writers) as well as on testing methods in cases where the writing material is very small (e.g., a few words).

References

1. G. Louloudis, N. Stamatopoulos, and B. Gatos, "ICDAR 2011 writer identification contest," in *Proceedings of the 11th International Conference on Document Analysis and Recognition* (ICDAR' 2011), Beijing, China, pp. 1475–1479, September 18–21, 2011.
2. G. Louloudis, B. Gatos, and N. Stamatopoulos, "ICFHR2012 competition on writer identification — Challenge 1: Latin/Greek documents," in *Proceedings of the 13th International Conference on Frontiers in Handwriting Recognition* (ICFHR' 2012), Bari, Italy, pp. 825–830, September 18–20, 2012.
3. G. Louloudis, B. Gatos, N. Stamatopoulos, and A. Papandreou, "ICDAR 2013 competition on writer identification," in *Proceedings of the 12th International Conference on Document Analysis and Recognition* (ICDAR' 2013), Washington, DC, USA, pp. 1397–1401, August 25–28, 2013.
4. S. Srihari, S. Cha, H. Arora, and S. Lee, "Individuality of handwriting," *Journal of Forensic Science*, vol. 47, no. 4, pp. 856–872, 2002.
5. L. Schomaker, "Advances in writer identification and verification," *Proceedings of the 9th International Conference on Document Analysis and Recognition* (ICDAR'2007), Parana, Brazil, pp. 1268–1273, September 23–26, 2007.
6. ICDAR 2011 benchmarking dataset: http://users.iit.demokritos.gr/~louloud/Writer_Identification_Contest/Benchmarking_Dataset.rar.
7. ICFHR 2012 benchmarking dataset: http://users.iit.demokritos.gr/~louloud/WritIdentCont2012/benchmarking_dataset_2012.rar.
8. ICDAR 2013 benchmarking dataset: http://users.iit.demokritos.gr/~louloud/ICDAR2013WriterIdentificationComp/icdar2013_benchmarking_dataset.rar.
9. A. Schlapbach, M. Liwicki, and H. Bunke, "A writer identification system for on-line whiteboard data," *Pattern Recognition Journal*, vol. 41, no. 7, pp. 2381–2397, 2008.
10. L. Schomaker and M. Bulacu, "Automatic writer identification using connected-component contours and edge-based features of uppercase western script," *IEEE Transactions on Pattern Analysis and Machine Intelligence*, vol. 26, no. 6, pp. 787–798, 2004.
11. C. Djeddi, I. Siddiqi, L. Souici-Meslati, and A. Ennaji, "Text-independent writer recognition using multi-script handwritten texts," *Pattern Recognition Letters*, vol. 34, no. 10, pp. 1196–1202, 2013.
12. E.N. Zois and V. Anastasopoulos, "Morphological waveform coding for writer identification," *Pattern Recognition Journal*, vol. 33, no. 3, pp. 385–398, 2000.

13. M. Bulacu and L. Schomaker, "Text-independent writer identification and verification using textural and allographic features," *IEEE Transactions on Pattern Analysis and Machine Intelligence*, vol. 29, no. 4, pp. 701–717, 2007.

14. S. Al-Ma'adeed, E. Mohammed, and D. Al Kassis, "Writer identification using edge-based directional probability distribution features for Arabic words," *IEEE International Conference on Computer Systems and Applications* (AICCSA' 2008), Doha, Qatar, pp. 582–590, March 31–April 4, 2008.

15. S. Al-Ma'adeed, A. Al-Kurbi, A. Al-Muslih, R. Al-Qahtani, and H. Al Kubisi, "Writer identification of Arabic handwriting documents using grapheme features," *IEEE International Conference on Computer Systems and Applications* (AICCSA' 2008), Doha, Qatar, pp. 923–924, March 31–April 4, 2008.

16. L. Xu, X. Ding, L. Peng, and X. Li, "An improved method based on weighted grid micro-structure feature for text-independent writer recognition," *Proceedings of the 11th International Conference on Document Analysis and Recognition* (ICDAR' 2011), Beijing, China, pp. 638–642, September 18–21, 2011.

17. http://www.kaggle.com/c/WIC2011/Data.

18. R. Jain and D. Doermann, "Offline writer identification using K-adjacent segments," in *Proceedings of the 11th International Conference on Document Analysis and Recognition* (ICDAR'2011), Beijing, China, pp. 769–773, September 18–21, 2011.

19. C. Djeddi and L. Souici-Meslati, "A texture based approach for Arabic writer identification and verification," in *Proceedings of the International Conference on Machine and Web Intelligence* (ICMWI' 2010), Algiers, Algeria, pp. 115–120, October 3–5, 2010.

20. A. Hassaïne, S. Al-Ma'adeed, J. Mohamad Alja'am, A.M. Jaoua, and A. Bouridane, "The ICDAR2011 Arabic writer identification contest," in *Proceedings of the 11th International Conference on Document Analysis and Recognition* (ICDAR'2011), Beijing, China, pp. 1470–1474, September 18–21, 2011.

21. R. Jain and D. Doermann, "Writer identification using an alphabet of contour gradient descriptors," in *Proceedings of the 12th International Conference on Document Analysis and Recognition* (ICDAR' 2013), Washington, DC, USA, pp. 550–554, August 25–28, 2013.

22. S. Fiel and R. Sablatnig, "Writer identification and writer retrieval using the Fisher vector on visual vocabularies," in *Proceedings of the 12th International Conference on Document Analysis and Recognition* (ICDAR'2013), Washington, DC, USA, pp. 545–549, August 25–28, 2013.

23. K.H. Steinke, M. Gehrke, and R. Dzido, "Writer recognition by combining local and global methods," in *Proceedings of the 2nd International Congress on Image and Signal Processing* (CISP'2009), pp. 1–6, 2009.

24. A. Hassaïne, S. Al-Maadeed, and A. Bouridane, "A set of geometrical features for writer identification," *Neural Information Processing, Lecture Notes in Computer Science*, vol. 7667, pp. 584–591. Berlin, Heidelberg, Springer, 2012.

25. S. Al-Maadeed, W. Ayouby, A. Hassaine, and J. Aljaam, "QUWI: An Arabic and English handwriting dataset for offline writer identification," in *Proceedings of the 13th International Conference on Frontiers in Handwriting Recognition* (ICFHR'2012), Bari, Italy, pp. 746–751, September 18–20, 2012.

26. C. Djeddi, L. Souici-Meslati, and A. Ennaji, "Writer recognition on Arabic handwritten documents," in *Proceedings of the 5th International Conference on Image and Signal Processing* (ICISP'2012), *Lecture Notes in Computer Science*, vol. 7340, pp. 493–501. Berlin, Heidelberg, Springer, 2012.

27. Z. Daniels and H. Baird, "Discriminating features for writer identification," in *Proceedings of the 12th International Conference on Document Analysis and Recognition* (ICDAR'2013), Washington, DC, USA, pp. 1385–1389, August 25–28, 2013.

28. X. Wu, Y. Tang, and W. Bu, "Offline text-independent writer identification based on scale invariant feature transform," *IEEE Transactions on Information Forensics and Security*, vol. 9, no. 3, pp. 526–536, 2014.

29. S. Fiel and R. Sablatnig, "Writer identification and retrieval using a convolutional neural network," in *Proceedings of the 16th International Conference on Computer Analysis of Image and Patterns* (CAIP'2015), *Lecture Notes in Computer Science*, vol. 9257, pp. 26–37. Berlin, Heidelberg, Springer, 2015.

30. Y.J. Xiong, Y. Wen, P.S.P. Wang, and Y. Lu, "Text-independent writer identification using SIFT descriptor and contour-directional feature," in *Proceedings of the 13th International Conference on Document Analysis and Recognition* (ICDAR'2015), Tunis, Tunisia, pp. 91–95, August 23–26, 2015.

31. R. Jain and D. Doermann, "Combining local features for offline writer identification," in *Proceedings of the 14th International Conference on Frontiers in Handwriting Recognition* (ICFHR'2014), Heraklion, Greece, pp. 583–588, September 1–4, 2014.

32. V. Christlein, D. Bernecker, F. Honig, and E. Angelopoulou, "Writer identification and verification using GMM supervectors," *IEEE Winter Conference on Applications of Computer Vision* (WACV'2014), Steamboat Springs, CO, USA, pp. 998–1005, March 24–26, 2014.

33. A. Nicolaou, A.D. Bagdanov, M. Liwicki, and D. Karatzas, "Sparse radial sampling LBP for writer identification," in *Proceedings of the 13th*

International Conferences on Document Analysis and Recognition (ICDAR' 2015), pp. 716–720, 2015.

34. V. Christlein, D. Bernecker, and E. Angelopoulou, "Writer identification using VLAD encoded contour-Zernike moments," in *Proceedings of the 13th International Conference on Document Analysis and Recognition* (ICDAR' 2015), Tunis, Tunisia, pp. 906–910, August 23–26, 2015.

Chapter 6

Arabic Writer Identification Using AHTID/MW and KHATT Database

Fouad Slimane and Sameh Awaida

6.1 Introduction

Handwritten text can serve as a biometric identifier and provide forensic information in a similar way to someone's face or fingerprints [1]. Typically, experts are consulted to examine or verify the authorship of the handwritten text. However, searching to identify a particular individual within a large data corpus may make a manual inspection unfeasible [2]. Writer identification refers to the task of determining the authorship of a sample of handwriting from a set of writers and samples. This has been an active research area during the last decade [3, 4]. Numerous identification systems producing good results have been reported in the literature. There are two types of writer identification procedures — online and offline — depending on the type of database. Offline writer identification relies solely on the handwritten text, generally from scanned documents, without any additional information. However, online writer identification is used when the database contains temporal information about the text's formation.

Readers are referred to [5] for a comprehensive survey of the writer identification of Arabic text and recent advances in the field of writer identification.

In this chapter, we present the offline writer identification systems evaluated using the AHTID/MW and KHATT database. We address the following question: Is it possible to develop a powerful system for Arabic writer identification using only word images, text-line, or paragraph images, and recognize the writer with only one handwritten word, text-line, or paragraph image?

The chapter is organized as follows. Section 6.2 presents some related work. Section 6.3 summarizes the main characteristics of the text databases used in this work. Section 6.4 is dedicated to describing the competitions organized, while Section 6.5 gives a brief description of the systems evaluated using the Arabic Handwritten Text Images Database written by Multiple Writers (AHTID/MW) and the KFUPM Handwritten Arabic TexT (KHATT) databases. The evaluation of the systems is discussed in Section 6.6, followed by the conclusions and recommendations.

6.2 Related Work

Over the past two decades, automatic offline writer identification has enjoyed renewed interest. One of the driving forces behind this surge is forensic document examiners' increasing need for writer identification techniques to identify criminals' scripts based on their handwriting [6]. Furthermore, threats of terrorist attacks have increased the use of writer identification and other biometric recognition techniques to identify potential or actual assailants [7].

The main databases used for the writer identification and verification of handwritten Latin and other western scripts are addressed. The CEDAR letter was developed at the University of Buffalo, New York [8], and is considered one of the first large databases developed for the writer identification and the verification of handwritten scripts using the Latin alphabet. The CEDAR letter, as shown in Figure 6.1, is concise (it has just 156 words); yet, every letter of the alphabet occurs at the beginning of a word as either a capital or a lower case letter, and as a lower case letter in the middle and at the end of a word. In addition, it also contains punctuation,

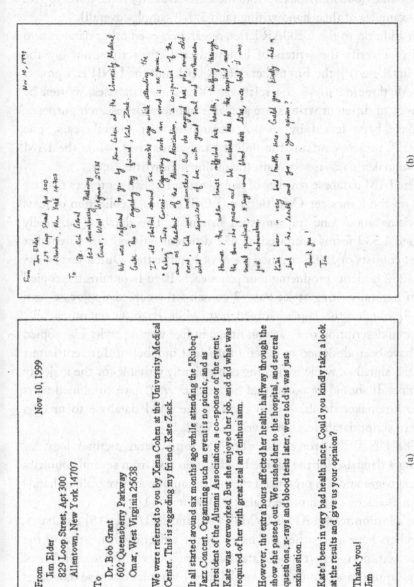

Figure 6.1. CEDAR letter: (a) source document and (b) scanned sample.

numerals, and some letter and numeral combinations (for example, ff, tt, oo, 00). Around 1,000 individuals wrote the CEDAR letter three times to give three examples of their handwriting (and 3,000 samples overall).

In addition to the CEDAR letter, researchers used other databases to identify or verify the writers of handwritten Latin scripts, notably, the IAM database [9], the Firemaker dataset [10], and the UNIPEN project [11]. All three databases are relatively large-scale databases, written by hundreds of different writers, are available publicly for research purposes, and have been tested by several researchers over several years. The UNIPEN project contains the online handwritten text, while the IAM and Firemaker databases contain the offline handwritten text.

The IAM database consists of handwritten English sentences that are based on the Lancaster-Oslo/Bergen (LOB) corpus, a collection of texts comprising about one million word instances. The database originally included 1,539 forms produced by 657 different writers. The Firemaker dataset consists of 1,008 scanned pages of handwritten Dutch texts written by 252 students producing four pages each. Page 1 contains the copied text in natural writing style; Page 2 contains the copied uppercase text; Page 3 contains the copied forged text, while Page 4 contains a self-generated description of a cartoon image in free writing style. The copied texts have been designed to cover a sufficient number of different letters from the alphabet, while remaining conveniently writable for the majority of writers. It should be noted that Schomaker *et al.* have combined parts of the Firemaker database with parts of the IAM database to make a Western script database of 900 writers [5, 12, 13].

The UNIPEN project describes the format and methodology for creating a database for the online handwritten text from several countries and languages and has organized the collection of over five million handwritten characters from more than 2,200 writers [11].

In addition to the AHTID/MW [14] and KHATT [15] databases, researchers have used other databases for the writer identification of the Arabic text, noting that most databases were limited in size, number of writers, application, domain, or availability. Examples of these databases include the Institute for Communications Technology (IFN)/Ecole Nationale d'Ingénieur de Tunis (ENIT) database [16], the Arabic Handwriting Data Base for Text Recognition (AHDB) [17], and Srihari *et al.* [18].

The IfN/ENIT database consists of 26,459 images of the 937 names of cities and towns in Tunisia, written by 411 different writers. Up to now, this database has been widely used by many researchers into the Arabic handwritten text recognition (more than 100 research groups from more than 30 countries) and has appeared in several global competitions. Due to its public availability, researchers have also used the IfN/ENIT database for Arabic text writer identification, although it is limited to city names and thus contains restricted vocabulary.

The AHDB contains Arabic words and texts written by about 100 writers. It also contains the most popular words in Arabic as well as sentences used in Arabic bank cheques. Finally, it contains free handwriting pages on a topic of interest to the writer. The form is designed with five pages. The first three pages are filled with 96 words, 67 of which are handwritten numbers as words as they would be used in handwritten cheques. The other 29 words are from the most popular written words in Arabic. The fourth page contains three sentences of handwritten words representing the numbers and quantities that can be written on cheques. The fifth page is lined and designed to be completed by the writer in freehand on any subject of his choice, as shown in Figure 6.2. Further information like the availability of the dataset is not clear from the authors published work.

Srihari *et al.* used a limited database for writer identification of Arabic handwritten text prepared from 10 different writers, each contributing 10 different full-page documents in handwritten Arabic for a total of 100 documents [18].

6.3 Databases Used

In this section, we present the well-known Arabic handwritten text databases: AHTID/MW [14] and KHATT [15].

6.3.1 *The AHTID/MW Database*

The AHTID/MW was built at the Multimedia, Information Systems and Advanced Computing Laboratory (MIRACL) Lab, and University of Sfax, Tunisia in joint collaboration with the Institute for Communications Technology (IfN), Technische Universität Braunschweig,

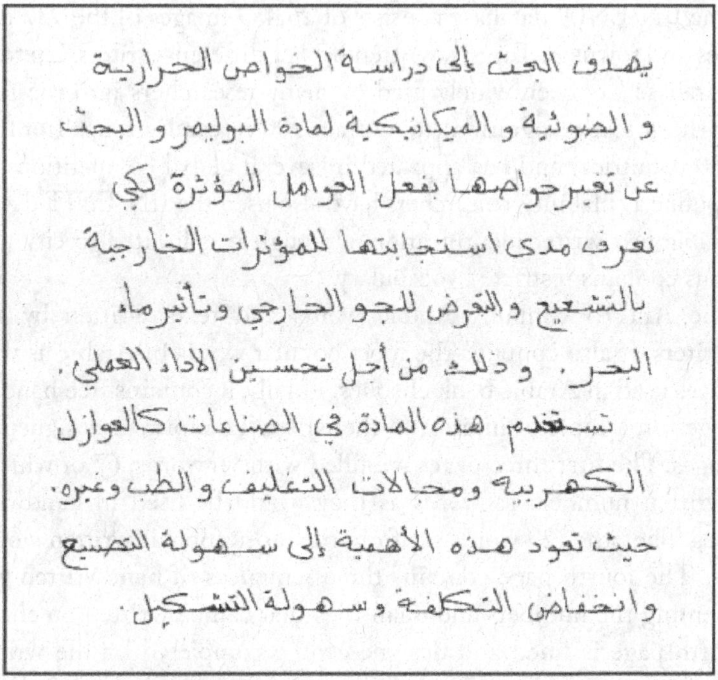

يهدف البحث الى دراسة الخواص الحرارية
و الضوئية و الميكانيكية لمادة البوليمر و البحث
عن تغير خواصها بفعل العوامل المؤثرة لكي
نعرف مدى استجابتها للمؤثرات الخارجية
بالتشعيع و التعرض للجو الخارجي و تأثير ماء
البحر . و ذلك من أجل تحسين الاداء العملي .
نستخدم هذه المادة في الصناعات كالعوازل
الكهربية و مجالات التغليف و الطب و غيره .
حيث تعود هذه الأهمية إلى سهولة التصنيع
و انخفاض التكلفة و سهولة التشكيل .

Figure 6.2.   Free handwriting sample from the AHDC dataset.

Germany. A variety of Arabic handwriting styles are found in the AHTID/MW dataset as illustrated in Figure 6.3. It can be used for research into Arabic handwritten text recognition, word segmentation, word spotting, and writer identification.

The AHTID/MW contains 3,710 text lines and 22,896 words written by 53 native writers of Arabic. These images are divided into five equal sets. The first four are available to the scientific community and the fifth set is kept internally for the potential future evaluation of systems in blind mode. Each word/line image in the AHTID/MW database is fully described using an XML file containing ground-truth information. The database is freely available for researchers worldwide. In fact, the AHTID/MW database is used by many groups worldwide working on Arabic handwritten text recognition. For more details, please refer to [14].

Figure 6.3.   Arabic handwritten word and text-line images from AHTID/MW database produced by different writers.

6.3.2 *The KHATT Database*

KHATT is a large and real-life Arabic handwritten text database, collected from 1,000 writers of different origins. Each writer wrote six paragraphs, including a paragraph (written twice) that contains all the shapes of the Arabic characters and two free form paragraphs on topics chosen by the writers themselves. Figure 6.4 illustrates the paragraph forms from one writer in the KHATT database. The database is highly suited to research in both Arabic writer identification and handwriting recognition. More details of the database can be found in [19]. The KHATT database can be downloaded from khatt.ideas2serve.net.

The KHATT database was first presented in ICFHR 2012 [15] and received the Best Poster Award. It was later selected for publication (an extended and enhanced version) in *Pattern Recognition* as one of the selected best papers of ICFHR 2012 [19]. The database is designed for tasks that are of central interest to the ICFHR community, such as writer identification, line segmentation, and binarization and noise removal techniques, as well as handwritten text recognition. A number of research groups around the world are using KHATT for their research purposes.

Figure 6.4.   Samples of paragraphs from the KHATT database.

6.4 Competition Using the AHTID and KHATT Databases

A competition was organized using the two famous databases during the *14th International Conference on Frontiers in Handwriting Recognition* (ICFHR2014) [20]. It was organized by Fouad Slimane,[a] Sameh Awaida,[b] Anis Mezghani,[c] Mohammad Tanvir Parvez,[d] Slim Kanoun,[e] Sabri A. Mahmoud,[d] and Volker Märgner[e] as a joint collaboration project between their Institutes. The scientific objectives of the competition were to measure the capacity of recognition systems to identify a writer using word, text-line, and paragraph images to allow researchers working in writer identification or related fields to compare the performances of their systems on new databases. The main difficulties faced in the competition were the similarities between the writer styles, the large number of writers — particularly in the KHATT database — the quality of the

---

[a]Digital Humanities Laboratory (DHLab), Ecole Polytechnique Fédérale de Lausanne (EPFL).

[b]Computer Engineering Department, Qassim University, Saudi Arabia.

[c]MIRACL Lab, ISIMS, University of Sfax, Tunisia.

[d]Information and Computer Science Department, King Fahd University of Petroleum & Minerals, Saudi Arabia.

[e]Institute for Communications Technology (IfN), Technische Universität Braunschweig, Germany.

scanned images, and the ability to recognize writers using one word, one line, or one paragraph images.

The rest of this section presents more details about the evaluation procedure and the proposed tasks of the ICFHR 2014 competition.

6.4.1 *Modalities of the Evaluation*

The evaluation was organized using a blind procedure. The participants were allowed to train their systems using the available sets of AHTID/MW and KHATT databases. Four sets are available from the AHTID/MW database. However, for the KHATT database, for each of the 1,000 writers, four paragraph images (like the ones in Figure 6.4) were provided as training and validation sets along with the verified ground-truth values. The participants used these paragraph images to train and test their writer identification systems. Two of these paragraph images are text dependent and two are text independent, which helped the competition participants develop both text-dependent and text-independent writer identification systems.

At a given date, the participants sent their executable systems that were run on an unseen data set. The competition organizers (see Figure 6.4) tested the submitted systems to this competition on Set 5 (Tasks 1 and 2) and 1,822 hidden paragraph images (Task 3), a maximum of two paragraph images per writer, like those in Figure 6.4. The systems produced the IDs of the 10 most probable writers for each image, sorted in descending order of likelihood (from Top-1 most probable writer ID to Top-10 least probable writer ID).

6.4.2 *Competition Tasks*

Three tasks were set in the ICFHR 2014 competition:

1. Writer identification using handwritten Arabic words with the AHTID/MW database
2. Writer identification using handwritten Arabic text lines with the AHTID/MW database
3. Writer identification using handwritten Arabic paragraphs with the KHATT database.

The participants were allowed to submit one, two, or three executable systems depending on whether they chose to participate in all the tasks or only one or two of them.

6.5 Evaluated Systems

The following section gives a short description of the systems evaluated using the AHTID/MW and KHATT databases.

6.5.1 *The WILL/SP System*

The WILL/SP (Writer Identification Line Level/Steerable Pyramids) system was submitted in the ICFHR 2014 Arabic writer identification competition for Task 2 by Faten Kallel Jaiem and Slim Kanoun, the members of MIRACL.[f] The WILL/SP system is based on steerable pyramids, using the Backpropagation Artificial Neural Network (BpANN) as a classifier.

In the feature extraction phases, each line image is normalized with a new of size 1024×1024. Then, the steerable pyramid is applied to all the images, with four orientations ($0°, 45°, 90°,$ and $135°$) at seven levels. The feature vector is constructed based on the calculated variance V for each level:

$$V = \sqrt{\frac{\sum_i \sum_j \left(d(i,j) - m\right)^2}{N}} \tag{6.1}$$

In the training phase, a three-layer feed-forward neural network classifier using a back-propagation method was used to evaluate the performance of the proposed system. The size of the input layer (first layer) as the dimension of the feature vector and the number of hidden layer units are calculated by Equation (6.2); however, the output layer

---

[f]Multimedia, Information systems and Advanced Computing Laboratory, University of Sfax, Tunisia.

has the same number of units as the class numbers (number of different writers):

$$N_h = \sqrt{N_i^2 + N_o^2} \qquad (6.2)$$

where N_h is the number of hidden layer units, N_i is the number of input layer units, and N_o is the number of output layer units. For more details about this system, please refer to [21].

6.5.2 The EMR System

EMR (edge-hinge and multi-scale run-length) feature-based system for Arabic writer identification was entered into the ICFHR 2014 Arabic writer identification competition for Task 3 by Chawki Djeddi,[g] Labiba Souici-Meslati,[h] Imran Siddiqi,[i] Abdellatif Ennaji,[j] and Haikal El Abed[k] as a joint collaboration project between all their laboratories.

This method is based on the combination of two types of features: edge-hinge features and multiscale run-length features. The edge-hinge features estimate the joint distribution of edge angles in a writer's handwriting. They are constructed by performing an edge detection using a Sobel kernel on the input images, and subsequently measuring the angles of both edge segments that emanate from each edge pixel.

The multiscale run-length features [22] are determined on the binary image, taking into consideration both the black pixels corresponding to the ink trace and the white pixels corresponding to the background. The probability distribution of black and white run-lengths was used. There are four scanning methods: horizontal, vertical, left-diagonal, and right-diagonal. The run-length features were calculated using the gray-level

[g]The LAMIS Laboratory, University of Tebessa, Tebessa, Algeria.
[h]The LISCO Laboratory, Badji Mokhtar-Annaba University, Annaba, Algeria.
[i]The Computer Science Department, Bahria University, Islamabad, Pakistan.
[j]The LITIS Laboratory, Rouen University, Rouen, France.
[k]The Technical Trainers College, German International Cooperation, Riyadh, Kingdom of Saudi Arabia.

run-length matrices, and the histogram of run-lengths has been normalized and interpreted as a probability distribution. The method considers horizontal, vertical, left-diagonal, and right-diagonal white run-lengths as well as horizontal, vertical, left-diagonal, and right-diagonal black run-lengths extracted from the original image. A detailed description of the features used along with the results achieved on the KHATT database can be found in [23].

6.5.3 *The GMMS System*

The GMMS (GMM supervector) system was entered in the ICFHR 2014 Arabic writer identification competition for Task 3 by Vincent Christlein, David Bernecker, Florian Hönig, and Elli Angelopoulou, all members of the Pattern Recognition Labs of the Friedrich-Alexander University Erlangen, Germany and the Friedrich-Alexander University, Nuremberg, Germany. The method is based on [13], in which the authors proposed to use GMMS to encode the features of a document. First, RootSIFT descriptors are extracted for each document. RootSIFT is a variant of SIFT in which the features are additionally normalized using the square root (Hellinger) kernel. The descriptors from the training set are used to train a Gaussian mixture model (GMM).

The GMM parameters are estimated using the expectation-maximization (EM) algorithm. This GMM serves as a universal background model (UBM) from which document-specific GMMs can be computed. The UBM adapts to the features of the query document by means of one maximum-a-posteriori (MAP) step, followed by a mixing step. In the MAP step, the new statistics up to the second order are computed, and then they are mixed (using a relevance factor) with the parameters of the UBM to create the document-specific GMM. The parameters of this newly created GMM are concatenated to form a supervector. After a normalization step, this high-dimensional supervectors are used for comparison using the cosine distance. For classification, a 1-nearest-neighbor classifier is used, i.e., each document's GMM supervector is computed and compared to all the GMM supervectors in the training set. (Thus, apart from the GMM, no training is involved.) Note that, in contrast to [24], the orientation information from the SIFT key points has been dropped. Furthermore, instead of a power normalization of the GMM supervectors, a component-wise L2 normalization is applied before the global L2 normalization.

6.5.4 *The OBI/SIFT System*

This system was submitted in the ICFHR 2014 Arabic writer identification competition for Task 3 by Daniel Fecker,[l] Abedelkadir Asi,[m] Volker Märgner,[l] Jihad El-Sana,[m] and Tim Fingscheidt[l] as a joint collaboration project between their Institutes.

The system uses a combination of two potent feature extraction techniques. The first approach is the oriented basic image (OBI) feature extraction technique [25], which works on the textual level. Multiscale symmetry and orientation features are computed for each pixel of the query document image using a Gaussian derivative filter pyramid. With these features, a histogram is generated as the feature vector for the writer's identification. The second feature extraction technique is a new approach utilizing key point-based descriptors (SIFT), presented in [26]. Here, a feature vector is generated by computing the distances between all the elements of all extracted SIFT-descriptor vectors of a query document image. The cosine-distance metric is employed to do this. The OBI features are extracted from binarized images employing Otsu's method, and the SIFT-based features use gray-scale images. Both features achieve a relatively good performance on their own with slightly better results for the SIFT-based features.

The classifier uses a late fusion scheme to combine these two multi-dimensional features. The classification is done using a special k-nearest-neighbor approach which first normalizes the distances of a query document to the k-nearest neighbors in the training data set. This is done separately for each feature domain similar to Equation (13) in [26]. As a result, the minimum distance has the absolute value of 1, and all others have smaller values. Afterward, these normalized distances, also weighted by the solo performance of each feature, are used to create a histogram

---

[l]Institute for Communications Technology (IfN), Technische Universität Braunschweig — Germany.
[m]Ben-Gurion University of the Negev, Beer Sheva — Israel.

whose entries belong to unique writers. The index with the maximum value in this histogram corresponds to the classified writer of the query document. The other entries in the ranked list for calculating the Top-5 and Top-10 potential IDs consist of the results of the single features employed alternately. In the final system, $k = 3$ and $\sigma = 2.5$ were used as the bases for the Gaussian derivative filter pyramid of the OBI features. Furthermore, χ^2-distance is used as a distance metric for the classification.

6.5.5 *The GMM-based System*

The GMM-based writer identification system was published by Slimane and Märgner [27]. It is inspired from Slimane *et al.* [28]. GMMs are used as the core of the system with only 21 features. They provide a powerful representation of the distribution of features extracted using a fixed-length sliding window from the text lines and words of a writer. The window moves from right to left on binarized images according to Arabic writing orientation. For more details, please refer to [27].

For each writer, a GMM is built and trained with the EM algorithm using the word and text-line images of that writer. In the recognition phase, the system returns log-likelihood scores. The GMM model(s) with the highest score(s) is(are) selected depending on whether the score is computed in Top-1 or Top-n level.

Experiments are based on word and text-line images using the AHTID/MW database.

6.5.6 *SRS–LBP System*

The method is based on a variant of the local binary pattern (LBP) descriptor modified to encapsulate the texture of textual images and is called sparse radial sampling LBP (SRS–LBP) [3]. The LBP operator encodes signs of the differences between each pixel and the pixels sampled on a circle around it as a bit-string, which is interpreted as the patterns integer label. The SRS variant adds a constant K to every pixel when comparing it to the samples on the circle, and instead of encoding the sign, encodes significantly darker pixels than the central pixel as 0, and the others as 1. The constant K is computed by clustering all the differences between the central and peripheral pixels in the image area with Otsu's method. The sampling of the neighborhood is done with the bilinear interpolation of eight points on a circle around each pixel of the radius r. The LBP transformation from gray levels to integer labels is computed for radii r 1 to 12 pixels. Histograms of LBP patterns are computed over the regions for each of the 12 label images and concatenated to provide a feature vector.

The specific pipeline was developed for writer identification given unsegmented text blocks containing several lines of text, and to avoid all segmentation issues, global pooling into histograms was preferred. It can be observed that text-as-texture classification on pipelines based on the SRS–LBP benefits from pooling words and text-line images in horizontal zones. All the pixels associated with plateaus in the original image produce the LBP of all 0; these patterns are suppressed for every radius. The zero-pattern suppression makes the feature representation invariant to plateaus, which, in the case of text, are associated with background-only areas in the image.

Furthermore, the histograms of each radius are normalized to a sum of 1, and, thus, the descriptor becomes invariant to the quantity of text. The feature vector consists of $256 \times 12 = 3,072$ dimensions. PCA computed on the training set is employed to reduce the dimensionality of the feature vectors to 200. As the final step, the Hellinger kernel is applied to the features, which are then L2 normalized. A KNN classifier implemented with quad-trees and $K = 11$ is constructed from the training set and classifies the test set. The pipeline is exactly the same as in Nicolaou *et al.* [3], with the exception of K, which was set to 11 instead of 1.

The SRS–LBP can accommodate both classification and retrieval modalities. PCA can be considered as unsupervised learning of feature-space transformation. Given enough samples per class, discriminative supervised learning can increase the classification accuracy dramatically; supervised metric learning could also be used to improve results for scenarios where only a few samples per class are available. The proposed method is highly generic; the SRS–LBP features have been used in a broad range of text-as-texture recognition tasks such as scene-text script identification, handwritten visual language recognition, video-text script identification, and document-ID-type classification. The 0 SRS–LBP won the first place (out of 8) in the ICDAR 2015 multiscript gender classification competition and the second place (out of 5) in the multiscript writer identification competition [29].

6.6 Evaluation

The AHTID/MW database has fewer writers than the KHATT database (53 writers). However, the difficulties of writer identification using handwritten Arabic words and lines from the AHTID/MW database come from the limited information provided for each writer (one or a few handwritten words). The KHATT database provides full handwritten paragraphs to select features from content to identify the writers. However, the difficulty of writer identification using handwritten Arabic paragraphs from the KHATT database comes from the very large number of writers (1,000 writers) in the training set. This unique combination makes the challenge more suited to real-life applications, and hence the less-than-perfect results from some of the systems presented later. All the systems were evaluated using the ICFHR 2014 Arabic writer identification competition datasets under the same conditions.

6.6.1 Writer Identification Using Handwritten Arabic Words with the AHTID/MW Database

As pointed out before, Arabic writer identification based only on words is difficult. Two systems have been evaluated using the AHTID/MW database: the GMM-based system proposed by Slimane and Märgner [27] and the SRS–LBP system proposed by Nicolaou et al. [3]. Table 6.1 presents the results. The accuracy with the GMM-based system is 23.03%, 49.84%, and 63.99%, respectively, for Top-1, Top-5, and Top-10. On the other hand, the identification rate with the SRS–LBP system is 28.94%,

Table 6.1.   Results of writer identification using handwritten Arabic words with the AHTID/MW database.

	Top-1	Top-5	Top-10
The GMM-based system	23.03	49.84	63.99
The SRS–LBP system	28.94	62.30	75.05

Table 6.2. Results of writer identification using handwritten Arabic text lines with the AHTID/MW database.

	Top-1	Top-5	Top-10
The WILL/SP system	37.51	61.27	73.81
The GMM-based system	59.05	76.69	84.35
The SRS–LBP system	63.04	87.01	91.68

62.30%, and 75.05%, respectively, for Top-1, Top-5, and Top-10. From these results, we conclude that the SRS–LBP system can perform significantly better than the GMM-based system.

6.6.2 *Writer Identification Using Handwritten Arabic Text Lines with the AHTID/MW Database*

Table 6.2 presents the results of the WILL/SP system, the GMM-based system, and the SRS–LBP system. The writer identification rates in Top-5 are 61.27%, 76.69%, and 87.01%, respectively, for the WILL/SP, GMM-based, and SRS–LBP systems. The SRS–LBP system had better results compared to the GMM-based system and the WILL/SP system, and the writer identification rates are less than 64% in Top-1 and 92% in Top-10, which confirms the difficulty in identifying a writer using one text line.

6.6.3 *Writer Identification Using Handwritten Arabic Paragraphs with the KHATT Database*

Three systems were evaluated using Arabic paragraphs from the KHATT database. Table 6.3 presents the results for the test set from the KHATT database. The best result is marked in bold. This test set contains two types of handwritten Arabic text paragraphs: some were written on ruled lines and the others were written without ruled lines. A total of 1,822 paragraphs were used while testing the systems, containing an almost equal number of paragraphs from each of the two types. In Table 6.3, writer identification performances are reported for each type of paragraphs separately.

Table 6.3.   Results of writer identification using handwritten Arabic text paragraphs with the KHATT database.

	Top-1	Top-5	Top-10
The EMR system (para. w/o ruled lines)	49.1	69.3	76.2
The EMR system (para. with ruled lines)	0.6	4.2	7.4
The GMMS system (para. w/o ruled lines)	**73.4**	**84.3**	**87.6**
The GMMS system (para. with ruled lines)	9.4	18.7	24.7
The OBI/SIFT system (para. w/o ruled lines)	63.2	77.9	83.3
The OBI/SIFT system (para. with ruled lines)	0.5	1.8	4.4

Table 6.3 shows that the evaluated systems generally perform better on paragraphs written without ruled lines. The performances of the systems go down significantly with the paragraphs with ruled lines. This behavior of the systems is because the training set provided to the competition participants did not contain any paragraphs written on ruled-lines.

The GMMS system generally performed best across the two types of paragraphs. As can be seen from Table 6.3, the best identification accuracy is 73.4% in Top-1 and 87.6% in Top-10 for handwritten paragraphs without ruled lines, while the accuracy goes down to 9.4% in Top-1 and 24.7% in Top-10 for paragraphs with ruled lines.

The OBI/SIFT and EMR systems perform slightly worse in Top-10 compared to the GMMS system, but all systems need to improve their performance for real biometric and forensic applications.

This rather low accuracy leaves room for researchers to improve their systems using the AHTID/MW and KHATT databases.

6.7 Conclusions and Recommendations

Six Arabic writer identification systems were evaluated using AHTID/ MW and KHATT databases. The results show the difficulties involved in building an accurate writer identification system.

On the one hand, the SRS–LBP system developed by Nicolaou *et al.* [3] performed the best of all the systems evaluated using word and text line with the AHTID/MW database. On the other hand, the GMMS system performed best among the systems using Arabic text paragraphs with the KHATT database, with 73.4% accuracy in Top-1 using paragraphs written without ruled lines and 9.4% using paragraphs with ruled lines. The GMMS system was the winner of the ICFHR 2014 Arabic writer identification competition using AHTID/MW and KHATT databases. The performances of the evaluated systems are rather low for the two databases used, which provides opportunities to researchers to further improve their systems for Arabic writer identification.

Acknowledgments

We would like to thank all participants of the ICFHR 2014 competition on Arabic Writer Identification using AHTID/MW and KHATT databases, and all the people who contributed to the success of this work. This work has been partially supported by the Swiss National Science Foundation fellowship project PBFRP2_145898 and by Qassim University Scientific Research Project #2812.

References

1. A. Hassaïne and S. Al Maadeed, "ICFHR 2012 competition on writer identification challenge 2: Arabic scripts," in *2012 International Conference on Frontiers in Handwriting Recognition (ICFHR' 2012)*, Bari, Italy, pp. 835–840, September 18–20, 2012.
2. V. Christlein, D. Bernecker, and E. Angelopoulou, "Writer identification using VLAD encoded contour-Zernike moments," in *13th International Conference on Document Analysis and Recognition (ICDAR' 2015)*, Tunis, Tunisia, pp. 906–910, August 23–26, 2015.
3. A. Nicolaou, A.D. Bagdanov, M. Liwicki, and D. Karatzas, "Sparse radial sampling LBP for writer identification," in *13th International Conference on Document Analysis and Recognition (ICDAR' 2015)*, Tunis, Tunisia, pp. 716–720, August 23–26, 2015.
4. C. Adak and B.B. Chaudhuri, "Writer Identification from Offline Isolated Bangla Characters and Numerals," in *13th International Conference on Document Analysis and Recognition (ICDAR' 2015)*, Tunis, Tunisia, pp. 486–490, August 23–26, 2015.

5. S. Awaida and S. Mahmoud, "State of the art in off-line writer identification of handwritten text and survey of writer identification of Arabic text," *Educational Research and Reviews*, vol. 7, no. 20, pp. 445–463, 2012.

6. D. Zhang, A. Jain, M. Tapiador, and J. Sigüenza, "Writer identification method based on forensic knowledge–Biometric authentication," in *Lecture Notes in Computer Science*, vol. 3072, pp. 555–561. Berlin, Heidelberg, Springer, 2004.

7. A. Schlapbach, "Writer identification and verification," *PhD dissertation*, Institute of Computer Science and Applications of Mathematics, Bern University, The Netherlands, p. 161, 2007.

8. S.-H. Cha and S.N. Srihari, "Writer identification: Statistical analysis and dichotomizer," *Advances in Pattern Recognition*, vol. 1876, pp. 123–132, 2000.

9. U. Marti and H. Bunke, "The IAM-database: An English sentence database for offline handwriting recognition," *International Journal on Document Analysis and Recognition*, vol. 5, no. 1, pp. 39–46, 2002.

10. L. Schomaker and L. Vuurpijl, "Forensic writer identification: A benchmark data set and a comparison of two systems," *Research Report,* Nijmegen, 2000.

11. I. Guyon, L. Schomaker, R. Plamondon, M. Liberman, and S. Janet, "UNIPEN project of on-line data exchange and recognizer benchmarks," *International Conference on Pattern Recognition*, vol. 2, pp. 29–33, 1994.

12. A. Brink, M. Bulacu, and L. Schomaker, "How much handwritten text is needed for text-independent writer verification and identification," in *Proceedings of the 19th International Conference on Pattern Recognition (ICPR' 2008),* Tampa, FL, USA, pp. 1–4, December 8–11, 2008.

13. L. Schomaker, K. Franke, and M. Bulacu, "Using codebooks of fragmented connected-component contours in forensic and historic writer identification," *Pattern Recognition Letters*, vol. 28, no. 6, pp. 719–727, 2008.

14. A. Mezghani, S. Kanoun, M. Khemakhem, and H.El Abed, "A database for Arabic handwritten text image recognition and writer identification," in *2012 International Conference on Frontiers in Handwriting Recognition (ICFHR' 2012),* Bari, Italy, pp. 399–402, September 18–20, 2012.

15. S.A. Mahmoud, I. Ahmad, M. Alshayeb, W. Al-Khatib, M.T. Parvez, G.A. Fink, V. Märgner, and H.El Abed, "KHATT: Arabic offline handwritten text database," in *2012 International Conference on Frontiers in Handwriting Recognition (ICFHR' 2012),* Bari, Italy, pp. 449–454, September 18–20, 2012.

16. M. Pechwitz, S. Maddouri, V. Märgner, N. Ellouze, and H. Amiri, "IFN/ ENIT—Database of handwritten Arabic words," in *Francophone International Conference on writing and Document (CIFED' 2002),* Hammamet, Tunisia, pp. 129–136, 2002.

17. S. Al-Ma'adeed, D. Elliman, and C. Higgins, "A data base for Arabic handwritten text recognition research," *The International Arab Journal of Information Technology*, vol. 1, no. 1, pp. 117–121, 2004.

18. S. Srihari and G. Ball, "Writer verification of Arabic handwriting," in *the 8th IAPR International Workshop on Document Analysis System (DAS' 2008)*, Nara, Japan, pp. 28–34, September 16–19, 2008.

19. S.A. Mahmoud, I. Ahmad, W. Al-Khatib, M. Alshayeb, M.T. Parvez, V. Märgner, and G.A. Fink, "KHATT: An open Arabic offline handwritten text database," *Pattern Recognition*, vol. 47, no. 3, pp. 1096–1112, 2014.

20. F. Slimane, S. Awaida, A. Mezghani, M.T. Parvez, S. Kanoun, S.A. Mahmoud, and V. Märgner, "ICFHR 2014 competition on Arabic writer identification using AHTID/MW and KHATT databases," in *14th International Conference on Frontiers in Handwriting Recognition (ICFHR' 2014)*, Heraklion, Greece, pp. 797–802, September 1–4, 2014.

21. F. Kallel Jaiem, S. Kanoun, and V. Eglin, "Arabic Font Recognition based on a priori Approach," in *14th International Conference on Frontiers in Handwriting Recognition (ICFHR' 2014)*, Heraklion, Greece, pp. 673–677, September 1–4, 2014.

22. C. Djeddi and L. Souici-Meslati, "A texture based approach for Arabic writer identification and verification," in *2010 International Conference on Machine and Web Intelligence (ICMWI' 2010)*, Algiers, Algeria, pp. 115–120, October 3–5, 2010.

23. C. Djeddi, L. Souici-Meslati, I. Siddiqi, A. Ennaji, H.El Abed, and A. Gattal, "Evaluation of texture features for offline Arabic writer identification," in *2014 11th IAPR International Workshop on Documet Analysis System (DAS' 2014)*, Tours, France, pp. 106–110, April 7–10, 2014.

24. V. Christlein, D. Bernecker, F. Hönig, and E. Angelopoulou, "Writer identification and verification using GMM supervectors," in *2014 IEEE Winter Conference on Applications of Computer Vision (WACV'2014)*, pp. 998–1005, March 24–26, 2014.

25. A.J. Newell and L.D. Griffin, "Natural image character recognition using oriented basic image features," in *2011 International Conference on Digital Image Computing Techniques and Applications (DICTA'2011)*, Noosa, QLD, Australia, pp. 191–196, December 6–8, 2001.

26. D. Fecker, A. Asi, V. Märgner, J. El-Sana, and T. Fingscheidt, "Writer identification for historical Arabic documents," in *22nd International Conference on Pattern Recognition (ICPR' 2014)*, Stockholm, Sweden, pp. 3050–3055, August 24–28, 2014.

27. F. Slimane and V. Märgner, "A new text-independent GMM Writer identification system applied to Arabic handwriting," in *14th International*

Conference on Frontiers in Handwriting Recognition (ICFHR' 2014), Heraklion, Greece, pp. 708–713, August 24–28, 2014.

28. F. Slimane, S. Kanoun, A.M. Alimi, R. Ingold, and J. Hennebert, "Gaussian mixture models for arabic font recognition," *ICPR*, pp. 2174–2177, 2010.

29. C. Djeddi, S. Al-Maadeed, A. Gattal, I. Siddiqi, L. Souici-Meslati, and H.El Abed, "ICDAR2015 competition on multi-script writer identification and gender classification using 'QUWI' database," in *13th International Conference on Document Analysis and Recognition (ICADR' 2015), Tunis, Tunisia*, pp. 1191–1195, August 23–26, 2015.

30. G. Louloudis, B. Gatos, and N. Stamatopoulos, "ICFHR 2012 competition on writer identification challenge 1: Latin/Greek documents," *2012 International Conference on Frontiers in Handwriting Recognition (ICFHR' 2012)*, Bari, Italy, pp. 829–834, September 18–20, 2012.

31. V. Märgner and H.El Abed, "Arabic handwriting recognition competition," *ICDAR*, pp. 1274–1278, 2007.

32. F. Slimane, S. Kanoun, H.El Abed, A.M. Alimi, R. Ingold, and J. Hennebert, "ICDAR 2011 — Arabic recognition competition: Multi-font multi-size digitally represented text," in *2011 International Conference on Document Analysis and Recognition (ICDAR' 2011)*, Beijing, China, pp. 1449–1453, September 18–21, 2011.

33. F. Slimane, S. Kanoun, H.El Abed, A.M. Alimi, R. Ingold, and J. Hennebert, "ICDAR 2013 competition on multi-font and multi-size digitally represented Arabic text," in *12th International Conference on Document Analysis and Recognition (ICDAR' 2012)*, Washington, DC, USA, pp. 1433–1437, August 25–28, 2013.

34. F. Slimane, S. Kanoun, J. Hennebert, A.M. Alimi, and R. Ingold, "A study on font-family and font-size recognition applied to Arabic word images at ultra-low resolution," *Pattern Recognition Letters*, vol. 34, no. 2, pp. 209–218, 2013.

Chapter 7

Signature Verification: Recent Developments and Perspectives

Muhammad Imran Malik, Sheraz Ahmed,
Andreas Dengel, and Marcus Liwicki

7.1 Introduction

Signature verification is the process of establishing whether or not a signature belongs to the person who claims to be the owner of the signature [1]. It is considered as a classical 1 to 1 pattern classification problem: either a signature is verified to belong to a given person or it is not. More specifically, the pattern recognition (PR) community defines signature verification as follows: given an input feature vector F_s, obtained from a signature s, and a claimed identity I, determine whether (I, F_s) belongs to class k_1 or to class k_2 [2, 3]. Here, class k_1 indicates that the signature is from the original author, while k_2 indicates that the signature is not from the original author. The feature vector F_s is compared with M_I, i.e., the model corresponding to the author I, to find whether to assign it to class k_1 or to class k_2. Therefore, we can write

$$(I, F_s) \in \begin{cases} k_1, & if\ f\left(M_I, F_s\right) \geq \theta \\ k_2, & otherwise \end{cases}$$

where the function $f(M_I, F_s)$ returns a similarity score sc $\in \mathbb{R}$, indicating the similarity of F_s and model M_I of author I and $\theta \in \mathbb{R}$, which is a predefined threshold. As we increase θ, the chances of the input signature being classified as not belonging to the authentic author increase.

If a signature is verified to belong to the claiming person, the signature is said to be genuine/authentic, and the person is called a *client* or *authentic/target/specimen* author or writer. Otherwise, the signature is called a *forgery* or simulation and the person who wrote it an *impostor/ forger or nonspecimen writer* [2, 4]. In PR research, a forgery/simulation is usually categorized in any of the following types [5].

- Random forgery/simple forgery: where the forger has not seen the genuine signatures of the authentic author.
- Unskilled forgery: where the forger has seen the original signatures of a person but has not practiced to forge the signatures.
- Skilled forgery: where the forger has seen and practiced to forge the genuine signature of a person. The forger may make use of various devices for observing the signature and practice forging it.

The signature data can be present in an online or an offline format. In online verification, a time-ordered sequence of coordinates, representing the pen movement, is available. This can be produced by any electronic sensing device, such as electronic pens or digitizing tablets. In offline verification, only image of a signature is available, which usually is scanned or photographed from paper. The temporal information adjunct with the writing style of a person, his/her angle of grasping the pen, direction of movement, etc., simplifies the task verification to some extent.

Whether verification is performed on offline or online data, the basic architecture of a verification system is similar. The following section provides an overview of a general signature verification system.

7.1.1 *General Signature Verification Steps*

A signature verification system is usually divided into consecutive units which iteratively process the input data to finally accept or reject a

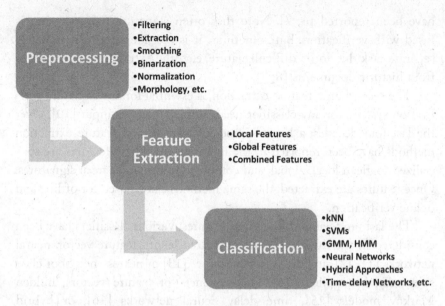

Figure 7.1.   General signature verification steps.

signature. The main units are illustrated in Figure 7.1 and summarized in this subsection. Note that there are differences between offline and online processing, but the underlying principles are the same. Only the methodology of performing the individual steps differs.

The first unit is the preprocessing unit, where the input is raw signature data and the output consists of signatures that have undergone some initial processing like binarization and size/skew normalization. The amount of effort that has to be invested into preprocessing depends on the given data. If the data have been acquired from a system that does not produce much noise, there is not much to do in this step. However, the data usually contain noise, which has to be removed to improve the quality of the data, or are available with some background information, e.g., on a bank check where we need to extract the signature from its background. However, there is an argument about the requirement of preprocessing and how it affects the possible outcomes, especially in forensic cases where sometimes lives are at stake [6]. Over the last few years, different systems capable of performing signature preprocessing have been reported [6, 7]. Note that often signature preprocessing is fused with verification, but sometimes it is considered as a completely separate task due to its difficult nature, e.g., the extraction of signatures from historic documents [8, 9].

The second unit, feature extraction, is essential for any signature verification system, for any classifier needs numeric data as input [10]. Over the last four decades, a large number of features and feature extraction methods have been reported in the literature [8]. These features are specialized to glean local, global, and combined information from signatures. Once features are extracted, the same methods can be used for offline and online verification.

The last unit classifies the input features. Various classifiers have been considered in the literature, e.g., for a fixed length feature vector, neural networks [11, 12] support vector machines [13] or nearest-neighbor classifiers can be applied [14]. For sequences of feature vectors, hidden Markov models [15], time delay neural networks [16], or hybrid approaches [17, 18] are generally used for classification [10]. The classification unit generally reports the final classification results, e.g., a binary decision or a similarity-based score/probability.

Most recently, the signature verification research has been largely influenced by the work of Forensic Handwriting Examiners (FHEs). Various signature verification workshops, e.g., *International Workshop on Automated Forensic Handwriting Analysis* (AFHA)-2011, -2013, -2014, and -2015, have been organized in order to make PR researchers aware about the work of FHEs and the signature features which are exclusively considered by FHEs. Furthermore, different signature verification competitions have been organized jointly by experts from PR community and forensic handwriting examination community. This is substantial as the forensic handwriting examination community is in search of automated signature verification systems that can be used in their routine casework. This chapter provides detailed insights into the reasons why these competitions were organized, and to which extent the participating systems are applicable in real-world forensic scenarios. It also describes various future perspectives that are worth considering when developing automatic signature verification systems, particularly for forensic environments.

7.1.2 Background

FHEs usually perform signature verification by the visual comparison of the known signature samples with the questioned signature. The FHE weighs the observations in light of the following two hypotheses H1 versus H2.

H1: The questioned signature is an authentic signature normally used by the reference writer;

H2: The questioned signature is not authentic but
   a. it is simulated by another writer than the reference writer;
   b. it is disguised by the reference writer;

As forensic signature verification is performed in a highly subjective manner, the discipline is in need for a scientific, objective base. The use of automatic signature verification tools can objectify the FHEs opinion about the authenticity of a questioned signature. So the questions are:

- What types of signing behaviors (e.g., genuine vs. forged) should an automated system consider while performing verification?
- What should an automated signature verification system output in order to be successfully applicable in forensic casework?

To answer these questions and to provide a better understanding of forensic casework, various competitions were organized in the recent past. These primarily focused on the needs of FHEs and demanded the participating systems to fulfill these needs. The aims, details, database access, and the mechanics of competing systems in each of these competitions are provided in the following sections.

7.2 Signature Verification Competition (SigComp2009)

The SigComp 2009 [21] focused both on-line and off-line signature verification. The participating systems reported similarity scores and were ranked by Equal Error Rate (EER). The conclusions were presented in a probabilistic way [20].

7.2.1 Data

Two unpublished signature datasets were used, both containing on-line and off-line data. The training dataset comprised 1920 images where 12 authentic writers contributed 5 genuine signatures each and 31 forgers provided 5 forgeries per genuine signature (1860 forgeries and 60 genuine signatures). The test/evaluation dataset consisted of 1200 genuine signatures by 100 newly introduced writers and forged signatures from 33 writers. Altogether, the test dataset had 1953 signatures available in on-line and off-line formats.[a]

7.2.2 Submitted Systems

Eight systems participated for the offline task and 15 systems participated for the online task. Since the space is limited and offline verification is more interesting for FHEs, we detail only the offline systems in this section. Detailed information on online systems appear in [21]. System 1 was based on global [22] and local [23] analyses and combines them with the linear combination of the individual scores. Linear regression is then used to compute the optimal fusion weights. System 13 uses a unique approach as it is only based on color information. Both Systems 14 and 15 are based on neural networks to define their optimal feature set. System 16 uses gradient, structure, and concavity features [25]. System 17 is based on the blurred shape model [26] and on the contour features [27]. Finally, Systems 18a and 18b use Gaussian mixture models and hidden Markov models, respectively, for classification. Nevertheless, both systems use the same localized feature vector sequences [28, 29].

7.2.3 Evaluation

For the off-line case, the task was to identify correctly the 6527 genuine and 9360 forgery cases. The evaluation was based on the Equal Error Rate (EER: the point where False Acceptance Rate (FAR) equals the False Rejection Rate (FRR)), and Detection Error Tradeoff (DET) curves are

---

[a]These data are available at http://www.iapr-tc11.org/mediawiki/index.php/ICDAR_2009_Signature_Verification_Competition_(SigComp2009).

Table 7.1. Evaluation of SigComp2009 offline systems with EER (%).

System-ID	EER (%)	95(%) Conf. Int.
13	**9.15**	**(8.72–9.68)**
14	15.50	(14.86–1625)
18(b)	15.78	(15.05–16.34)
18(a)	16.10	(15.47–16.84)
1	18.27	(17.60–18.88)
16	23.00	(22.29–23.70)
17	41.12	(40.25–41.91)
15	43.02	(42.21–43.88)

Note that since it is not straightforward whether an EER of, e.g., 3% is significantly better than an EER of 5%, therefore, nonparametric bootstrapping was used to obtain 95% confidence intervals for the EERs [30]. System with ID 13 gives the lowest EER in offline verification, i.e., 9.15%. Table 7.1 shows the results of this competition (winning system depicted in bold).

generated for each system. Furthermore, non-parametric bootstrapping was used to obtain 95% confidence intervals for the EERs [Alberink and Ruifrok, 2008]. System with ID 13 gives the lowest EER in off-line verification, i.e., 9:15%. Table 7.1 shows the results of this competition (winning system depicted in bold).

7.3 Forensic Signature Verification Competition (4NSigComp2010)

This is the second competition organized jointly by PR experts and FHEs. Two scenarios were defined. One scenario focused on the detection of skilled versus nonskilled simulations [31]. Its aim was to evaluate various automated systems in security-less critical environments. It considered classification among genuine signatures, random, and unskilled forgeries. The GPDS-960 [32] data set was used and the performance was reported using the overall error (based on the FRR and FAR for simulated and random forgeries). Here, the best system got an overall error of 8.94%. This chapter will focus the second scenario [33] which is more closely relevant to forensic applications. The second scenario included the category of disguised signatures (where authentic authors tried to simulate their own signatures). The systems had to detect skilled forgeries and disguised signatures from genuine signatures of a reference writer. To the best of author's knowledge, this was the first time ever when disguised signatures were exclusively included in a competition training and test data [33].

7.3.1 Data

The signatures were collected under the supervision of Bryan Found and Doug Rogers in the years 2002 and 2006, respectively [34]. The training set contained 209 images. It comprised 85 genuine, 104 forged, and 20 disguised signatures. The test set contained 125 signatures. It comprised 28 genuine, 90 forged, and 7 disguised signatures.[b]

7.3.2 Submitted Systems

In total, seven systems participated in this competition. System 1 is based on the fusion of two machine experts: one based on the local analysis of the image [23] and another approach based on allographic analysis [24]. System 2 uses a dynamic time-warping (DTW) similarity on their projections obtained by Mojette transform. To answer the nature of the signature (naturally written or not), the similarity matrix on the given reference signatures is computed. Systems 3 and 7 compute several features based on the number of connected components, number of holes, moments, projections, distributions, position of barycenter, number of branches in the skeleton, Fourier descriptors, directions, curvatures, and chain codes. System 4 is a commercial product, and its working details were not provided by the participants. System 5 tessellates the image into a fixed number of zones using polar coordinate representation and extracts gradient information in each zone. System 6 opted to remain anonymous and did not provide a description.

---

[b]These data are available at http://www.iapr-tc11.org/mediawiki/index.php/ICFHR_ 2010_Signature_Verification_Competition_(4NSigComp2010).

7.3.3 Evaluation

The systems presented their opinion by means of a probability value P between 0 and 1 for each of the questioned signatures. The probability value P was compared to a predefined threshold t. A higher value ($P > t$) indicated that the questioned signature was most likely a genuine one. A lower value ($P < t$) indicated that the questioned signature was not genuine, meaning that it was not written by the reference author. A probability value of ($P = t$) was considered as inconclusive. A summary of the results is given in Table 7.2 (winning system depicted in bold).

A crucial observation is that most of the systems could not handle disguised signatures. There was only one system (System-ID 6 in Table 7.2) that performed well on the disguised signatures, but this system showed a large error rate in detecting simulated signatures, which hints the difficult nature of disguised signatures.

7.4 Signature Verification Competition (SigComp2011)

Traditionally, automatic signature verification systems report their decisions in a Boolean manner, i.e., if enough evidence of a forgery is present, a system reports a "reject," otherwise an "accept." Though this is quite objective and may be significant in some fields like real-time application, e.g., banking, but a Boolean answer of genuine or forged is not adequate for the

Table 7.2. Summary of 4NSigComp2010 results.

| System-ID | Wrongly classified | | | Acc. | FAR | FRR | EER |
	D	F	G				
1	7	1	2	90.0	1.1	90	80
2	7	37	2	54.0	41.1	90	58
3	7	18	0	75.0	20.0	70	70
4	7	0	1	92.0	0.0	80	70
5	**7**	**12**	**1**	**80.0**	**13.3**	**80**	**55**
6	1	79	0	20.0	87.0	10	60
7	7	1	1	91.0	1.1	80	70

Note: FRR: false rejection rate, FAR: false acceptance rate, D: disguise, F: forged, G: genuine.

FHEs. They are interested to exactly know how close a questioned signature to a genuine signature is when it is declared as forged and vice versa.

A solution, therefore, is that automatic systems should produce some continuous similarity/difference scores (that may vary between any two extremes like, 0:001 to 1000) which would be converted into evidential value/likelihood ratios (LRs) according to the Bayesian approach [36]. The scores can be converted into LRs by a so-called calibration procedure [37], such as the one implemented in the FoCal toolkit.[c]

The SigComp2011 [19] competition applied such an evaluation scheme by using the FoCal toolkit. Note that the said scheme is suitable not only for FHEs, but it also provides objective values ($\hat{C}_{cllr}^{min}$) of system performances which are generally required in PR to find out the standing of a system in comparison to other systems, e.g., in a competition.

7.4.1 *Data*

This competition provided signature data in two languages, i.e., Dutch and Chinese. Signatures were either genuine or forged/simulated. For both, Dutch and Chinese signatures, data from 10 reference writers were provided to the participants. Each writer contributed with 12 reference signatures and 12 questioned genuine signatures for both modes: offline and online. Furthermore, 36 forgeries were produced by three forgers for each reference writer. The data for evaluation were similar. The only difference was that, for Chinese, just the data of 10 writers were used, while for Dutch, the data of 54 writers were used, leading to more representative results.[d] More details are presented in [19].

7.4.2 *Submitted Systems*

In total, 13 systems were submitted for this competition. System 1 tessellates the signature into a fixed number of zones using polar coordinate representation and extracts gradient information in each zone. The

---

[c]http://focaltoolkit.googlepages.com.
[d]These data are available at http://www.iapr-tc11.org/mediawiki/index.php/ICDAR_2011_Signature_Verification_Competition_(SigComp2011).

extracted features of the query signature are classified using a user-dependent support vector machine (SVM) that is trained with the reference signatures of the user and negative examples. System 2 preferred remaining anonymous. System 3 includes two main phases: the evidence estimation phase and the calibration phase. For every two signatures, two types of descriptors, a local (at every sampled point based on the gradient in the gray scale image) and a global (in a skeleton image by using shape context) are computed. In the second phase, the FoCal framework [37] is used to calibrate the evidence score. Systems 4 and 5 are commercial products and from the same participant. Systems 6 and 7 use edge-based directional probability distribution features [39] and grapheme features [38]. System 8 is based on the methods introduced in Daramola [40]. System 9 remained anonymous and did not provide any description. While Systems 1, 6, 7, and 9 were submitted for online and offline signatures, Systems 4 and 5 for online data only, and Systems 3, 4, and 8 for offline data only.

7.4.3 *Evaluation*

Four different signature verification tasks/scenarios were defined for the said competition, i.e., Chinese offline, Dutch offline, Chinese online, and Dutch online signature verification. The systems were evaluated according to several measures. First, Receiver Operating Characteristic (ROC) curves were generated to see at which point the EER is reached. At this specific point, the accuracy was also measured, i.e., the percentage of correct decisions with respect to all questioned signatures. The uniqueness of the said competition and associated evaluation was that the participants were required to report continuous scores that can be converted into LRs or log LRs (LLRs) by various calibration procedures. One such calibration using the FoCal toolkit [37] was carried out in this competition where first the cost of the log-likelihood ratios (LLRs) $\hat{C}_{llr}$ was measured and then the minimum possible value of $\hat{C}_{llr}$, i.e., $\hat{C}_{llr}^{min}$. where $\hat{C}_{llr}$ is the cost due to the lack of discrimination and calibration associated with an automatic system. The greater a system misclassified or the greater a system classified signatures on the opposite side, i.e., classify forgeries as genuine and genuine as forgeries, the greater will be $\hat{C}_{llr}$. The $\hat{C}_{llr}^{min}$ is used as the final assessment value of a system's performance.

Note that a smaller value of $\hat{C}_{llr}^{min}$ denotes a better performance of the method. The results of this competition appear in Table 7.3 (winning systems depicted in bold). An interesting observation can be made when having a closer look at Table 7.3. A good EER does not always result in a good $\hat{C}_{llr}^{min}$, e.g., System 9(b) performs quite well on online Chinese data when looking at the EER but has the worst $\hat{C}_{llr}^{min}$. This might be explained by the fact that even a few large misleading answers spoil the overall performance with $\hat{C}_{llr}^{min}$. Note that this reflects the practice, i.e., a system should not produce a high likelihood for a wrong decision, as this might result in wrong judgment with severe outcomes.

7.5 Forensic Signature Verification Competition (4NSigComp2012)

This competition [54] focused on the automatic classification of disguised signatures along with genuine and forged signatures, and the results were reported using the LRs so that to be more informative for FHEs. A larger and more diverse data set is used in this competition. Note that the participating systems this time had the possibility of training on the complete data from 4NSigComp2010, and this has helped the systems improve results.

7.5.1 *Data*

The data contain only offline signature samples. The training set of 4NSigcomp2012 comprised the training and the test set of the 4NsigComp2010. The test set of the 4Nsigcomp2012 was a mixture of genuine signatures, disguised signatures, and skilled forgeries for three reference authors as given in Tables 7.4 and 7.5.[e]

7.5.2 *Submitted Systems*

In total, five systems from five institutes participated in this competition.

System 1 employs the Gaussian grid feature extraction technique by dividing the signature contour into $m \times n$ zones [41]. System 2 computes

---

[e]These data are available at http://www.iapr-tc11.org/mediawiki/index.php/ICFHR_2012_Signature_Verification_Competition_(4NSigComp2012).

Table 7.3. SigComp2011: Evaluation.

System-ID	Accuracy (%)	FRR	FAR	$\hat{C}_{llr}$	$\hat{C}_{llr}^{min}$
			Task 1: Chinese offline verification		
1(a)	80.84	21.01	19.62	0.76	0.69
2	73.10	27.50	26.70	3.06	0.77
3	72.90	27.50	26.98	1.13	0.79
6(a)	56.06	45.00	43.60	1.26	0.89
7(a)	51.95	50.00	47.41	3.22	0.95
8	62.01	37.50	38.15	1.57	0.93
9(a)	61.81	38.33	38.15	6.23	0.92
			Task 2: Dutch offline verification		
1(a)	82.91	17.93	16.41	0.73	0.57
2	77.99	22.22	21.75	2.46	0.67
3	87.80	12.35	12.05	0.42	0.39
6(a)	95.57	4.48	4.38	0.71	0.13
7(a)	97.67	2.47	2.19	0.90	0.08
8	75.84	23.77	24.57	1.66	0.72
9(a)	71.02	29.17	28.79	4.13	0.79
			Task 3: Chinese online verification		
1(b)	84.81	12.00	16.05	0.57	0.35
4	93.17	6.40	6.94	0.41	0.22
5	93.17	6.40	6.94	0.42	0.22
6(b)	82.94	16.80	17.14	1.05	0.50
7(b)	85.32	13.60	14.97	0.91	0.46
9(b)	80.89	9.26	8.14	6.21	0.73
			Task 4: Dutch online verification		
1(b)	93.49	7.56	7.69	0.50	0.24
4	96.27	3.70	3.76	0.26	0.12
5	96.35	3.86	3.44	0.35	0.12
6(b)	91.82	8.33	8.02	0.53	0.29
7(b)	92.93	7.25	6.87	0.60	0.24
9(b)	88.56	11.11	11.27	6.43	0.40

Table 7.4.   Overview of the test data 4NsigComp2012.

No. of signatures	Author "A1"	Author "A2"	Author "A2"
Reference	20	16	15
Questioned	250	100	100

Table 7.5.   Breakup of test set questioned signatures.

No. of signatures	Author "A1"	Author "A2"	Author "A2"
Disguised	47	08	09
Forged	160	42	71
Genuine	43	50	20

several features based on the number of connected components, number of holes, moments, projections, distributions, position of barycenter, number of branches in the skeleton, Fourier descriptors, tortuosities, directions, curvatures, and chain codes. System 3 tessellates the image into a fixed number of zones using polar coordinate representation and extract gradient information in each zone. System Anonym-I is based on various grid features, including size of grid/cell, it's center of mass, centroid, and the angles of inclinations each black pixel makes with the corners of the corresponding cell [40]. System Anonym-II uses a sliding window approach. The width of the window is varied from one to three pixel, and following geometrical features are computed at each window position; the mean pixel gray value, the centroid, vertical, and horizontal second-order moments, the locations of the uppermost, and lowermost black pixel, and their positions and gradients with respect to the neighboring windows, the black to white transitions present within the entire window, the number of black–white transitions between the uppermost and lowermost pixels in an image column, and the proportion of black pixels to the number of pixels between the uppermost and lowermost pixels.

7.5.3 *Evaluation*

The experiments were divided into two evaluation categories. The evaluation 1 for all the experiments considered genuine, forged, and disguised signatures. The evaluation 2 for all the experiments considered only

Table 7.6.   Summary of 4NSigComp2012 results.

System-ID	Accuracy (%)	FAR	FRR	EER	EER w/o disguised
Griffith	**85.11**	**15.82**	**15.82**	**15.82**	**14.16**
Nifi-Full	77.88	23.16	23.16	21.62	16.48
Sabanci	78.89	21.47	21.47	20.88	13.19
Anonym-I	71.11	28.81	28.81	28.81	20.35
Anonym-I	30.67	62.71	62.71	62.71	68.14

Note: FRR: false rejection rate, FAR: false acceptance rate, EER: equal error rate.

genuine and forged signatures. A summary of these results is given in Table 7.6 (winning system depicted in bold). The results show that the grid-based features which actually focus on many small regions of the signature seem to be the most efficient features for this data set. However, we can also observe that the effectiveness of the features vary from one writer to another. Thus, it is hard to draw some general conclusions out of these results. Note that the System Anonym-II also uses features from many small regions; however, instead of using a static grid, it applies a more sophisticated method, which finally works worse on this data set.

7.6 Signature Verification and Writer Identification Competitions (SigWiComp2013)

The signature verification community was again motivated to enable their systems compute the LRs instead of just computing the evidence. The tasks this time were more challenging as more diverse forensic signature data (Japanese and Dutch) were available to the participants [55]. There were three tasks of signature analysis, i.e., Dutch offline, Japanese offline, and Japanese online signature verification.

7.6.1 *Data*

The Dutch signatures were collected by FHEs at the Netherlands Forensic Institute (NFI). The Japanese signatures were collected by PR researchers at the Human Interface Laboratory, Mie University, Japan. The Dutch offline signatures (both training and test) were available in

Table 7.7.   Dutch signatures.

Mode	Training A*			Training B*			Test		
	A	G	F	A	G	F	A	G	F
Offline	12	60	1,860	54	1,296	648	27	270	972

Note: A: authors, G: genuine signatures, F: forged signatures, A*: SigComp2009 data, B*: SigComp2011 data.

Table 7.8.   Japanese signatures.

Mode	Training			Test		
	A	G	F	A	G	F
Offline	11	462	396	20	840	720
Online	11	462	396	20	840	720

Note: A: authors, G: genuine signatures, F: forged signatures.

the offline format only. The training set comprised of signatures from training and test set of the SigComp2009 and SigComp2011. The evaluation set for this task was comprised of 27 authors where each author contributed 10 of her/his genuine signatures. There were 36 skilled forgeries on average available for each genuine author (varying from minimum 25 to maximum 60 forgeries per genuine author. The data breakup is provided in Table 7.7.[f] The training sets for both Japanese online and offline tasks comprised of 11 authors with 42 genuine signatures and 36 forgeries per author. The test sets for both Japanese online and offline tasks comprised of 20 authors with 42 genuine signatures each and 36 corresponding forgeries per author. The data breakup is provided in Table 7.8.

7.6.2 *Submitted Systems*

Ten systems participated for offline and three system for online signature verification tasks. System 1 uses signatures' baselines and loops, and then

---

[f]These data are available at http://tc11.cvc.uab.es/datasets/SigWiComp2013_1.

generalizes the distribution of these features in all the genuine signatures. A similar process is repeated with forgeries, and finally classification is performed using various distribution analysis methods [42]. Systems 2, System 3, and System 4 are from the same participant. The system, in general, uses two complementary features from each signature: histogram of oriented gradients (HOGs) and local binary patterns (LBPs). HOG features are extracted in the Cartesian and polar coordinates, LBP features are extracted only in the Cartesian coordinates, resulting in three kinds of features in total. For classification, SVMs are used [43]. System 5 combines through a logistic regression classifier the geometrical features based on the number of holes, moments, projections, distributions, position of barycenter, number of branches in the skeleton, Fourier descriptors, tortuosities, directions, curvatures, chain codes, and edge-based directional features. System 6 is based on edge-based directional features. The method starts with conventional edge detection that generates a binary image in which only the edge pixels are "on." Then each edge pixel is considered in the middle of a square neighborhood and checked in all directions emerging from the central pixel and ending on the periphery of the neighborhood for the presence of an entire edge fragment. All the verified instances are counted into a histogram that is finally normalized to a probability distribution which gives the probability of finding in the image an edge fragment oriented at the angle measured from the horizontal. For comparison purposes, the Manhattan distance metric is used. System 7 is based on the edge-hinge features which estimate the joint distribution of edge angles in a writer's handwriting. They are constructed by performing an edge detection using a Sobel kernel on the input images, and subsequently, measuring the angles of both edge segments that emanate from each edge pixel. To compare the signatures, the Manhattan distance metric is used. System 8 is based on multiscale run-length features [44] which are determined on the binary image taking into consideration both the black pixels corresponding to the ink trace and the white pixels corresponding to the background. The probability distribution of black and white run-lengths has been used. There are four scanning methods: horizontal, vertical, left-diagonal, and right-diagonal. The run-length features are calculated using the gray-level run-length matrices, and the histogram of run-lengths is normalized and interpreted as a probability distribution. The method considers horizontal, vertical, left-diagonal, and right-diagonal white run-lengths as well as horizontal, vertical, left-diagonal, and right-diagonal black run-lengths extracted from the original image. To compare the signatures, the Manhattan distance metric is used. System 9 is based on the combination of both types of features used by the previous systems: multiscale edge-hinge features and multiscale run-length features. Again for this method, the Manhattan distance metric is used. System 10 is based on the combination of three types of features used by the Systems 6, 7, and 8: multiscale edge-hinge features, multiscale run-length features, and the edge-based directional features. Again for this method, the Manhattan distance metric is used to compare signatures. Systems 11, 12, and 13 perform online verification only and therefore tested for Japanese only. System 11 computes differences between the features of the questioned signature and the reference signatures at the signal level as well as the histogram level [45]. Those features include the x and y coordinates, pressure, directions, angles, speed, and angular speed. System 12 is the DTW-based system described in [46], where the DTW score is slightly adjusted to obtain user-based thresholds and capture some new forgery clues. This adjustment is made by analyzing the reference signatures and the alignment of the query to the references. System 12 is similar to System 13 with the exception that pressure is also included in the DTW algorithm.

7.6.3 *Evaluation*

The results of the three defined tasks are given in Tables 7.9–7.11 (winning systems depicted in bold). As shown, different systems performed best on different tasks. A few interesting observations can be made when having a closer look at the tables. Similar to the Sigcomp2011, it is obvious from the results that the system with the best FRR and FAR always turned out to have the best value of $\hat{C}_{llr}^{min}$, but a good EER does not always result in a good $\hat{C}_{llr}^{min}$, e.g., System 3 performs quite well for Task 1 when looking at the EER as compared to that of System 4 on the same data, but the $\hat{C}_{llr}^{min}$ of System 4 is better than that of System 3. This might be explained by the fact that a few large errors might spoil the overall performance with $\hat{C}_{llr}^{min}$. Similar is the case with Systems 8 and 9 on the

Table 7.9. Results for Task 1: Dutch offline signature verification.

System-ID	Accuracy (%)	FRR	FAR	$\hat{C}_{Ur}$	$\hat{C}_{Ur}^{min}$
1	67.90	31.85	32.14	2.005070	0.863449
2	**76.83**	**23.70**	**23.10**	**0.880048**	**0.642632**
3	75.56	24.44	24.44	1.086197	0.706733
4	74.93	25.19	25.05	0.979237	0.698044
5	73.76	26.67	26.18	3.941330	0.732123
6	72.14	27.41	27.93	0.966780	0.739129
7	70.87	29.63	29.06	1.103572	0.776319
8	69.16	31.11	30.80	1.021834	0.742239
9	70.15	29.63	29.88	1.053304	0.744848
10	72.95	27.41	27.00	1.023746	0.728198

Table 7.10. Results for Task 2: Japanese offline signature verification.

System-ID	Accuracy (%)	FRR	FAR	$\hat{C}_{Ur}$	$\hat{C}_{Ur}^{min}$
1	72.70	27.23	27.36	4.692036	0.778976
2	**90.72**	**9.74**	**9.72**	**0.796040**	**0.339265**
3	89.82	10.23	10.14	0.814598	0.349146
4	86.95	13.04	13.06	0.831630	0.400977
5	66.67	33.33	33.33	0.940937	0.833182
6	76.70	23.60	23.06	0.980174	0.665241
7	73.98	26.07	25.97	1.021412	0.720444
8	68.33	31.35	31.94	1.006464	0.758588
9	72.10	27.89	27.92	1.013250	0.717454
10	74.59	25.41	25.42	1.002516	0.694036

Table 7.11. Results for Task 3: Japanese online signature verification.

System-ID	Accuracy (%)	FRR	FAR	$\hat{C}_{Ur}$	$\hat{C}_{Ur}^{min}$
11	70.55	29.56	30.22	1.176164	0.884223
12	**72.55**	**27.56**	**27.36**	**1.089183**	**0.744544**
13	72.47	27.56	27.50	1.114015	0.744793

same task. This is an important observation as it gives a clue that the evaluation metric used in this competition, i.e., $\hat{C}_{llr}^{min}$ not only looks into the number of errors but is also influenced by the severity of respective errors, and this makes the metric ($\hat{C}_{llr}^{min}$) well suited for the forensic casework.

7.7 Signature Verification and Writer Identification Competition (SigWiComp2015)

This competition [56] further strengthened a paradigm shift in automatic signature verification (introduced in the SigComp2011, and tested heavily in 4NSigComp2012 and SigWiComp2013) from the "decision paradigm" to an "evidential value paradigm." This time, however, three signature analysis tasks were defined, i.e., Italian offline, Bangla offline, and German online signature verification.

7.7.1 *Data*

The signature data were available in Italian, Bangla, and German.[g] The Italian offline signatures were collected at the University of Salerno from the University employees and students. Two unique aspects of these data are as follows: these are actual signatures that were provided by individuals while filling various forms and applications at the University, and the signatures collection span over a period of time that is between 3 and 5 years depending on the subject. The forgeries are also made by students where they were allowed to practice the forgery as many times as they liked, and then they produced skilled forgeries. For training, a set of 50 specimen genuine authors, with 5 reference signatures from each specimen author, was provided to the participants in a binarized form. For evaluation, the same 50 specimen authors, with 10 new (previously unknown) corresponding questioned signatures each, containing genuine signatures and skilled forgeries in a binarized form. Detailed breakup is provided in Table 7.12. The Bangla/Bengali offline signatures were collected from different parts of the West Bengal, a state

---

[g]These data are available at http://tc11.cvc.uab.es/datasets/.

Table 7.12. Italian offline signature data.

Data	Authors	Genuine	Forged	Total
Training	50	250	0	250
Testing	50	229	249	478

Table 7.13. Bengali offline signature data.

Data	Authors	Genuine	Forged	Total
Training	10	120	0	120
Testing	10	120	300	420

of India. The majority of the signatures were contributed by students. A total number of 240 genuine signatures were collected from 10 contributors (24 genuine signatures by each). For each contributor, all genuine specimens were collected in a single day's writing session. In order to produce the forgeries, the imitators were allowed to practice forgeries as long as they wished. A total number of 300 (30 signatures, 10 individuals) forged signatures were collected. The images were captured in 256 level gray scale at 300 dpi and stored in the TIFF format (Tagged Image File Format). A detailed breakup is provided in Table 7.13. The German online signatures were collected at the German Research Center for Artificial Intelligence, Germany. A unique aspect of these data is that the data have been collected using a digitized pen rather than a tablet, i.e., by Anoto Pen [48]. This pen specializes in providing the look and feel of regular pens. It only demands to add the Anoto dot pattern to any paper and data can be digitized seamlessly. The Anoto pattern makes it possible for the Anoto pen built-in camera to detect strokes and record signatures. The signature data were collected from employees of different financial institutions and students of University of Kaiserslautern who also participated in the generation of skilled forgeries. The data set consists of ASCII files with the format: X, Y, and pressure with the sampling rate of 75 Hz and the resolution of 85 dpi. For training, 30 specimen genuine authors were selected, from whom each one provided 10 genuine reference signatures. For evaluation, data

Table 7.14.   German online signature data.

Data	Authors	Genuine	Forged	Total
Training	30	300	0	300
Testing	30	150	300	450

from the same 30 specimen genuine authors, with 15 corresponding questioned signatures each, containing genuine signatures and skilled forgeries were used. Detailed data breakup is provided in Table 7.14.

7.7.2 Submitted Systems

A total of 30 systems from 13 different institutions participated. The details are as follows: 9 systems for offline Italian signature verification, the same 9 systems optimized for offline Bengali signature verification, and 12 system for the online German signature verification. System 1 uses HOG and LBP extracted from local regions, together with the user-based and global SVM classifiers and a sophisticated classifier combination. Systems 2–6 are the same systems which participated in the SigWiComp2013 (Systems 6, 7, 8, 9, and 10), but this time optimized for Italian and German data. Systems 7 and 8 combine through a logistic regression classifier the geometrical features described in [45]. Those features are based on the number of holes, moments, projections, distributions, position of barycenter, number of branches in the skeleton, Fourier descriptors, tortuosities, directions, curvatures, chain codes, and edge-based directional features. The two systems differ in weighting the features they are built on. System 9 has four main modules. The first one identify and extracts the signature from the image page. The second module applies filtering and other preprocessing on the extracted signature. The third module extracts various spatial, geometric, morphological, and statistical features. The last module allows the combination of multiple classifiers and uses DTW, Pearson correlation, and Euclidean distance combined by an MLP neural network to make the final decision.

The same nine systems (Systems 1–9) have participated for both Italian and Bengali tasks (when optimized for the specific task); their details are therefore omitted. For German online signature verification systems, 10–14 are from the same academic organization, and they have requested not to mention their identities. All of these systems are based on DTW on various time functions derived from the position trajectory and the pressure information. These five systems differ in the specific functions considered and the type of score normalization applied. System 15 is based on the DTW algorithm and uses both global features (e.g., total writing time) and local features (e.g., pressure in a given point). If the total writing time of the signature to be verified is acceptable, for each local feature f (such as X–Y coordinates, pressure), the DTW distance between the time series related to the authentic signature and to the signature to be verified is computed. Then, DTW distances are combined with a weighted sum by giving a weight to each of the different kinds of features. The similarity score is computed accordingly. In System 16, multiple time series representation of signature, including time series of X-coordinate, Y-coordinate, pressure, speed, and centroid distance are computed. Verification of genuine and forged signature is done using the adaptation of multivariate m-mediod-based classification and anomaly detection approach as presented in [47]. Systems 17 and 18 are commercial products designed by Cursor Insight. These systems specialize in calculating more than 70,000 movement characteristics of each hand-written sample. For further details, refer to Cursor Insight.[h] System 19 compares the signatures using statistical data as well as a time-based model. It extracts the changes of several dynamic features (direction, pressure, and speed) over time. The statistical data contain static information like the duration of the signature or duration and time of pen liftings. The reference signatures are compared against each other to define the validity space of the model. The similarities of the features are combined into a final score using different weightings. System 20 computes differences between the features of the questioned signature and the reference signatures at the signal level as well as the histogram level [45]. Those features include the x and y coordinates, pressure, directions, angles, speed, and angular speed. System 21 only uses the "x" and "y" coordinates as features and DTW as the matching algorithm. Normalization of the query scores

---

[h]www.cursorinsight.com

is done based on reference signature statistics. Details of this system can be found in [46].

7.7.3 Evaluation

The systems were evaluated according to the cost of the LLRs $\hat{C}_{llr}$ using the FoCal toolkit [37], and finally the minimal possible value of $\hat{C}_{llr}$, i.e., $\hat{C}_{llr}^{min}$ as the final assessment value. A smaller value of $\hat{C}_{llr}^{min}$ denotes a better performance of the method. Important observations about the signature verification tasks for different data are as follows. For Italian offline signatures, the system using a combination of local and global features outperformed all other systems (mostly based on global features) by a large margin; for Bengali offline signatures, most of the systems performed good and there was not much variance among the results which might indicate that the systems which were originally designed for western languages were able to adapt well on an Indic language provided better training; for German online signatures, the systems had to face difficulties as these data were collected by specialized electronic pen Anoto. The Anoto pen also records position and pressure similar to standard data capturing tablets, however, with different internal data capturing mechanism. Since the use of electronic pens is increasing, the PR research should also consider these data and optimize the systems accordingly. The results are summarized in Tables 7.15, 7.16, and 7.17 (winning systems depicted in bold), respectively.

Table 7.15.   Results for Task 1: Italian offline signature verification.

System-ID	Participant	$\hat{C}_{Ur}$	$\hat{C}_{Ur}^{min}$
1	**Sabanci university**	**0.655109**	**0.021358**
2	Tebessa university	0.993189	0.893270
3	Tebessa university	1.065696	0.952499
4	Tebessa university	1.074474	0.880930
5	Tebessa university	1.065475	0.901003
6	Tebessa university	1.041895	0.901003
7	Qatar university	8.901864	0.972708
8	Qatar university	13.111064	0.960163
9	Commercial system	1.003786	0.988845

Table 7.16. Results for Task 2: Bengali offline signature verification.

System-ID	Participant	$\hat{C}_{Ur}$	$\hat{C}_{Ur}^{min}$
1	Sabanci university	0.68895	0.052485
2	Tebessa university	0.933750	0.154390
3	Tebessa university	0.939850	0.116541
4	**Tebessa university**	**0.923886**	**0.039721**
5	Tebessa university	0.931253	0.060248
6	Tebessa university	0.929922	0.55556
7	Qatar university	1.161387	0.973043
8	Qatar university	2.839290	0.297842
9	Commercial system	0.998630	0.893893

Table 7.17. Results for Task 3: German online signature verification.

System-ID	Participant	$\hat{C}_{Ur}$	$\hat{C}_{Ur}^{min}$
10	Anonymous	0.948878	0.680014
11	Anonymous	0.944402	0.688105
12	Anonymous	0.855595	0.576762
13	Anonymous	0.874655	0.577098
14	Anonymous	1.262207	0.684602
15	Anonymous	0.996586	0.839468
16	Baharia university	1.025046	0.772073
17	**Cursor insight**	**1.243891**	**0.290158**
18	Cursor insight	1.496257	0.540563
19	Commercial system	0.807276	0.465681
20	Qatar university	3.345016	0.854712
21	Sabanci university	0.873383	0.304159

7.8 Discussions and Future Perspectives

This chapter has introduced the particular document analysis problem of
signature verification and has summarized the results of several signature
verification competitions organized jointly by PR researchers and FHEs.
The data used in these competitions have also been described and links to
these data are provided.

In 2009, the SigComp2009 evaluated automated systems on the data collected by FHEs from forensic-like cases. An important observation on these data was that they contained only five genuine signatures per reference author (for 100 authors). Now if at least three of these genuine signatures are used for training, the remaining set is too small to gauge the performance of competing systems effectively.

In 2010, along with the more traditional genuine versus forged paradigm, the 4NSigComp2010 included disguised signatures (where genuine author imitates their own signature). This was the first competition ever when disguised signatures were also present in the data set. It took automated systems more close to forensic casework. However, an observation about this competition is the limited amount of data (which, of course, is caused by the difficulty of getting genuine, forged, and disguised signatures from forensic-like scenarios).

In 2011, the SigComp2011 focused on the issue that automated systems when applied in forensic scenarios do not produce output as required by FHEs. Therefore, the systems were required to produce a comparison score, e.g., a degree of similarity or difference, and the evidential value of that score.

This evidential value of score was expressed as the LR. Reporting the results this way took the automated signature verification systems one step closer to the forensic casework. This time large data sets of Chinese and Dutch signatures (online and offline) were provided, thereby ensuring that the systems would be effectively evaluated.

In 2012, the 4NSigComp2012 focused on providing more disguised signature data, and the evaluation was performed in terms of LRs. This time the participating systems had a possibility to train on the previously available disguised signatures data from 4NSigComp2010, which significantly improved the results.

In 2013, more signature data in Japanese and Dutch were provided. Evaluations were again based on LRs. In 2015, even more signature data were made available publicly. This competition offered novel data in Italian, Bangla, and German. The online data were captured using a novel digitizing pen, Anoto pen, and the offline data were collected from real-world situations (e.g., students registering with a university in Italy). This has helped even better evaluation of the systems.

Note that in every competition, the focus was either a bit broadened (e.g., the inclusion of disguised signatures, likelihood-based evaluations) or more data were provided in more languages/scripts. Further, every time, the evaluation protocol, the results, and most importantly the data have been made publicly available. This has not only helped the overall PR community in better understanding the nature of forensic signature examination but has also motivated forensic examiners to look into the possibilities of using automated signature verification systems during their routine casework.

Furthermore, some very important considerations are highlighted in these competitions. First, the PR community should also consider the novel/forgotten types of signatures (e.g., disguised signatures) when developing systems for real-world applications, particularly involving forensic scenarios. Second, these systems should report LRs. The concern is not to replace the existing evaluation methods in the PR community. Rather, providing likelihoods in addition to the well-known error rates will increase the acceptability of automatic signature verification systems in forensic casework.

Third, fictitious cases (random forgeries/genuine signatures of any person other than the reference author) should be handled with caution as they tend to artificially lower the error rate [50]. If random forgeries are used for specific purposes (e.g., while training) and for specific application domain, their results must be reported separately [49].

Fourth, the forgeries (be it random or otherwise) should not be used while training a system for application in the real world. Note that for all of the signature verification tasks, no forgeries were provided for training (see, e.g., Tables 7.12–7.14). This is important as in the real world one can never limit the forgery set since every signature other than the genuine signature written naturally by the authentic author can be a forgery, and also when forgeries are used for training, there is always a chance that an automatic system may learn to declare signatures as forgeries when they are coming from the forgers for whom the system is trained with [51–53]. This introduces an artificial bias in the system which should be avoided.

In future, it would be desirable if FHEs could provide PR researchers with freely available realistic data collected from forensic situations. It may need some ethical considerations but freely available data sets with the large number of realistic skilled forgeries and disguised signatures would help the PR researchers better optimize their systems for forensic scenarios.

Noteworthy, a fundamental limitation with the current data sets is that forgeries are done by "genuine" people. Real "fraudsters" may have unique behavior like nervousness. Creating such data sets may be difficult but should be addressed by FHEs so that to test the state-of-the-art automatic methods on "true" data. In the future, there should also be cases where automatic systems are applied to detect forgeries that are in fact/perfect copies" of original signatures. This would help in identifying the cases where fraudsters/forgers might have taken the genuine signatures of an authentic author and pasted somehow to pass automatic signature verification.

Another important observation made through the course of competitions reported here, and various other experiments carried out on the data of these competitions, is that automatic signature analysis systems based on local/part-based features generally produce better results for cases involving disguised signatures. Though a lot more data and experiments are required to establish this thoroughly, some initial proof of concept has been made available in these competitions and later experiments [51–53].

References

1. R. Plamondon and G. Lorette, "Automatic signature verification and writer identification the state of the art," *Pattern Recognition*, vol. 22, no. 2, pp. 107–131, 1989.
2. A. Schlapbach, "Writer identification and verification," Chapter 1, pp. 2–4. Clearway Logistics Phase 2–3, 1013 BG Amsterdam, The Netherlands, 2007.
3. A.K. Jain, A. Ross, and S. Prabhakar, "An introduction to biometric recognition," *IEEE Transactions on Circuits and Systems for Video Technology*, vol. 14, no. 1, pp. 4–20, 2004.
4. G. Chollet and F. Bimbot, "Assessment of speaker verification systems," *Handbook of Standards and Resources for Spoken Language Systems*, Chapter 11, pp. 408–480. Berlin, Germany, Mouton de Gruyter, 1997.
5. M. Hanmandlu, M. Hafizuddin Mohd Yusof, and V. Krishna Madasu, "Offline signature verification and forgery detection using fuzzy modeling," *Pattern Recognition*, vol. 38, no. 3, pp. 341–356, 2005.

6. S. Ahmed, M. I. Malik, M. Liwicki, and A. Dengel, "Signature segmentation from document images," in *International Conference on Frontiers in Handwriting Recognition*, IEEE, September 18–20, 2012, pp. 425–429.

7. R. Mandal, P.P. Roy, and U. Pal, "Signature segmentation from machine printed documents using conditional random field," in *International Conference on Document Analysis and Recognition*, IEEE, September 18–21, 2011, pp. 1170–1174.

8. D. Impedovo and G. Pirlo, "Automatic signature verification: The state of the art," *IEEE Transactions on Systems, Man, and Cybernetics, Part C: Applications and Reviews*, vol. 38, no. 5, pp. 609–635, 2008.

9. J. Llados and G. Sanchez, "Indexing historical documents by word shape signatures," in *International Conference on Document Analysis and Recognition*, IEEE, September 23–26, 2007, pp. 362–366.

10. M. Liwicki, "Recognition of whiteboard notes online, offline, and combination," PhD Thesis, Institut für Informatik und angewandte Mathematik, Bern University, 2007.

11. H. Baltzakis and N. Papamarkos, "A new signature verification technique based on a two-stage neural network classifier," *Engineering Applications of Artificial Intelligence*, vol. 14, no. 1, pp. 95–103, 2001.

12. R. Bajaj and S. Chaudhury, "Signature verification using multiple neural classifiers," *Pattern Recognition*, vol. 30, no. 1, pp. 1–7, 1997.

13. E. Ozgunduz, T. Senturk, and E. K. Arsligil, "Off-line signature verification and recognition by support vector machine," in *European Signal Processing Conference*, Eusipco, Curran Associates Inc., September 4–8, 2005, pp. 113–116.

14. M.K. Kalera, S. Srihari, and A. Xu, "Online signature verification and identification using distance statistics," *International Journal of Pattern Recognition and Artificial Intelligence*, vol. 18, no. 7, pp. 1339–1360, 2004.

15. J. Fierrez, J. Ortega-Garcia, D. Ramos, and J. Gonzalez-Rodriguez, "HMM-based on-line signature verification: Feature extraction and signature modeling," *Pattern Recognition Letters*, vol. 28, no. 16, pp. 2325–2334, 2007.

16. J. Bromley, I. Guyon, Y. Lecun, E. Sckinger, and R. Shah "Signature verification using a "siamese" time delay neural network," in *Neural Information Processing Systems*, Morgan-Kaufmann, pp. 737–744, 1993.

17. G.S. Eskander, R. Sabourin, and E. Granger, "Hybrid writer independent–writer-dependent off-line signature verification system," *IET Biometrics*, vol. 2, no. 4, pp. 169–181, 2013.

18. Z.-H. Quan and K.-L. Liu, "On-line signature verification based on the hybrid HMM/ANN model," *International Journal of Computer Science and Network Security*, vol. 7, no. 3, 2007.

19. M. Liwicki and M. I. Malik and C. E. van den Heuvel, X. Chen, C. Berger, R. Stoel, M. Blumenstein, and B. Found, "Signature verification competition for online and offline skilled forgeries (SigComp2011), in *International Conference on Document Analysis and Recognition*, IEEE, 18–21 September 2011, pp. 1480–1484.

20. W. Evett, "Bayesian inference and forensic science: Problems and perspectives," *Journal of the Royal Statistical Society, Series D, The Statistician*, vol. 36, no. 2/3, Special Issue: Practical Bayesian Statistics, pp. 99–105, 1987.

21. V. L. Blankers, C. E. van den Heuvel, K.Y. Franke, and L.G. Vuurpijl, "ICDAR 2009 signature verification competition," in *Proceedings of the International Conference on Document Analysis and Recognition*, IEEE, July 26–29, 2009, pp. 1403–1407.

22. J. Fierrez-Aguilar, N. Alonso-Hermira, G. Moreno-Marquez, and J. Ortega-Garcia, "An off-line signature verification system based on fusion of local and global information," in D. Maltoni and A. K. Jain, Eds., *Biometric Authentication, Lecture Notes in Computer Science*, vol. 3087, pp. 295–306. Berlin, Heidelberger, Springer-Verlag, 2004.

23. A. Gilperez, F. Alonso-Fernandez, S. Pecharroman, J. Fierrez, and J. Ortega-Garcia, "Off-line signature verification using contour features," in *International Conference on Frontiers in Handwriting Recognition*, IEEE, Online, 6 pages, August 19–21, 2008.

24. M. Bulacu and L. Schomaker, "Text-independent writer identification and verification using textural and allographic features," *IEEE Transactions on Pattern Analysis and Machine Intelligence*, vol. 29, no. 4, pp. 701–717, 2007.

25. S.N. Srihari, H. Srinivasan, S. Chen, and M.J. Beal, "Machine learning for signature verification," in *Machine Learning in Document Analysis and Recognition*, pp. 387–408. Berlin, Heidelberg, Springer, 2008.

26. A. Fornés, S. Escalera, J. Lladós, G. Sánchez, and J. Mas, "Hand drawn symbol recognition by blurred shape model descriptor and a multiclass classifier," in W. Liu, J. Lladós, and J.-M. Ogier, Eds., *Graphics Recognition. Recent Advances and New Opportunities, Lecture Notes in Computer Science*, vol. 5046, pp. 29–39. Berlin, Heidelberg, Springer, 2008.

27. M. A. Ferrer, J. B. Alonso, and C. M. Travieso, "Off-line geometric parameters for automatic signature verification using fixed-point arithmetic," in *IEEE Transactions on Pattern Analysis and Machine Intelligence*, vol. 27, no. 6, pp. 993–997, 2005.

28. M. Liwicki, A. Schlapbach, H. Bunke, S. Bengio, and J. Richiardi, "Writer identification for smart meeting room systems," in *IAPR Workshop on Document Analysis Systems*, Lecture Notes in Computer Science, vol. 3872, pp. 186–195, Berlin, Heidelberg, Springer, 2006.

29. A. Schlapbach, M. Liwicki, and H. Bunke, "A writer identification system for on-line whiteboard data," *Pattern Recognition*, vol. 41, no. 7, pp. 2381–2397, 2008.

30. I. Alberink and A. Ruifrok, "Repeatability and reproducibility of earprint acquisition," *Journal of Forensic Sciences*, vol. 53, no. 2, pp. 325–330, 2008.

31. M. Blumenstein, M. A. Ferrer and J. F. Vargas "The 4NSigComp2010 off-line signature verification competition: Scenario 2," *Proceedings of the International Conference on Frontiers in Handwriting Recognition*, IEEE, 16–18 November, 2010, pp. 721–726.

32. F. Vargas, M. Ferrer, C. Travieso, and J. Alonso, "Off-line handwritten signature GPDS-960 corpus," in *Proceedings of the International Conference on Document Analysis and Recognition*," IEEE, September 23–26, 2007, pp. 764–768.

33. M. Liwicki, C.E. van den Heuvel, B. Found, and M.I. Malik, "Forensic signature verification competition 4NSigComp2010 — detection of simulated and disguised signatures," in *Proceedings of the International Conference on Frontiers in Handwriting Recognition*, IEEE, November 16–18, 2010, pp. 715–720.

34. C. Bird, B. Found, and D. Rogers, "Forensic document examiners' opinions on process of production of disguised and simulated signatures," in *Proceedings of the International Conference of Graphonomics Society*," IEEE, November 11–14, 2007, pp. 171–174.

35. M. Liwicki and M.I. Malik, "Surprising power of local features for automated signature verification," in *Proceedings of the International Conference of Graphonomics Society*, IEEE, June 12–15, 2011, pp. 18–21.

36. J. Gonzalez-Rodrigues, J. Fierrez-Aguilar, D. Ramos-Castro, and J. Ortega-Garcia, "Bayesian analysis of fingerprint, face and signature evidences with automated biometric systems," *Forensic Science International*, vol. 155, no. 2–3, pp. 126–140, 2005.

37. N. Niko Brummer and J. du Preez, "Application-independent evaluation of speaker detection," *Computer Speech and Language*, vol. 20, no. 2–3, pp. 230–275, 2006.

38. S. Al-Ma'adeed, A.-A. Al-Kurbi, A. Al-Muslih, R. Al-Qahtani, and H. Al Kubisi, "Writer identification of Arabic handwriting documents using grapheme features," in *Proceedings of the IEEE/ACS International Conference*

on Computer Systems and Applications, IEEE, 31 March–4 April, 2008, pp. 923–924.

39. S. Al-Ma'adeed, E. Mohammed, and D. Al Kassis, "Writer identification using edge-based directional probability distribution features for Arabic words," in *Proceedings of the IEEE/ACS International Conference on Computer Systems and Applications*, IEEE, 31 March–4 April, 2008, pp. 582–590.

40. S.A. Daramola and I. Samuel, "Novel feature extraction technique for off-line signature verification system," *International Journal of Engineering Science and Technology*, vol. 2, no. 7, pp. 3137–3143, 2010.

41. V. Nguyen and M. Blumenstein, "An application of the 2D Gaussian filter for enhancing feature extraction in off-line signature verification," in *Proceedings of the International Conference on Document Analysis and Recognition*, IEEE, September 18–21, 2011, pp. 339–343.

42. B. Kovari and H. Charaf, "A study on the consistency and significance of local features in off-line signature verification," *Pattern Recognition Letters*, vol. 34, no. 3, pp. 247–255, 2013.

43. M.B. Yilmaz, B. Yanikoglu, C. Tirkaz, and A. Kholmatov, "Off-line signature verification using classifier combination of hog and LBP features," in *Proceedings of the International Joint Conference on Biometrics*, IEEE, October 11–13, 2011, pp. 1–7.

44. C. Djeddi, I. Siddiqi, L. Souici-Meslati, and A. Ennaji, "Text-independent writer recognition using multi-script handwritten texts," *Pattern Recognition Letters*, vol. 34, no. 10, pp. 1196–1202, 2013.

45. A. Hassaine, S. Al-Maadeed, and A. Bouridane, "A set of geometrical features for writer identification," in T. Huang, Z. Zeng, C. Li, and C.S. Leung, Eds., in *Neural Information Processing (ICONIP'2012), Lecture Notes in Computer Science*, vol. 7667, pp. 584–591. Berlin, Heidelberg, Springer, 2012.

46. A. Kholmatov and B. Yanikoglu, "Identity authentication using improved on-line signature verification method," *Pattern Recognition Letters*, vol. 26, no. 15, pp. 2400–2408, 2005.

47. S. Khalid and S. Razzaq, "Frameworks for multivariate m-mediods based modeling and classification in Euclidean and general feature spaces," *Pattern Recognition*, vol. 45, no. 3, pp. 1092–1103, 2012.

48. M. I. Malik, S. Ahmed, A. Dengel, and M. Liwicki, "A signature verification framework for digital pen applications," in *Proceedings of the 10th IAPR International Workshop on Document Analysis Systems (DAS'2012)*, IEEE, March 27–29, 2012, pp. 419–423.

49. M. I. Malik and M. Liwicki, "From terminology to evaluation: Performance assessment of automatic signature verification systems," in *Proceedings of*

the International Conference on Frontiers in Handwriting Recognition, pp. 613–618, 2012.

50. M. I. Malik, M. Liwicki, A. Dengel, and B. Found, "Man vs. machine: A comparative analysis for signature verification," *Journal of Forensic Document Examination*, vol. 24, no. 1, pp. 21–35, 2014.

51. M. I. Malik, M. Liwicki, and A. Dengel, "Part-based automatic system in comparison to human experts for forensic signature verification," in *Proceedings of the International Conference on Document Analysis and Recognition*, IEEE, August 25–28, 2013, pp. 872–876.

52. M. I. Malik, M. Liwicki, and A. Dengel, "Freak for real time forensic signature verification," in *Proceedings of the International Conference on Document Analysis and Recognition*, IEEE, August 25–28, 2013, pp. 971–975.

53. M. I. Malik, L. Alewijnse, M. Liwicki, and M. Blumenstein, "Signature verification tutorial," in *the 2nd International Workshop and Tutorial on Automated Forensic Handwriting Analysis*, CEUR-WS, August 22–23, 2013.

54. M. Liwicki, M. I. Malik, L. Alewijnse, C. E. van den Heuvel, and B. Found, "ICFHR 2012 competition on automatic forensic signature verification (4NSigComp2012), in *International Conference on Frontiers in Handwriting Recognition*, IEEE, 18–20 September 2012, pp. 823–828.

55. M. I. Malik, M. Liwicki, L. Alewijnse, W. Ohyama, M. Blumenstein, and B. Found, "ICDAR 2013 competitions on signature verification and writer identification for on- and offline skilled forgeries (SigWiComp2013), in *International Conference on Document Analysis and Recognition*, IEEE, 25–28 August 2013, pp. 1477–1483.

56. M. I. Malik, S. Ahmed, A. Marcelli, U. Pal, M. Blumenstein, L. Alewijns, and M. Liwicki, "ICDAR2015 competition on signature verification and writer identification for on- and off-line skilled forgeries (SigWIcomp2015), in *International Conference on Document Analysis and Recognition*, IEEE, pp. 1186–1190, 23–26 August 2015.

Part IV
Text Recognition

Chapter 8

Handwritten Text Recognition Competitions With the tranScriptorium Dataset

Joan Andreu Sánchez, Verónica Romero,
Alejandro H. Toselli, and Enrique Vidal

8.1 Introduction

There is an increasing interest worldwide to digitally preserve and provide access to historical document collections residing in libraries, museums and archives. Such documents constitute a unique public asset, forming the collective and evolving memory of our societies.

Many institutions, all over the word, have already undertaken mass digitization of paper documents, which are then stored in digital libraries[a] and usually made web accessible to the public. This paper-to-image conversion ensures long-term preservation of documents that, in some cases, were in advanced degradation state with a high risk of loss of information. Of course, these efforts are leading to a major advance over the previous "paper-era" situation. But in the horizon of one decade, the new challenge is to automatically extract the textual contents from these digital text images. This is the aim of research areas such as Document Image Analysis and Handwritten Text Recognition (HTR).

---

[a]http://www.europeana.eu/.

The nowadays prevalent technology for HTR borrows concepts and methods from the field of Automatic Speech Recognition, such as Hidden Markov Models (HMM), N-Grams and neural network (NN) [1, 2, 4, 12, 16, 22, 25, 27, 31, 37, 38]. Using these technologies, accuracy rates as high as 50–90%, has been reported with more or less unrestricted text images.

In recent years, several international competitions have been organized to allow fair comparisons of the proposed approaches and to thereby foster technological improvements in the HTR field [9, 19, 34, 35]. In this chapter, we focus on the competitions carried out in the framework of the two major international conferences devoted to document image processing, namely, ICDAR and ICFHR. In the last editions of these conferences, two contests have been organized, aiming at precisely and robustly transcribing handwritten documents from the so-called *Bentham collection*, which is one of the main collections considered in the tranScriptorium project.

8.1.1 *The TranScriptorium Project*

The tranScriptorium project[b] [33] was an EU-funded project, developed between January 2013 and December 31, 2015. In this project, innovative, cost-effective solutions were developed for the indexing, search and full transcription of historical handwritten document images, using HTR technology. TranScriptorium tried to turn HTR into a mature technology by addressing the following objectives:

1. Enhancing HTR technology for efficient transcription. Departing from state-of-the-art HTR approaches, tranScriptorium capitalized on interactive-predictive techniques for effective and user-friendly computer-assisted transcription.

    Bringing the HTR technology to users. Two kinds of users were mainly considered: (a) individual researchers in humanities, with experience in handwritten documents transcription, generally interested in transcribing specific documents and (b) volunteers which collaborated in large transcription projects.

---

[b]http://transcriptorium.eu/.

2. Integrating the HTR results in public web portals. This way, HTR technology can become an increasingly important support in the digitization of the handwritten materials.

Within the tranScriptorium project span, HTR technology was developed and applied to the automatic and assisted transcription of several collections of historical documents in cursive handwriting. TranScriptorium mainly focused on four languages: Spanish, German, English, and Dutch. This not only aimed to illustrate the applicability of the technology to different languages, but also at stimulating the uptake and validation of the technology for a wider audience.

Among these historical collections, the largest, more ambitious, and challenging one was the *Bentham collection*. It was the source, from which the datasets used in the competitions described in this chapter, were extracted.

8.2 The Bentham Datasets Used in the HTR Contests

In tranScriptorium, a large set of manuscripts written in English by the renowned philosopher and reformer Jeremy Bentham (1748–1832) [11] was considered. The Bentham papers include manuscripts written by Bentham himself over a period of 60 years, as well as fair copies written by Bentham's secretarial staff. Many of these manuscripts are plenty of crossed-out words and lines, but most of them are still readable. The transcription of this collection was being carried out at the tranScriptorium time span by amateur volunteers, participating in the award-winning, crowd-sourcing initiative known as "Transcribe Bentham".[c] For this crowd-sourcing effort, assistive HTR technologies developed in tranScriptorium were adopted.

Page images of the Bentham collection generally entail important layout analysis difficulties (see examples in Figures 8.1 and 8.2), such marginal notes, fainted writing, stamps, skewed images, lines with different slope in the same page, slanted lines, interline sentences, etc. They are also difficult from the HTR point of view. They are written by several hands, there are many crossed-out words, hyphenated words, punctuation symbols, footnote symbols, etc. Even with these difficulties, most of these

---

[c]http://blogs.ucl.ac.uk/transcribe-bentham/.

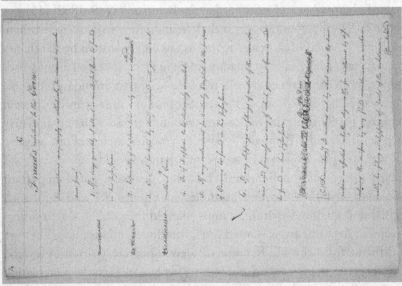

Figure 8.1.   Document samples of the Bentham dataset used in tranScriptorium.

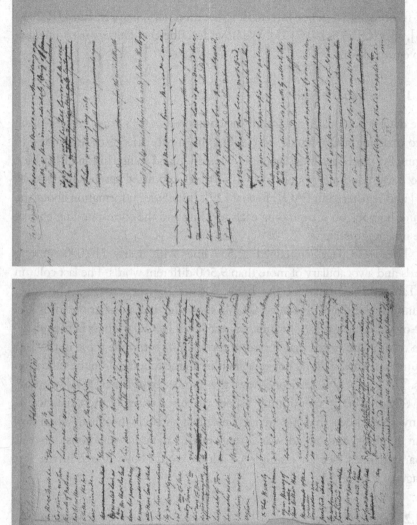

Figure 8.2. Document samples of the Bentham dataset used in tranScriptorium.

page images are readable for human beings. HTR results in a representative, but easy set of the Bentham collection were reported in [14] by using some of the HTR techniques previously mentioned.

Two HTR contests were organized with Bentham datasets, both in the framework of major international conferences, namely, ICFHR 2014 [34], and ICDAR 2015 [35]. We now describe the datasets used in these two competitions.

8.2.1 *First Dataset Issue*

The dataset for this first edition was composed of 433-page images,[d] each encompassing of a single text block in most cases (see examples in Figure 8.1) and entailing diverse line detection and transcription difficulties. The corresponding ground truth (GT) was produced semi-automatically [14] and registered in PAGE format [29]. It includes information about the bounding polygon surrounding each text line and the corresponding correct line image transcript.

These 433 pages contained 11,537 lines with nearly 110,000 running words and a vocabulary of more than 9,500 different words. The last column in Table 8.1 summarizes the basic statistics of these pages. The rows, "Running word" and "Running OOV," show the total number of words and out-of-vocabulary (OOV) words, respectively. The OOV words in the validation column are words that appear in the training set, while those in the Test column are words that do not appear either in the training or in the validation sets. The row "OOV Lexicon" shows the number of *different* OOV words.

A noteworthy mentioning aspect of this dataset is the existence of many short lines that are mainly, numbers, section headers, subsection item symbols, and added words that, in this dataset, were considered as separated lines (see an example of added word above line 7 in the left image of Figure 8.1).

8.2.2 *Second Dataset Issue*

Taking into account the experience of the previous contest edition [34], as well as the works being carried out in tranScriptorium, more difficult

---

[d]http://transcriptorium.eu/datasets/bentham-collection/.

Table 8.1. The Bentham dataset used in the 2014 HTR contest edition.

Number of	Training	Validation	Test	Total
Pages	350	50	33	433
Lines	9,198	1,415	860	11,473
Running words	86,075	12,962	7,868	106,905
Lexicon	8,658	2,709	1,946	9,716
Running OOV	—	857	417	—
OOV Lexicon	—	681	377	—
Character set size	86	86	86	86
Run. Characters	442,336	67,400	40,938	550,664

challenges were considered in the second contest edition. Figure 8.2 shows two examples of the images used in this edition.

The dataset was chosen according to the following challenges[e]:

Challenge 1. A usual circumstance in HTR is that when the transcription of a collection is tackled, it is possible to have transcripts available for some portions of the collection. These transcripts can be used for training both optical and language models (LMs). For training optical models (OMs), it is necessary to align the transcripts with the line images. Automatic methods have been researched for this purpose with good results [5, 14]. In this edition, such a scenario was simulated: a portion of the training data was provided as raw page images with transcripts including line breaks roughly aligned with image lines.[f] The entrants could use this data to obtain additional training data aligned at line level with their own methods.

Challenge 2. Another usual challenge, when the transcription of a collection starts, is to decide which criterion should be used for sorting the documents to be transcribed. Possible alternatives are: according to the page numbering, the glossaries first and then the other pages, in increasing

---

[e]http://transcriptorium.eu/datasets/bentham-collection/.
[f]Note that line breaks were also useful to know the number of lines to be detected in the page image.

difficulty for transcribing, in increasing difficulty in the layout, combinations of the previous alternatives, etc. In the second edition, we decided to choose the images according to the same criterion decided in tranScriptorium [14], that is, the pages were selected and sorted in increasing layout complexity.

Challenge 3. As mentioned in the introduction, several techniques exist for HTR, and the machinery in each of them can be very diverse. Therefore, comparing different techniques can be sometimes difficult. To allow for more detailed comparison of techniques, in the second edition, a track with restricted training data conditions was mandatory for all participants.

Challenge 4. The transcription difficulty of the test images was significantly increased in this edition. Accordingly, the organizers decided to deliver it to the participants several days in advance to the deadline (12 days). However, with this decision, the entrants had sufficient time to excessively adjust their system parameters to the test data. To counteract this possibility, the test set was divided into two parts, and the second, a smaller part was delivered only three days in advance to the deadline. Both parts were equally difficult in terms of expected recognition error rate.

The dataset for the second competition was composed of 796-page images. As in HTRtS-14, most of these images encompass a single text block each, but in this edition, many pages included plenty of marginal notes and added interlines. As in the previous edition, these pages entailed many line detection and transcription difficulties, the GT was produced semi-automatically and manually reviewed [14] (see examples of extracted lines in Figure 8.3) and the GT information was also registered in PAGE format.

These 796 pages contained 21,752 lines with nearly 186,500 running words and a vocabulary of more than 17,500 different words. The last column in Table 8.2 summarizes the basic statistics of these pages.

The dataset was divided into two subsets for training and testing, respectively encompassing 746 and 50 images. The training set, in turn, consisted of two batches. The first batch was composed of 433-page images (Train-B1 column in Table 8.2). This was the full (training, validation, and test) set used in the 2014 contest edition. The GT was annotated at line level in the PAGE format files. The second batch was composed of

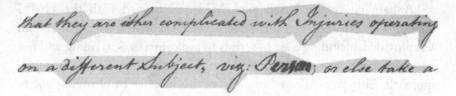

Figure 8.3.   Sample lines such as they were provided for experimentation.

Table 8.2.   The Bentham dataset used in the 2015 HTR contest edition.

Number of	Train-B1	Train-B2	Training	Test	Total
Pages	433	313	746	50	796
Lines	11,473	8,947	20,420	1,332	21,752
Running words	106,905	70,447	177,203	9,440	186,643
Lexicon	9,716	11,152	16,881	2,493	17,948
Running OOV	—	—	—	1,169	—
OOV Lexicon	—	—	—	1,067	—
Character set size	86	87	87	84	87
Running Characters	550,674	357,672	874,369	47,286	92,165

313 new and more challenging page images (Train-B2 column in Table 8.2). The GT in this batch was also in PAGE format but it was annotated only at text block level (no line detection or segmentation was provided). Line-by-line transcripts for the blocks were provided in a separated file, with a newline character at the end of each line (*Challenge 1*). Train-B2 had more layout difficulties than Train-B1 (*Challenge 2*). The test set was divided, in turn, also into two subsets for checking possibly excessive system tuning to the test set (*Challenge 4*).

8.3 Contest Protocol and Evaluation Methodology

The same general protocol and methodology were adopted for the two competition editions considered here. The training set was provided to the participants as soon as the competition became open, while the test part was kept unpublished and released in due time just to obtain the results to be evaluated and compared.

A baseline system based on HMM and trained with the HMM Toolkit[g] (HTK) and *N*-gram models trained with the SRILM[h] toolkit was provided, including a set of scripts to perform a basic training and test experiment. The participants could use this baseline system as an initial approach. They were allowed to improve this baseline by changing one or several of the training and/or recognition steps.

The participants had to send the output transcripts for the test set. Several results per participant were allowed, corresponding to different runs of their own systems, and all the results were considered for the final decision. Output transcripts were expected with correct capitalization and punctuation.

The evaluation metric was the Word Error Rate (WER) between the reference transcripts of the test set and the recognition results. The winner would be the participant that obtained the least WER. A web-based platform was available for the participants to submit their recognition results.

Two tracks were planned in both competitions; these are as follows:

- *Restricted track.* Participants were allowed to use just the data provided by the organizers for training and tuning their systems.
- *Unrestricted track.* Participants were allowed to use any data of their choice.

The purpose of defining two tracks was to have the possibility of comparing techniques with respect to the amount of training data used (*Challenge 3*). Whereas in the first content, the entrants could choose to participate only in the unrestricted track or in both, in the second contest, the entrants had to participate necessarily in the restricted track.

When the competition closed, the competitors were informed only about their own results and they were asked for submitting a description of the system for which they obtained their best results. These descriptions are summarized in subsections 8.5.2 and 8.5.3.

In the next subsection, the typical details of each contest are described.

---

[g] http://htk.eng.cam.ac.uk.
[h] http://www.speech.sri.com/projects/srilm/.

8.3.1 *First Edition of the HTR Contest*

In this contest, the training data was divided into training and validation and, as previously commented, were provided to the participants as soon as the competition became open. The training and validation data available for the participants consisted of the following:

- The original images of all the training and validation pages.
- The PAGE file corresponding to each page image (For each text line in this image, the PAGE file contained a bounding polygon and the corresponding correct transcript).
- The preprocessed and extracted line images for all the lines of the training and validation sets in grayscale (see examples in Figure 8.3).
- The corresponding transcripts of each of these lines (These transcripts had the punctuation symbols separated from words, and the final results on the test set had to be submitted in the same way).

The first pair of items was redundant with the second and was provided for those who wished to try improving results by using specific image preprocessing and line extraction tools. Note that the purpose of providing the lines correctly detected was to focus the contest on HTR and not in layout analysis and line detection and extraction. The test images, with the transcript fields empty in the PAGE file, were eventually provided in the same (redundant) formats for evaluation purposes.

8.3.2 *Second Edition of the HTR Contest*

The training set described in the previous section was provided to the participants as soon as the competition became open. The training data available for the participants consisted of the following:

- The original page images of all the training.
- The PAGE file corresponding to each page image for Train-B1 (For each text line in this image, the PAGE file contained a bounding polygon and the corresponding correct transcript. A PAGE file just with the textual regions and the corresponding transcripts with line breaks were provided for Train-B2).

- The preprocessed and extracted line images for all the lines of the Train-B1 set in grayscale (see examples in Figure 8.3).
- The corresponding transcripts of each of these lines for Train-B1 (As in the first contest, these transcripts had the punctuation symbols separated from words, and the final results on the test set had to be submitted in the same way).

The test images, with the transcript fields empty in the PAGE file, were also eventually provided in the same formats as in the Train-B1 set for evaluation purposes.

The competition was planned in such a way that the participants had about 10 weeks for preparing their systems before the test set was provided. Then, they had 12 days for sending their transcription results on the test set. As discussed in Subsection 8.2.1, a smaller subset (aiming at checking the successive tuning on test data) was released three days before the deadline (*Challenge 4*).

8.4 Existing State-of-the-Art Approaches

In handwritten documents, it is generally impossible to reliably isolate the characters or even the words that compose a cursive handwritten text. Therefore, the required technology should be able to recognize all text elements (sentences, words, and characters) as a whole, without any prior segmentation of the image into these elements. Moreover, these systems should be also able to be trained on unsegmented text (line) images. This technology is generally referred to as "*offline HTR*."

In the current state of the art of this technology, intermediate steps for text line extraction are needed. These steps consist of text/graphic segmentation, text block detection, and text line extraction. The main difficulty in text/graphic separation is found in separating overlapping elements [21, 32]. A slightly similar problem is text block detection and text line segmentation in document images.

Once text blocks are located, text line segmentation in handwritten documents is one of the major issues. This directly influences the accuracy of the modern HTR systems. Handwritten text lines entail different factors that make their extraction more difficult: variable interline spacing, overlapping strokes of adjacent handwritten lines, influence of document level degradation, etc.

Once the text lines have been segmented, the next step is to recognize the handwritten text. Two main approaches are widely addressed in the HTR field: the ones based on N-gram LM and *HMM* with *Gaussian Mixtures* emission probabilities (HMM–GMM) and the ones based on NNs. In what follows, we described these two approaches in relation to what were employed in/submitted to the HTR contest.

8.4.1 *HTR Based on N-Gram/HMM–GMM*

The fundamentals of HTR based on N-gram/HMM–GMM were originally presented in [1] and further developed in [37, 40] among others. Recognizers of this kind accept an input text line image, represented as a sequence of feature vectors $\mathbf{x} = \vec{x}_1, \vec{x}_2, ..., \vec{x}_n, \vec{x}_i, \in \Re^D$ most likely word sequence $\hat{\mathbf{w}} = \hat{w}_1 \hat{w}_2 ... \hat{w}_l$, according to

$$\hat{\mathbf{w}} = argmax_w \, P(w|x) = argmax_w P(w) \, P(x|w) \tag{8.1}$$

The prior probability $P(w)$ and the conditional density $P(x|w)$ are approximated, respectively, by an N-gram LM and by "optical" word models (OM) consisting in the concatenation of character HMMs [22].

The decoding problem in equation (8.1) can be solved by the Viterbi algorithm [22] (also called "token passing" in recent works).

8.4.1.1 *Preprocessing and Feature Extraction*

Text line images constitute here the basic input of the HTR process. They can be obtained from each document image by means of conventional text line detection and segmentation techniques [7, 8, 24]. The extracted line images are first processed to correct line skew as well as to normalize slant and size handwriting attributes [31, 37].

A simple, intuitively appealing feature extraction approach is the one described in [39]. A narrow sliding window is horizontally applied to the preprocessed line image. For each window position i, $1 \leq i \leq n$, 60D feature vector $\vec{x}_i$ is obtained by computing three kinds of features: normalized vertical gray levels for 20 evenly distributed vertical positions and horizontal and vertical gray level derivatives at each of the these vertical positions.

The baseline result reported in subsection 8.6.1 was obtained using this feature extraction approach. However, recent works have shown that HTR accuracy can be significantly improved by using more sophisticated feature extraction techniques [23]. It is also based on sliding window analysis, but rather than computing raw gray levels and their gradients, geometric moments are used to perform some geometric normalizations to the images within each analysis window. For each window position, i, moment-based geometric normalizations are performed and a high-dimensional vector is obtained just by stacking the (normalized) gray-level values of all the pixels within the window. Then, each of these vectors is reduced to a 20D feature vector, $\vec{x}_i$, by means of principal component analysis (PCA). Finally, local variability of the position, size, and shape of the strokes and/or blobs within each window (which was greatly deemed by the moment-based normalization) is modeled independently by retaining second-order moment information into four new features, which are added to the previous PCA-projected 20 components [23].

It should be mentioned that the implicit geometry normalization entailed by this approach allows useful simplifications in the preprocessing phase. More specifically, skew and size normalization proved largely unnecessary and slant correction was the only image normalization step actually applied before using this feature extraction approach.

8.4.1.2 *Lexicon and Language Modeling*

Standard N-Gram LM training is adopted here to approximate $P(w)$ in equation (8.1). It requires a lexicon or set of "words" to be previously defined, where each word is represented in terms of its constituent *alphabet elements*. The alphabet includes all the different characters, punctuation marks, etc., along with one or more elements representing white space. Each *lexical entry* or "word", v, acts as a single, unique LM item and the word HMM for v is obtained by combining the HMMs of the alphabet elements defined for v in the lexicon. Each item w_i of a word sequence w in equation (8.1) corresponds to some lexical entry, v.

Lexical entries are obtained ("trained") by analyzing a corpus of text image transcripts. This analysis generally entails *tokenization* and *text normalization* steps to decide, among others, what are the allowed capitalizations of each word and how to model punctuation marks, hyphenated words, etc., how or to decide whether to train from line, paragraph or whole page transcripts.

8.4.1.3 *HMM–GMM Training*

According to equation (8.1) and the discussion in subsubsection 8.4.1.2, $P(x|w)$ is approximated by combining (generally just concatenating) the character HMMs of the words in w. Each character (alphabet element) is modeled by a continuous density left-to-right HMM, where a Gaussian mixture model (GMM) is used to account for the emission of feature vectors in each HMM state. Once a HMM "*topology*" (number of states and Gaussians and structure) has been adopted, the model parameters can be easily estimated by *maximum likelihood*. The required training data consists of continuous handwriting text line images (*without any kind of word or character segmentation*), accompanied by the transcription of this text into the corresponding sequence of characters. This training process is carried out using a well-known instance of the EM algorithm called *embedded Baum–Welch re-estimation* [22].

Maximum-likelihood parameter estimation is the simplest, most basic training approach for HMMs. This was the training method used in the baseline system provided to the entrants of the ICFHR-2014 HTR contest, and it was employed to obtain the baseline result reported in subsection 8.6.1.

8.4.2 *HTR Based on Neural Networks*

Systems based on NNs have been gaining increasing attentions in the HTR field because of their good recognition results. Most popular architectures include hybrid systems, using (deep) multilayer perceptrons to model the emission probability of traditional HMMs [6, 12] (hereafter referred to as DNN), and systems using the *bidirectional long short-term memory* NN units (referred to as BLSTM) [4, 6, 16, 27].

NN approaches like the ones described in [4, 6] are tested for two different feature extraction methods, called "raw pixel values" and "handcrafted features". Standard geometry corrections and other preprocessing steps are previously applied to each text line image: contrast enhancement, skew and slant correction, and size normalization, as described in [3, 10, 30] and [41], respectively. It was reported that (slightly) better results are consistently achieved with handcrafted features, which are geometrical and statistical features extracted with a sliding window of width 3px with a shift of 3px, resulting in 56D feature vectors [2].

Regarding DNN, parameters are trained using a training set created by forced-alignments provided by a traditional N-gram/HMM–GMM system, trained with the original training data. The network parameters are pre-trained with an unsupervised layer-wise training method [20], and fine-tuned with cross-entropy training and stochastic gradient descent.

On the other hand, BLSTM network parameters were trained with the *connectionist temporal classification* (CTC) objective function [15], using stochastic gradient descent and making use of the dropout technique described in [28], which proved effective to improve recognition accuracy.

LMs are also used in these approaches to HTR. In the case of DNN, they are used exactly as in traditional N-gram/HMM–GMM. For BLSTM systems, LMs can be applied by adapting the CTC algorithm [15] or, as in [6], by means of combining the N-grams with simplified HMMs which have just one state per character whose emission probability is obtained from the BLSTM output. In any case, N-gram (and lexicon) training is essentially as described in subsubsection 8.4.1.2.

8.5 HTR Approaches Employed in the Contests

8.5.1 *Baseline HTR Approach*

Baseline experiments in this case were carried out with the N-gram/HMM–GMM HTR approach described in subsection 8.4.1. Obtained results with this approach were aimed at being compared with recognizers presented in the *restricted track*s of the first and second editions of the HTR contests, described in subsections 8.3.1 and 8.3.2 respectively.

Table 8.3. Identifiers used to identify the best results that each partner submitted to each track.

	Restricted track	Unrestricted track
A2IA	—	A2IA-Un
CITlab	CITlab-Re	—
LIMSI	LIMSU-Re	LIMSI-Un

8.5.2 HTR Approaches Submitted to the First Edition of the Contest

Seven research groups registered at the contest and finally three of them submitted their official results. Two participants submitted results of several systems to just one track and one participant submitted results of several systems to the two tracks described in subsection 8.3.1. The three research groups were as follows (see Table 8.3):

- Artificial Intelligence and Image Analysis (A2IA).[i]
- Computational Intelligence Technology Laboratory (CITlab).[j]
- Spoken Language Processing Group at Laboratoire d'Informatique pour la Mécanique et les Sciences de l'Ingénieur (LIMSI).[k]

A2IA submitted results just to the unrestricted track, CITlab submitted results just to the restricted track and LIMSI submitted results both to the restricted and the unrestricted tracks.

- **A2IA-Un:** The OM was a multi-directional long short-term memory (MDLSTM) [17] NN, as described in [27]. The system used a hybrid word/character LM that comprised a top-level LM (3-gram on words/punctuation) for the most frequent words and a secondary-level character LM that dealt with OOV words [26]. CTC [15] and stochastic gradient descent were used to train the recurrent NN (RNN). The LM was trained with and additional Bentham dataset that was gathered through the web.[l] With this additional data the

---

[i] http://www.a2ia.com/en; http://www.a2ialab.com/doku.php.
[j] http://www.citlab.uni-rostock.de.
[k] http://www.limsi.fr/Scientifique/tlp/.
[l] http://oll.libertyfund.org/titles/bentham-works-of-jeremy-bentham-11-vols.

lexicon OOV decreased from 377 (see Table 8.1) to 275, and the running OOV decreased from 417 (5.3%) to 313 (4.0%).

- **CITlab-Re:** Optical modelling was carried out with NN. The lexicon was composed by all words in the training and validation sets and complemented by additional verbs with "-ing" and "-ed" endings. Hyphenated words were taken as one entire word instead of including its parts. CITlab used backpropagation through time (BPTT) [18] using the CTC algorithm [15] for network training.[m]

- **LIMSI-Re:** This system was, in fact, a systems combination, and therefore, this description summarizes the main characteristics of these systems. Hybrid NN/HMM models were used for modelling OMs. Two type of NN were considered and each system used just one of them: deep NN (DNN) and BLSTM NN. For training DNN, first a GMM–HMM system was used. The GMM–HMM system was trained with the standard EM algorithm. The forced alignment computed with the GMM–HMM was used to create a training set for DNNs. BLSTM–RNNs systems [17] were trained with the CTC objective function [15] and with the dropout technique [28]. For language modelling, Pyphen[n] was used for dealing with hyphenated words. It was used to generate hyphenated words from the most frequent word in the vocabulary and the obtained parts of the words were used to complete full words that were added to the LM as unigrams. Recognition was carried out at line level with a 4-gram. Lattices were generated with all systems, and a lattice-based system combination was carried out.

- **LIMSI-Un:** This system was also a system combination. The difference between this system and the previous system was that additional training data was used in this system. The Open American National Corpus (OANC)[o] was used as external resource for training the LM. The recognition was carried out at line level with a bigram, and then a rescoring with the lattices was carried out with a trigram. The combination included seven systems.

---

[m]The software modules behind that as well as the basic utility technologies are essentially powered by PLANET's ARGUS framework for intelligent text recognition and image processing.

[n]http://pyphen.org/.

[o]http://www.americannationalcorpus.org/OANC/index.html.

8.5.3 HTR Approaches Submitted to the Second Edition of the Contest

Nine research groups registered at the contest and finally three of them submitted results. Two participants submitted results of several systems to just one track and one participant submitted results of several systems to the two tracks described in subsection 8.3.2. The three research groups, listed in the same order they registered, were:

- Computational Intelligence Technology Lab (CITlab).
- Artificial Intelligence and Image Analysis (A2IA).
- Qatar Computing Research Institute (QCRI).[p]

The entrants submitted several transcripts that were obtained by several systems. The main characteristics of the best system for each entrant are the following:

CITlab-Re. For feature extraction, they used the same technique described in [15]. Optical modelling was carried out with NN. The lexicon was composed by all words in the training. CITlab used BPTT [18], using the CTC algorithm [15] for network training. For training, CITlab tried several alternatives with Train-B1 and Train-B2, and the best results were obtained by using Train-B1 and a large percentage (3,968 additional lines, 44% of Train-B2) of lines from Train-B2. In the decoding experiments, CITlab used system combinations (expert committee decoding [13]).

A2IA-Re. In the system developed by A2IA, three sort of features were used: (a) the feature vectors provided with the training data by the organizers; (b) feature vectors extracted with a sliding window containing geometrical and statistical features [2]; and (c) feature vectors containing raw pixel intensities in a sliding window. The OM was a MDLSTM [17] NN, as described in [27]. The system used a hybrid word/character LM that comprised a top-level LM (3-gram on words/punctuation) for the most frequent words and a secondary-level LM (7-gram on characters) that dealt with OOV words [26]. The Train-B2 set was used also for obtaining lines automatically [5] for training both the OM and the LM. CTC [15] and stochastic gradient descent were used for decoding and training.

---

[p] http://www.qcri.org.qa/.

A2IA-Un. This system had basically the same characteristics of the A2IA-Re system. The LM was trained with and additional Bentham dataset that was gathered through the web. This dataset amounted to 5.86M words, with a vocabulary of 57,324 word-tokens but the vocabulary was limited to the 50k most frequent words in the training data.

QCRI-Re. A sliding window in reading direction over the normalized text line image was used to extract features. Two different feature extraction methods used were raw pixel grayscale intensity values and segment-based features proposed in [36], which is a low-dimensional feature vector representation conveying enough information to fully recover the written script image. This system was trained exclusively with Train-B1 and Train-B2 provided in the competition. Train-B2 was used as follows: First, an initial recognizer was trained with Train-B1. Then, projection profiles of text areas in Train-B2 were fitted to sinus functions. The frequency of the sinus functions was then used to estimate the line heights and split the text areas into line images. Third, the resulting 6,882 line images were recognized with the initial system. The maligna tool[q] was used for lexicalized sentence-to-sentence alignment between the recognized sentences and the reference transcriptions. One-to-one alignments were selected and ended up with 4,246 lines which were added to the training data from the first batch. Finally, the complete system was retrained from scratch with the extended training set. One system used HMM with DNN and another system used HMM with LSTM NN, both trained with Kaldi.[r] System combination on the lattices was used. A word 4-gram LM was trained with Train-B1 and Train-B2.

8.6 Presentation and Analysis of HTR Contest Results

8.6.1 *Baseline Results*

In Table 8.4 are reported the baseline results for the restricted track of both contest editions, using the HTR approach depicted in subsection 8.5.1.

---

[q]http://align.sourceforge.net/.
[r]http://kaldi.sourceforge.net/dnn2.html.

Table 8.4. Best WER and CER obtained by the
baseline HTR approach on the restricted track.

1st HTR contest	2nd HTR contest
23.9/10.7	62.6/36.3

Table 8.5. Best WER and CER obtained by the participants
on each track.

	Restricted track	Unrestricted track
A2IA	—	8.5/2.9
CITlab	14.6/5.0	—
LIMSI	15.0/5.5	11.0/3.9

8.6.2 First HTR Contest: Results and Discussion

The best results obtained by each participant can be seen in Table 8.5. The results showed that a clear improvement was achieved when using more training data, as column, unrestricted track, illustrates. In the restricted track, both entrants obtained similar results. In the unrestricted track, A2IA clearly obtained the best result, even though the techniques used by both participants were quite similar. Such a significant improvement could be due to two important aspects: (a) the training of the OMs included a large dataset of historical documents and (b) the LM included transcripts from additional Bentham manuscripts.

Figure 8.4 shows the histogram of the positions of the errors with regard to the correct line transcripts. We used the lines with more than three words in the reference transcripts for computing this histogram. Note that most of the errors were concentrated in the initial and last parts of the lines for all results. Hyphenated words may have large influence in the errors. Note also that the LIMSI technique for dealing with hyphenated words seemed to have a positive effect when dealing with these hyphenated words as top and bottom plots show.

8.6.3 Second HTR Contest: Results and Discussion

The best results obtained by each participant can be seen in Table 8.6. In the restricted track, two entrants obtained similar results and the third entrant

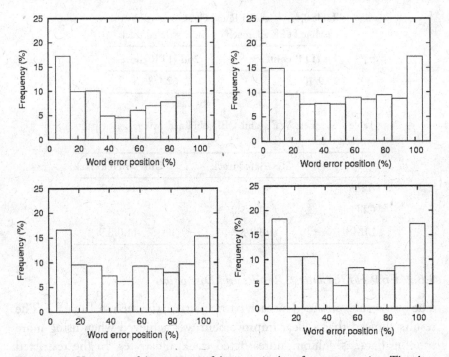

Figure 8.4.   Histogram of the positions of the errors in the reference transcripts. The plots from top to down and from left to right correspond to A2IA-Un, CITlab-Re, LIMSI-Re, and LIMSI-Un.

Table 8.6.   Best WER and CER obtained by the participants on each track.

	Restricted track	**Unrestricted track**
CITlab	30.2 ± 1.0/15.5 ± 0.4	—
A2IA	31.6 ± 1.0/14.7 ± 0.4	27.9 ± 1.0/13.6 ± 0.4
QCRI	44.0 ± 1.0/28.8 ± 0.5	—

obtained worst results. In the unrestricted track, A2IA clearly obtained the best result. Some conclusions can be obtained from these figures.

First, a great improvement was achieved when using external training text, as column, unrestricted track, shows for A2IA. Clearly, training the LM with in-domain transcripts from additional Bentham manuscripts (different from those used in the test set), led to a substantial reduction of the rate of OOV words, which largely explains the results.

Second, the results obtained by CITlab improved when system combination was used. The WER decreased from 33.9% achieved with the best system to 30.2% by combining the outputs of five systems.

Third, it becomes clear that current technology does allow to automatically obtain training data (line images and their corresponding transcripts) when just unsegmented page images and page transcripts are available (*Challenge 1*). The three entrants took profit (albeit not very significant) of the Train-B2 set. Thus, when using just the best system, CITlab improved the WER from 34.1% to 33.9% by adding to Train-B1 3,968 automatically obtained lines from Train-B2. Similarly, when the outputs of five systems were combined, the WER was improved from 31.8% down to 30.2%.

Figure 8.5 shows the transcripts of the best CITlab results for several lines, sorted according to their WER. Note that even for the line with the largest WER, the automatic transcript can be useful both for reading and

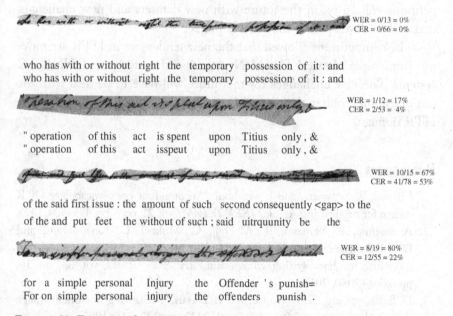

WER = 0/13 = 0%
CER = 0/66 = 0%

who has with or without right the temporary possession of it : and
who has with or without right the temporary possession of it : and

WER = 1/12 = 17%
CER = 2/53 = 4%

" operation   of this   act is spent   upon Titius only , &
" operation   of this   act isspeut   upon Titius only , &

WER = 10/15 = 67%
CER = 41/78 = 53%

of the said first issue : the amount of such   second consequently <gap> to the
of the and put feet   the without of such ; said uitrquunity be   the

WER = 8/19 = 80%
CER = 12/55 = 22%

for a simple personal Injury   the Offender 's punish=
For on simple personal injury   the offenders   punish .

Figure 8.5. Examples of test line images of increasing difficulty. The reference transcript and the CITlab system hypothesis are displayed (in this order) below of each image. The corresponding WER and CER figures are also shown on the right of each image.

for searching. Even some lines with all the words crossed-out can be acceptably transcribed, as the last line shows. Finally, we can see that if the line has a large WER but a low CER, sometimes the transcript can be more useful than if the WER is lower and the CER higher (see third and fourth lines). The average WER for the four lines is 40%.

8.7 Remarks and Conclusions

This chapter has included the main results obtained in two competitions on HTR with datasets that were prepared within the tranScriptorium project. The results obtained by the participant can be considered as very good. A fundamental contribution of these competitions is that they allowed bringing the HTR technology to its current cutting-edge status. Another important achievement of these competitions was the current availability of two comprehensive datasets for researching about HTR, which include a lot of effort for producing ground truth that can be used for many purposes about document image analysis and HTR. These competitions will go on in the future with new datasets and new challenges that will be developed in the READ project.[s]

The competitions showed that the new tendencies in HTR are moving from more classical HMM/N-gram based systems to DNN/CTC systems. The new challenges for the future will have to be deal with the line detection problem that currently can be considered a bottleneck in the HTR domain.

References

1. I. Bazzi, R. Schwartz, and J. Makhoul, "An omnifont open-vocabulary OCR system for English and Arabic," *IEEE Tr. PAMI*, vol. 21, no. 6, pp. 495–504, 1999.
2. A. Bianne, F. Menasri, R. Al-Hajj, C. Mokbel, C. Kermorvant, and L. Likforman-Sulem, "Dynamic and contextual information in hmm modeling for handwriting recognition," *IEEE Tr. PAMI*, vol. 33, no. 10, pp. 2066–2080, 2011.
3. D. S. Bloomberg, G. E. Kopec, and L. Dasari, "Measuring document image skew and orientation," *Proc. SPIE*, vol. 2422, pp. 302–316, 1995.

---

[s] http://read.transkribus.eu/.

4. T. Bluche, "Deep neural networks for large vocabulary handwritten text recognition," Ph.D. thesis, Ecole Doctorale Informatique de Paris-Sud — Laboratoire d'Informatique pour la Mcanique et les Sciences de l'Ingnieur, discipline: Informatique, 2015.

5. T. Bluche, B. Moysset, and C. Kermorvant, "Automatic line segmentation and ground-truth alignment of handwritten documents," in *ICFHR*, pp. 667–672, 2014.

6. T. Bluche, H. Ney, and C. Kermorvant, "The LIMSI/A2IA handwriting recognition systems for the HTRtS contest," in *ICDAR* (IEEE Computer Society, Gammarth, Tunisia), pp. 448–452, 2015.

7. V. Bosch, A. Toselli, and E. Vidal, "Statistical text line analysis in handwritten documents," in *ICFHR* (Bari, Italy), pp. 201–206, 2012.

8. V. Bosch-Campos, A. Toselli, and E. Vidal, "Semi-automatic text baseline detection in large historical handwritten documents," in *ICFHR*, pp. 690–695, 2014.

9. S. Brunessaux, P. Giroux, B. Grilheres, M. Manta, M. Bodin, K. Choukri, O. Galibert, and J. Kahn, "The Maurdor project-improving automatic processing of digital documents," in *DAS*, pp. 349–354, 2014.

10. R. Buse, Z. Liu, and T. Caelli, "A structural and relational approach to handwritten word recognition," *IEEE Transactions on Systems, Man, and Cybernetics, Part B* 27, no. 5, pp. 847–861, 1997.

11. T. Causer and V. Wallace, "Building a volunteer community: Results and findings from Transcribe Bentham," *Digital Humanities Quarterly*, vol. 6, no. 2, 2012.

12. S. España-Boquera, M. Castro-Bleda, J. Gorbe-Moya, and F. Zamora-Martínez, "Improving offline handwriting text recognition with hybrid HMM/ANN models," *IEEE Tr. PAMI*, vol. 33, no. 4, pp. 767–779, pp. 690–695, 2011.

13. J. Fiscus, "A post-processing system to yield reduced word error rates: Recognizer output voting error reduction (ROVER)," in *IEEE Workshop on ASRU*, 1997.

14. B. Gatos, G. Louloudis, T. Causer, K. Grint, V. Romero, J. A. Sánchez, A. H. Toselli, and E. Vidal, "Ground-truth production in the tranScriptorium project," in *DAS* (France), pp. 237–241, 2014.

15. A. Graves, S. Fernández, F. Gomez, and J. Schmidhuber, "Connectionist temporal classification: Labelling unsegmented sequence data with recurrent neural networks," in *ICML*, pp. 369–376, 2006.

16. A. Graves, M. Liwicki, S. Fernánandez, R. Bertolami, H. Bunke, and J. Schmidhuber, "A novel connectionist system for unconstrained handwriting recognition," *IEEE Tr. PAMI*, vol. 31, no. 5, pp. 855–868, 2009a.

17. A. Graves, M. Liwicki, S. Fernandez, R. Bertolami, H. Bunke, and J. Schmidhuber, "A novel connectionist system for unconstrained handwriting recognition," *IEEE Tr. PAMI*, vol. 31, no. 5, pp. 855–868, 2009b.

18. A. Graves, and J. Schmidhuber, "Offline handwriting recognition with multi-dimensional recurrent neural networks," in *NIPS*, pp. 545–552, 2008.

19. E. Grosicki, and H. E. Abed, "ICDAR 2009 handwriting recognition competition," in *ICDAR*, pp. 1398–1402, 2009.

20. G. Hinton, S. Osindero, and Y.-W. Teh, "A fast learning algorithm for deep belief nets," *Neural Computation*, vol. 18, no. 7, pp. 1527–554, 2006.

21. T. V. Hoang, and S. Tabbone, "Text extraction from graphical document images using sparse representation," in *International Workshop on Document Analysis Systems*, 2010.

22. F. Jelinek, *Statistical Methods for Speech Recognition* (MIT Press, 1998).

23. M. Kozielski, J. Forster, and H. Ney, "Moment-based image normalization for handwritten text recognition," in *ICFHR*, pp. 256–261, 2012.

24. L. Likforman-Sulem, A. Zahour, and B. Taconet, B, "Text line segmentation of historical documents: A survey," *IJDAR*, vol. 9(2–4), pp. 123–138, 2007.

25. U.-V. Marti and H. Bunke, "Using a statistical language model to improve the performance of an HMM-based cursive handwriting recognition system," *IJPRAI*, vol. 15, no. 1, pp. 65–90, 2001.

26. R. Messina and C. Kermorvant, "Over-generative finite state transducer *n*-gram for out-of-vocabulary word recognition," in *DAS*, pp. 212–217, 2014.

27. B. Moysset, T. Bluche, M. Knibbe, M. F. Benzeghiba, R. Messina, J. Louradour, and C. Kermorvant, "The A2iA multi-lingual text recognition system at the second Maurdor evaluation," in *ICFHR*, pp. 297–302, 2014.

28. V. Pham, C. Kermorvant, and J. Louradour, "Dropout improves recurrent neural networks for handwriting recognition," 2013. Available: http://arxiv.org/abs/1312.4569.

29. S. Pletschacher and A. Antonacopoulos, "The PAGE (page analysis and ground-truth elements) format framework," in *ICPR*, pp. 257–260, 2010.

30. P. Roeder, "Adapting the RWTH-OCR handwriting recognition system to French handwriting," Ph.D. Thesis, RWTH Aachen University, Aachen, Germany, human Language Technology and Pattern Recognition Group, 2009.

31. V. Romero, A. Toselli, and E. Vidal, "Multimodal interactive handwritten text transcription," *Series in Machine Perception and Artificial Intelligence*. New Jersey, World Scientific Publishing, 2012.

32. P. P. Roy, J. Llados, and U. Pal, "Text/graphics separation in color maps," in *International Conference on Computing: Theory and Applications*, 2007.

33. J. A. Sánchez, G. Mühlberger, B. Gatos, P. Schofield, K. Depuydt, R. Davis, E. Vidal, and J. de Does, "tranScriptorium: An European project on handwritten text recognition," in *DocEng*, pp. 227–228, 2013.

34. J. A. Sánchez, V. Romero, A. Toselli, and E. Vidal, "ICFHR2014 competition on handwritten text recognition on tranScriptorium datasets (HTRtS)," in *ICFHR*, pp. 181–186, 2014.

35. J. A. Sánchez, A. Toselli, V. Romero, and E. Vidal, "ICDAR 2015 competition HTRtS: Handwritten text recognition on the tranScriptorium dataset," in *ICDAR*, pp. 1166–1170, 2015.

36. F. Stahlberg and S. Vogel, "The QCRI recognition system for handwritten arabic," in *ICIAP*, pp. 1166–1170, 2015.

37. A. Toselli, A. Juan, D. Keysers, J. González, I. Salvador, H. Ney, E. Vidal, and F. Casacuberta, "Integrated handwriting recognition and interpretation using finite-state models," *IJPRAI*, vol. 18, no. 4, pp. 519–539, 2004.

38. A. Toselli, E. Vidal, and F. Casacuberta, *Multimodal Interactive Pattern Recognition and Applications*, 1st Edition. London, Springer, 2011.

39. A. H. Toselli, V. Romero, L. Rodríguez, and E. Vidal, "Computer assisted transcription of handwritten text," in *ICDAR*, pp. 944–948, 2007.

40. A. Vinciarelli, S. Bengio, and H. Bunke, "Off-line recognition of unconstrained handwritten texts using HMMs and statistical language models," *IEEE Tr. PAMI*, vol. 26, no. 6, pp. 709–720, 2004.

41 A. Vinciarelli and J. Luettin, "A new normalization technique for cursive handwritten words," *Pattern Recognition Letters*, vol. 22, no. 9, pp. 1043–1050, 2001.

Chapter 9

Multifont and Multisize Low-resolution Arabic Text Recognition Using APTI Database

Fouad Slimane and Christine Vanoirbeek

9.1 Introduction

Some Arabic characters change their shapes according to the place where they occur in the word. Most of them have four shapes: isolated, initial, medial, and final. Some Arabic letters include a "loop," generally called an "occlusion shape," which differs from one character to another. Figure 9.1 illustrates an example of an Arabic word with dots, occlusions, and pseudowords. The Arabic script is represented by a cursive script for printed as well as handwritten text, and is composed of interrelated characters written from right to left. This cursive nature of Arabic texts adds an inherent difficulty in segmenting them into characters. Thus, Arabic script recognition is a very complex task.

Text recognition is done to transform an image containing a printed or handwritten text into an editable text and a format that can be understood by a computer. For many applications, a robust printed Arabic text recognition system can be very useful for improving the man–machine interface. It can enable the conversion of huge amounts of scanned printed Arabic documents into an editable content.

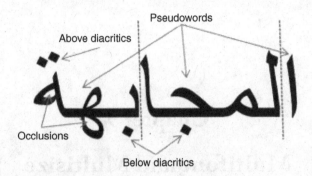

Figure 9.1. An example of Arabic words with dots, occlusions, and pseudowords.

The domain of Arabic text recognition can be segmented into printed text [1] and handwritten text [2]. Handwritten and printed Arabic text images can be acquired offline, typically from a scanner or a camera, or online with a graphical tablet or touchscreen. This chapter is focused on offline recognition. In addition, while previous research studies focused on high-resolution images typically acquired with scanners, this chapter addresses a low-resolution scenario. Low-resolution Arabic text images are becoming more frequent, either directly embedded in websites as menus or decorations, or resulting from screen capture tools on rendered documents. This chapter describes the well-known Arabic Printed Text Image (APTI) database [3], the organized competitions, and all the systems evaluated using this database.

The chapter is organized as follows. Section 9.2 summarizes the main characteristics of the APTI database. Section 9.3 is dedicated to the organized competitions using the APTI database. Sections 9.4, 9.5, and 9.6 present the systems evaluated with APTI for text recognition, text segmentation, and font identification, respectively. The evaluation and discussion of the results are presented in Section 9.7, followed by conclusions and recommendations.

9.2 The APTI Database

The APTI database was developed to promote the research and development of Arabic printed word recognition systems. Available from July 2009, APTI is freely distributed to the scientific community for

Figure 9.2. Fonts used to generate the APTI database: (A) Andalus, (B) Arabic Transparent, (C) Advertising Bold, (D) Diwani Letter, (E) DecoTypeThuluth, (F) Simplified Arabic, (G) Tahoma, (H) Traditional Arabic, (I) DecoTypeNaskh, and (J) M Unicode Sara.

benchmarking purposes [3]. At the time of writing this chapter, more than 100 research groups started using it.

The APTI database contains a mix of decomposable (generated from root Arabic verbs) and nondecomposable (formed by Arabic proper general names) word images. To generate the lexicon, the authors parsed different Arabic books, Arabic newspapers, articles taken from the Internet, and a large lexicon file. It was created at the word level in ultra-low-resolution "72 dot/inch" with a lexicon of 113,284 different Arabic words and 10 fonts, as presented in Figure 9.2. These fonts were selected to cover the different complexity of shapes of Arabic printed characters such as overlaps, ligatures, and flourishes. Different font sizes are also used in APTI: 6, 7, 8, 9, 10, 12, 14, 16, 18, and 24 points. Four different styles, namely, plain, italic, bold, and a combination of italic and bold were also used. These sizes, fonts, and styles are widely used on computer screens, Arabic newspapers, and many other documents. The combination of fonts, styles, and sizes guarantees a wide variability of images in the database. Images presented in Figure 9.3 illustrate the variability of APTI images with various combinations of fonts and sizes. Artifacts of the

Font/Size	6	8	10	12	18	24
Andalus	الآراء	الآراء	الآراء	الآراء	الآراء	الآراء
Image Resizing	21X13 to 81X49 pixels	28X17 to 81X49 pixels	34X21 to 81X49 pixels	41X25 to 81X49 pixels	61X37 to 81X49 pixels	81X49 to 81X49 pixels
Arabic Transparent	الآراء	الآراء	الآراء	الآراء	الآراء	الآراء
Image Resizing	22X12 to 85X45 pixels	29X16 to 85X45 pixels	36X19 to 85X45 pixels	43X23 to 85X45 pixels	64X34 to 85X45 pixels	85X45 to 85X45 pixels
Simplified Arabic	الآراء	الآراء	الآراء	الآراء	الآراء	الآراء
Image Resizing	22X12 to 85X46 pixels	29X16 to 85X46 pixels	36X19 to 85X46 pixels	43X23 to 85X46 pixels	64X34 to 85X46 pixels	85X46 to 85X46 pixels
Traditional Arabic	الآراء	الآراء	الآراء	الآراء	الآراء	الآراء
Image Resizing	17X10 to 64X39 pixels	22X13 to 64X39 pixels	36X19 to 64X39 pixels	43X23 to 64X39 pixels	48X29 to 64X39 pixels	64X39 to 64X39 pixels
Diwani Letter	الآراء	الآراء	الآراء	الآراء	الآراء	الآراء
Image Resizing	21X12 to 80X44 pixels	27X15 to 80X44 pixels	34X19 to 80X44 pixels	41X23 to 80X44 pixels	60X33 to 80X44 pixels	80X44 to 80X44 pixels
AdvertisingBold	الآراء	الآراء	الآراء	الآراء	الآراء	الآراء
Image Resizing	23X14 to 88X52 pixels	30X18 to 88X52 pixels	37X22 to 88X52 pixels	44X26 to 88X52 pixels	66X39 to 88X52 pixels	88X52 to 88X52 pixels
DecoType Naskh	الآراء	الآراء	الآراء	الآراء	الآراء	الآراء
Image Resizing	17X14 to 64X54 pixels	22X19 to 64X54 pixels	27X23 to 64X54 pixels	32X28 to 64X54 pixels	48X41 to 64X54 pixels	64X54 to 64X54 pixels
DecoType Thuluth	الآراء	الآراء	الآراء	الآراء	الآراء	الآراء
Image Resizing	21X12 to 83X46 pixels	28X16 to 83X46 pixels	35X20 to 83X46 pixels	42X23 to 83X46 pixels	62X34 to 83X46 pixels	83X46 to 83X46 pixels
M Unicode Sara	الآراء	الآراء	الآراء	الآراء	الآراء	الآراء
Image Resizing	15X11 to 57X40 pixels	20X14 to 57X40 pixels	24X17 to 57X40 pixels	29X20 to 57X40 pixels	43X30 to 57X40 pixels	57X40 to 57X40 pixels
Tahoma	الآراء	الآراء	الآراء	الآراء	الآراء	الآراء
Image Resizing	21X14 to 83X52 pixels	28X18 to 83X52 pixels	35X22 to 83X52 pixels	42X26 to 83X52 pixels	62X39 to 83X52 pixels	83X52 to 83X52 pixels

Figure 9.3.   APTI image sample on plain style and different fonts and sizes.

downsampling and the anti-aliasing filters, various forms of ligatures, and overlaps of characters are illustrated.

The total number of word images is above 45 million. Each word image in the APTI database is in gray and fully described using an XML file containing ground-truth information about the sequence of characters as well as information about its generation. All Arabic letters have a balanced distribution throughout the sets composing the database.

The database is divided into six comparable sets to allow for flexibility in the composition of development and evaluation partitions. For more details about APTI, see [3] and [4].

Some researchers have been inspired from the building of APTI and the ground-truthing method to build other databases and corpus such as the ALIF data set by Yousfi *et al.* [5], the AcTiV-DB by Zayene *et al.* [6], the MMA Corpus by Abdel Raouf *et al.* [7], the

AHTID/MW database by Mezghani *et al.* [8], and the APTID/MF database by Kallel Jaiem *et al.* [9].

9.3 Organized Competitions Using APTI Database

Two competitions were organized using the APTI database [10, 11] in a "blind" manner. These competitions were organized by Fouad Slimane,[a] Slim Kanoun,[b] Haikal El Abed,[c] Adel M. Alimi,[d] Rolf Ingold,[e] and Jean Hennebert[f] as a joint collaboration project between researchers. The testing data of the evaluation are composed of an unpublished set (the so-called Set 6 of APTI), which is kept secret for evaluation purposes. All evaluations were done using the writing style: plain and the font sizes: 6, 8, 10, 12, 18, and 24.

The participants were asked to send an executable version of their recognizer to the organizers who, in turn, arranged to run the systems against an unseen set of data. The participants were able to train and tune their systems using the public parts of APTI. All the systems were compared using the recognition rates at the character and word levels.

9.3.1 *ICDAR 2011*

In 2011, the first competition for multifont and multisize digitally represented Arabic text was presented at the *International Conference on Document Analysis and Recognition (ICDAR 2011)* [10].

The scientific objectives of this competition were to measure the impact of font size on recognition performance. This was evaluated in mono- and multifont contexts. The protocols were defined to evaluate the capacity of recognition systems to handle different sizes and fonts using digitally low-resolution images with the aim of looking for a robust

---

[a]MEDIA Research Lab, Ecole Polytechnique Fédérale de Lausanne (EPFL).
[b]MIRACL Lab, ISIMS, University of Sfax, Tunisia.
[c]The Technical Trainers College, German International Cooperation, Riyadh — Kingdom of Saudi Arabia.
[d]REGIM Lab. University of Sfax, National School of Engineers (ENIS), Tunisia.
[e]DIVA Research Group, Department of Informatics. University of Fribourg (unifr), Switzerland.

approach to screen-based OCR. Two groups submitted three systems to enter this competition.

Two protocols were proposed by the organizers in 2011:

- The APTI Protocol for Competition: APTIPC1-tested images generated with the font: Arabic Transparent.
- The APTI Protocol for Competition: APTIPC2-tested images generated with the fonts: Diwani Letter, Andalus, Arabic Transparent, Simplified Arabic, and Traditional Arabic.

9.3.2 *ICDAR 2013*

In 2013, the results of the second competition on multifont and multisize digitally represented Arabic text were presented at *the International Conference on Document Analysis and Recognition (ICDAR 2013)* [11].

This time, four groups with six systems participated in the competition. Compared to the first time, the systems were tested with more fonts and in different contexts in this second competition.

Four protocols were proposed by the organizers in 2013:

- Reference APTI Protocol for Competition: Ref. APTIPC-tested images generated with the font: Arabic Transparent.
  This protocol is the same as in the first edition of the competition. To participate to this protocol, the participants submitted six systems (one for each size) or one system using the parameter size.
- APTI Protocol for Competition: 1st APTIPC.
  This protocol uses the same font as in the reference protocol but independent of the size. The participants submitted one multisize system for this protocol (Font: Arabic Transparent).
- APTI Protocol for Competition: 2nd APTIPC-tested images generated with the font: DecoTypeNaskh.
  This protocol uses the ligatured font "DecoTypeNaskh" independent of the font size. The participants submitted one multisize system for this protocol.
- APTI Protocol for Competition: 3rd APTIPC-tested images generated with the following fonts: Andalus, Arabic Transparent, Advertising

Bold, Diwani Letter, DecoTypeThuluth, Simplified Arabic, Tahoma, Traditional Arabic, DecoTypeNaskh, and M Unicode Sara.

This protocol uses All APTI fonts independent of the font size. The competitors submitted one multifont and one multisize system.

9.4 Text Recognition Systems Evaluated with APTI

This section gives a short overview of the published text recognition systems evaluated using the APTI database.

9.4.1 *IPSAR System — ICDAR 2011*

The IPSAR system was submitted to the "ICDAR 2011 — Arabic recognition competition: Multifont multisize digitally represented text" by Samir Ouis, Mohammad S. Khorsheed, and Khalid Alfaifi, all members of the Image Processing and Signal Analysis & Recognition (IPSAR) Group. This group is part of the Computer Research Institute (CRI) at King Abdul Aziz City for Science & Technology (KACST) in the Kingdom of Saudi Arabia.

IPSARec is a cursive Arabic script recognition system where ligatures, overlaps, and style variation pose challenges for the recognition system. It is based on the hidden Markov model toolkit (HTK), a portable toolkit for speech recognition systems customized in this case, to recognize characters. IPSARec is an omnifont, unlimited vocabulary recognition system, which does not require segmentation. The proposed system has three main stages: it first extracts a set of features from the input images, then clusters the feature set according to a predefined codebook, and, finally, it recognizes the characters.

Each word/line image is transferred into a sequence of feature vectors. The features are extracted from overlapping vertical windows divided into cells, each containing a predefined number of pixels along the word/line image, which are then clustered into discrete symbols.

Stage 2 is performed within HTK and combines the feature vectors with the corresponding ground truth to estimate the character model's parameters. The final output of this stage is a lexicon-free system for recognizing cursive Arabic text. During the recognition process, an input pattern of discrete symbols representing the word/line image is injected into the global model, which then produces a stream of characters matching the text line. For more details of this system, please refer to [12].

9.4.2 UPV–BHMM Systems — ICDAR 2011

These systems entered the "ICDAR 2011 — Arabic recognition competition: Multifont multisize digitally represented text," by Ihab Alkhoury, Adrià Giménez, and Alfons Juan, from the Universitat Politècnica de València (UPV), Spain. They are based on Bernoulli HMMs (BHMMs), i.e., HMMs in which the conventional Gaussian mixture density functions are replaced by Bernoulli mixture probability functions [13]. Also, in contrast to the basic approach followed in [13], whereby narrow, one-column slices of binary pixels are fed into BHMMs, the UPV–BHMM systems are based on a sliding window of adequate width to better capture the image context at each horizontal position of the word image. This new, windowed version of the basic approach is described in [14].

The UPV–PRHLT systems were trained through input images scaled in height to 40 pixels (keeping the aspect ratio) after the addition of a number of white pixel rows to both the top and bottom of each image, and then binarized with the Otsu algorithm. A sliding window of width 9 was applied; consequently, the input (binary) feature vectors for the BHMMs had 360 bits. The number of states per character was adjusted to 5 states for images with a font size of 6, and 6 states for the other font sizes. Similarly, the number of mixture components per state was empirically adjusted to 64. The expectation-maximization (EM) algorithm was used for the estimation and recognition parameters.

Two systems were submitted: UPV–PRHLT-REC1 and UPV–PRHLT-REC2, and used for both tasks/protocols. In the first task (one style), there were no differences between the systems; one model for each font size was trained and later used to recognize the test corpus. In the second task, in the first system, a different model for each font style was trained for each font size. The test corpus was recognized on all models, and the recognized text word of the highest probability was selected. For the second task in the other system, a different character was considered for each style. A model for all the styles together was trained in order to recognize the test corpus.

9.4.3 *Siemens System — ICDAR 2013*

The Siemens System was submitted to the "ICDAR 2013 — Arabic recognition competition: Multifont multisize digitally represented text," by Marc-Peter Schambach, Joerg Rottland, and Sheikh Faisal Rashid, from Siemens AG and Image Understanding and Pattern Recognition (IUPR), University of Kaiserslautern, Germany. The system is based on the recurrent neural networks described by Alex Graves in [15, 16]. It is a multilayer neural network, which transforms a 2D pixel plane into a sequence of class probabilities by subsampling the input pixel planes in each layer and collapsing the final plane in the Y-direction, producing a sequence in the X-direction. Each layer is recurrent, with input not only from the input pixel but also from the neighboring cells within the layer. Cells are long short-term memory (LSTM) cells, containing rich structure with input, output, and forget gates. The network topology has three hidden layers, with 2, 10, and 50 cells each. The subsampling layers have the dimension 1 × 2 or 2 × 3 (depending on image size), with 6 and 20 cells. A separate network was trained for each font size of the reference task. For the multisize Tasks 1–3, the images were scaled to common heights for training purposes. Depending on the test image size, one of the multiple trained networks was chosen for the recognition task.

9.4.4 *UPV–BHMM Systems — ICDAR 2013*

The UPV–BHMM systems were submitted for the "ICDAR 2013 — Arabic recognition competition: Multifont multisize digitally represented text" by Ihab Alkhoury, Adrià Giménez, Jesús Andrés-Ferrer, and Alfons Juan, from the Universitat Politècnica de València (UPV), València, Spain.

This UPV–BHMM system is built from character-based windowed BHMMs (Bernoulli HMMs) adequately concatenated to produce a different word-level windowed BHMM for each word to be recognized

[1, 13, 14]. The text image of an unknown word is first transformed into a sequence of binary feature vectors by applying a sliding window at each horizontal position. The width of the sliding window is known to have a strong effect on the system's ability to capture local image distortions. However, local image distortions, and vertical distortions in particular, may not be correctly modeled when the sliding window is at a constant vertical position on the image. To overcome this limitation, the sliding window is repositioned (translated) before application. More precisely, the sliding window was repositioned to align its center with its mass center. More details concerning this idea are described in [17].

9.4.5 *SID Systems — ICDAR 2013*

The SID system was submitted to the "ICDAR 2013 — Arabic recognition competition: Multifont multisize digitally represented text" by Oussama Zayene, Najoua Essoukri Ben Amara, and Sameh Touj, members of the Signal, Image and Document team. This team is part of the SAGE (Systèmes Avancés en Génie Electrique) at the National Engineering School of Sousse, Tunisia. The SID system is based on the hidden Markov models (HMMs) using the HTK toolkit. It is an open vocabulary recognition system and does not require any character segmentation.

The system has two main stages: training and recognition. Preprocessing and feature extractions steps are common to both stages. A set of characteristics is extracted from each word image using the sliding window technique, in this case, with 6 pixels width and an overlap between two successive windows of 1 pixel. Each window is further divided vertically into nine cells, and each word image transformed into a matrix of values where the number of lines corresponds to the number of analysis windows, and the number of columns is equal to the number of feature coefficients in each feature vector. During the training phase, a right–left HMM corresponding to the known sequence of characters is prepared for each word associated with the features file. Once the HMM parameters have been initialized, an embedded iterative training for the character models is performed using a Baum–Welch procedure. Recognition is performed through applying the Viterbi algorithm to an ergodic HMM defined by the set of all the character models. More details about this system are presented in [18].

9.4.6 *THOCR Systems — ICDAR 2013*

THOCR systems were submitted to the "ICDAR 2013 — Arabic recognition competition: Multifont multisize digitally represented text" by Zhiwei Jiang, Xiaoqing Ding, Changsong Liu, and Liangrui Peng from the Center of Intelligent Image and Document Processing (CIDP), Department of Electronic Engineering at Tsinghua University in China.

The HMM is the core technique of all three systems, and the HTK is used for the training, decoding, and rescoring processes. The three systems follow the classic preprocessing procedure of HMM-based systems. First, a normalized image of 120 pixel height is sequenced for frames by an 8-pixel-width sliding window with 1-pixel steps. Next, a 28D feature is extracted frame by frame. Two-thirds of the features are statistical, while the remainder is structural. At the same time, the positions of the upper and lower baselines are also used to divide the image into different zones for statistical purposes. For each feature extracted, an additional 28D differential feature is calculated through the previous and immediate neighboring ones and added to the end of the original 28D feature. So a 56D feature is extracted in all THOCR systems.

The THOCR 1 system is a simple HMM-based one. The usual embedded Baum–Welch algorithm and Viterbi algorithm are used for training and decoding separately. All 128 Arabic letters and two kinds of spaces are illustrated by 67 models.

Similar letters share one model because the model can be trained to perform better with more sample data.

The THOCR 2 system includes nearly all the procedures of THOCR 1, but a 4-gram language model, which is trained with the ground truth of all training sets available in APTI, is used in THOCR 2. It rescores the path of state transition after the decoding is complete.

Both THOCR 1 and THOCR 2 were originally designed for single-font Arabic character recognition. The THOCR 3 system is quite different from the two mentioned above because it contains two HMMs inside for multifont Arabic character recognition.

Through analyzing the character recognition performance confusion matrix of 10-font samples, authors cluster 10 fonts into 6 groups and train 6 corresponding HMM-based font models first. Before carrying out character recognition, the THOCR 3 system identifies the font of the current sample using the HMM-based font system, and then the system works in the same way as THOCR 2 using the HMM-based character recognition system with a particular font.

Font recognition is also accomplished through the same 56D feature, but the model is trained by font-based ground truth instead.

9.4.7 *DIVA–REGIM System — 2012*

The DIVA–REGIM system is part of a joint collaboration between the DIVA (Document, Image and Voice Analysis) group of the university of Fribourg, Switzerland, and the REGIM (Research Group over Intelligence Machines) group from the university of Sfax, Tunisia. This system is called cascading and works in three steps: feature extraction, font recognition, and word recognition using font-dependent models.

The preprocessing phase aims at reducing the variability of character shapes due to misalignment on the Y-axis. The idea in this system is to detect a probable baseline region (here called *below*, *middle*, and *above* regions) using data-driven methods trained on local character features. Once a probable baseline region has been recognized by the Gaussian mixture models (GMM)-based system, the final position of the baseline is fine-tuned using the classical horizontal projection histogram, but limited to this region. The baseline recognition system is quite similar to the system presented in [19] for Arabic font recognition. For more details about the baseline system, please see [20].

The features are extracted using the sliding window technique from word images at the binary and gray levels. The used analysis window slides horizontally, from right to left, on the word image with a shift of s pixels, where s is an integer window equal to 1. As a result, no segmentation into letters is made, and the word image is transformed into a matrix of values, whereby the number of lines corresponds to the number of analysis windows, and the number of columns is equal to the number of coefficients in each feature vector.

The open vocabulary DIVA–REGIM word recognition system is based on the HMMs and its architecture is similar to that presented in [21]. In each training word image, the corresponding character submodels are connected to form a right–left HMM. The training procedure involves two steps iteratively applied to increase the number of Gaussian mixtures for a given M value (M is defined experimentally by the author maximizing the recognition rate). In the first step, a binary split procedure along the iteration process is applied to the Gaussians to increase their number. In the second step, the Baum–Welch re-estimation procedure is launched to estimate the parameters of the Gaussians. Recognition uses an ergodic HMM built from all the submodels. This is done by selecting the best state sequence in the HMM using a Viterbi procedure. For more details about the feature extraction, training, and recognition phases, please see [22].

9.4.8 *Su and Ding-2013 System*

Su and Ding use a model-based dimensionality reduction method for vector sequences, namely, a linear sequence discriminant analysis (LSDA) which attempts to find a subspace where sequences of the same class are projected together, while those of different classes are projected as far away as possible. An HMM is built from states whose statistics have been extracted for each sequence. The means of these states are linked to form a mean sequence, and the variance of the sequence class is defined as the sum of all variances of component states. LSDA then learns a transformation by maximizing the separability between the sequence classes, at the same time minimizing the within-sequence class scatter. The DTW distance between the mean sequences is used to measure the separability between sequence classes. The optimization problem can be approximately transformed into an Eigen decomposition problem. LDA can be seen as a special case of LSDA considering nonsequential vectors as sequences of length 1. This system is evaluated outside of the two competitions mentioned earlier. For more details, please refer to [22, 23].

9.4.9 *SOCR System*

In [24], Rosenberg proposed a method which segments words into letters and then identifies individual letters using multiple grids of SIFT descriptors as features. The system is called SOCR for "SIFT-based

OCR." To construct the classifier, the author does not use a large training set of images with their corresponding ground truth — a process usually done to construct a classifier — but, rather, an image containing all possible symbols is created and a classifier constructed by extracting the features of each symbol. To recognize the text inside an image, the image is split into "pieces of Arabic words" (paws), and then each paw is scanned with increasing window sizes. Segmentation points are set where the classifier achieves maximum confidence. From the fact that Arabic has four forms of letters (isolated, initial, medial, and final), the search space is narrowed down based on the location inside the paw. This system is evaluated outside of the two competitions mentioned previously. For more details, please refer to [24].

9.4.10 *Ahmad et al.-2015 System*

In [25], Ahmad *et al.* present a multifont printed Arabic text recognition system using the HMMs. Their method uses the sliding window technique for feature extraction. The size and position of the cells of the sliding window can adapt to the writing lines of Arabic text and ink-pixel distributions. A two-step approach is taken for mixed-font text recognition, whereby the input text-line image is first associated with the closest known font using simple and effective features for font identification. The text line is then recognized by the system trained for that particular font as the next step. This approach has proved to be more effective than text recognition, employing a recognizer trained on samples with multiple fonts. They also present a framework for the recognition of unknown fonts, which employs font association and HMM adaptation techniques. This system is evaluated outside of the two competitions as previously mentioned.

9.4.11 *Khorsheed and Ouis-2014 System*

In [26], Khorsheed and Ouis extracts statistical features that measure image characteristics by local scales. Their proposed approach encodes the features extracted from a sliding one-pixel width window along the X-axis of the word image, into 1D feature vectors. The feature vector set is then injected into a recognition engine that uses the robustness of HMMs through applying the HTK. In order to select the optimal parameters for the HMM classifier, the APTI training data set is further divided into a smaller training subset and a verification set. The estimated parameters are then used in the testing phase.

9.4.12 *Awaida and Khorsheed-2012 System*

In [27], a technique for the recognition of the unconstrained Arabic printed text is proposed. First, features measuring the image characteristics at local scales are applied. A line image is divided into a set of one-pixel width windows, which slides across that text line. Run-length encoding is used to extract the features from each window. A single method is chosen to select the best number of transitions for each window and to select the optimal parameters for feature extraction and the HMM classifier, the APTI training data set is further divided into a smaller training subset and a verification set. This system is evaluated outside of the two aforementioned competitions.

9.4.13 *UPV-2013 System*

In [28], a system based on windowed Bernoulli HMMs is described. This system is an extension of the previous UPV–PRHLT–REC-ICDAR 2011 and UPV–BHMM-ICDAR 2013 systems improved by repositioning and exhaustive experimentation to adjust the various key parameters and model topology (variable number of states). It is evaluated outside of the two aforementioned competitions.

9.4.14 *UPV-2014 System*

In [28], based on their work on handwriting recognition with vertical repositioning, a DNN hybrid HMM system and vertical repositioning is offered. Khoury *et al.* carried out a series of experiments using a subset of the APTI database and a deep neural network (DNN) hybrid HMM system, similar to the LSTM technique. It has been implemented in a recently released, open-source toolkit for automatic speech recognition called TLK toolkit. This system is evaluated outside of the two competitions mentioned earlier. More details are given in [28].

9.4.15 *Jiang et al. -2015 System*

In [29], an extension version of the THOCR systems — ICDAR 2013 is presented. Improvements came from the different levels listed below:

- The clustering feature of states in HMM through comparing the mechanism of the quadratic discriminant function (QDF) classifier and HMM.
- Through the clustering effect of Viterbi training and Baum–Welch training by proposing a clustering-based model pertaining approach.

9.4.16 *Adhitama et al.-2014 System*

In [30], printed Arabic text recognition is presented. The proposed system is based on HMM and postprocessing with the Levenshtein distance. The system is segmentation-based, hence requires the segmentation of Arabic words. Each character is recognized individually using an HMM classifier. Some characters are confused because of their similarity of shape; the difference is only being in their number of dots used above or below the character shape. The recognition and segmentation system performance has been improved by implementing the Levenshtein distance algorithm. The Levenshtein distance works by comparing a recognized word with every word in the dictionary. The system is evaluated outside of the two aforementioned competitions using APTI word images generated in six different fonts. These fonts are: Tahoma, Simlified Arabic, Traditional Arabic, Andalus, DecoTypeNaskh, and DecoTypeThuluth.

9.4.17 *KacemEchi et al. -2014 System*

In [31], the proposed system is based on three classifiers — transparent neuronal networks (TNN) — which exploit the morphological aspect of Arabic words and collaborate for better word recognition. The approach focuses on decomposable words derived from healthy tri-consonant roots and easy to prove decomposition. To perform word recognition, the system extracts a set of global structural features, and then learns and recognizes the roots, schemes, and conjugation elements that compose the word. To help the recognition process, some local perceptual information is used to mitigate ambiguities. This interaction between global recognition and local checking makes the recognition of complex scripts, such as Arabic, easier. Several experiments have been performed using a vocabulary of 5,757 words organized in a corpus of more than 17,200 samples. This system is evaluated outside of the two competitions mentioned earlier. For more details, please refer to [31].

9.5 Text Segmentation Systems Evaluated with APTI

To our knowledge, only one text segmentation system has been evaluated using the APTI database. In [32], a character segmentation algorithm is proposed for Arabic text. Referring to the authors in [32], as segmentation and recognition are closely dependent on each other, and segmentation is not the aim per se, the proposed approach defers the ligature problem to the recognition phase. The algorithm is tolerant of the slant and, to some extent, of the overlapping characters. However, it was unable to segment the characters "س" and "ش" which have three strokes segmented into three segments based on the strokes. The proposed algorithm was evaluated outside of the two competitions mentioned earlier using 1,000 images from APTI. A correct segmentation rate of about 91% was achieved.

9.6 Font-identification Systems Evaluated with APTI

This section gives a short description of the published Arabic font-identification systems evaluated using the APTI database. All systems were evaluated outside of the competitions mentioned earlier.

9.6.1 *Ahmad et al.-2015 System*

Ahmad *et al.* proposed a font-identification system based on the support vector machine (SVM) classifier with radial basis function (RBF) as the kernel. The font features are primarily dependent on the projection profile of the text-line image. These features were extracted from 15,000 word images in the training set (Set 1 of each font at 24-point size). For more details, please refer to [25].

9.6.2 *Nicolaou et al.-2014 System*

In [33], local binary pattern (LBP), a generic texture classification method, is used for optical font recognition (OFR). The authors stripped down the redundant oriented LBP (RO-LBP) method previously used in writer identification and applied it to OFR to create a generic method to classify text as the oriented texture. The proposed LBP method can operate directly on text regions without the need for any specific word and text-line segmentation. It can consequently be used at earlier stages of the document image analysis (DIA) pipeline.

9.6.3 *Slimane et al.-2013 System*

The GMM–OFR system has two main parts (training and classification). A complete description of how the feature extraction works is available in [19] and [34]. The GMMs assess the likelihood of 10 font classes. The EM algorithm is used in training to iteratively refine the component weights, means, and variances, and thus monotonically increase the chances of the training feature vectors being in place. The experiments used the EM algorithm to construct the models, in two steps, through a simple binary splitting procedure after every 10 iterations to increase the Gaussian mixtures to as many as 2,048. A total of 2,048 Gaussians were experimentally determined to be optimal in terms of the recognition rate; no prior knowledge of class distribution contributed to the decision process. At the recognition step, the GMMs are fed in parallel with the features extracted from the image. Recognition is achieved through the comparison of simple class scores. The highest score model is chosen, which thus determines the font hypothesis. The performance is evaluated according to the classification rates when using an unseen set of line or word images. For more details about the use of GMMs, please see [34].

9.7 Evaluation

This section describes the results of all the systems described previously. They were evaluated using part of the APTI database. The APTI database has six equilibrated sets (in terms of the number of words and characters) to allow flexibility in the composition of the development and evaluation partitions. While the words in each set are different, the distribution of all the used letters is almost the same in each set. Some results have been computed on Set 6, Set 5, or on part of the five sets available to the scientific community. As the sets have almost equal numbers of words and equal distribution of letters, and based on experiments with the APTI data, it is assumed that the results are all comparable, even though each system was not tested using the same sets. They were evaluated in terms of their word, character, and font recognition rates. This chapter gives the results of the writing style: plain and the font sizes (6, 8, 10, 12, 18, and 24). The best recognition rate each experiment achieved is marked in **bold**.

The results are given according to the seven following categories.

9.7.1 *Mono-size Arabic Transparent Word Recognition Results*

The systems in this category were all evaluated using APTI-generated images with the "Arabic Transparent" font. Each system was tested in a mono-size context like the first and the reference protocols proposed in the ICDAR 2011 and ICDAR 2013 competitions (one system for each size, six in total).

Table 9.1 shows the results of the 23 systems evaluated using mono-size "Arabic Transparent" APTI word images. Most had good results at the word and character levels.

Around 13 systems had a higher than 90% word recognition rate, and 10 systems achieved above 99% character recognition rate. The best recognition rate for both word and character was obtained with the "Siemens System-ICDAR 2013," which won the ICDAR 2013 competition.

9.7.2 *Multisize Arabic Transparent Word Recognition Results*

All the systems in this category were evaluated using images from Set 6 of APTI generated using the "Arabic Transparent" font. Each was tested

Table 9.1.   Mono-size "Arabic Transparent" word recognition results.

System/Size		6	8	10	12	18	24	Mean
IPSAR System — ICDAR 2011*	WRR	5.7	73.3	75.0	83.1	77.1	77.5	65.3
	CRR	59.4	94.2	95.1	96.9	95.7	96.8	89.7
UPV-PRHLT-REC1 — ICDAR 2011*	WRR	94.5	97.4	96.7	92.5	84.6	84.4	91.7
	CRR	99.0	99.6	99.4	98.7	96.9	96.0	98.3
UPV-PRHLT-REC2 — ICDAR 2011*	WRR	94.5	97.4	96.7	92.5	84.6	84.4	91.7
	CRR	99.0	99.6	99.4	98.7	96.9	96.0	98.3
UPV-BHMM systems — ICDAR 2013*	WRR	97.25	99.67	99.78	99.88	99.9	99.9	99.4
	CRR	99.48	99.93	99.96	99.96	99.96	99.96	99.88
SID systems — ICDAR 2013*	WRR	94.3	96.23	98.18	98.78	96.6	97.41	96.92
	CRR	99.66	99.95	99.96	99.91	99.97	99.99	99.91
THOCR 1 system — ICDAR 2013*	WRR	75.97	88.06	89.08	87.73	88.97	91.77	86.93
	CRR	97.9	99.13	98.93	98.93	98.92	98.95	98.79
THOCR 2 system — ICDAR 2013*	WRR	89.47	95.83	94.8	92.48	94.57	95.03	93.70
	CRR	98.28	99.46	99.15	99.07	99.13	99.19	99.05
DIVA-REGIM system-2012*	WRR	97.47	98.67	99.02	99.32	99.44	99.76	99.21
	CRR	99.74	99.82	99.86	99.92	99.94	99.97	99.91
PCA-Su and Ding-2013-system	WRR	—	—	—	—	—	78.04	—
	CRR	—	—	—	—	—	95.17	—

State-LDA–Su and Ding-2013 system	WRR	—	—	—	—	—	83.91	—
	CRR	—	—	—	—	—	96.78	—
LSDA–Su and Ding-2013 system	WRR	—	—	—	—	—	85.05	—
	CRR	—	—	—	—	—	96.95	—
Siemens System — ICDAR 2013*	**WRR**	**99.87**	**99.92**	**99.95**	**99.94**	**99.96**	**99.97**	**99.94**
	CRR	**99.98**	**99.99**	**99.99**	**99.99**	**100**	**100**	**99.99**
SOCR	WRR	23.5	61.9	63.5	71.2	84.0	97.0	66.85
	CRR	64.7	90.1	92.7	93.2	97.1	99.2	89.50
SOCR Ignore Alif variation	WRR	27.6	78.9	89.8	94.0	99.0	98.5	81.3
	CRR	68.2	94.4	97.5	97.6	99.8	99.6	92.8
Ahmad *et al.*-2015 system†	WRR	—	—	—	—	—	97.88	—
	CRR	—	—	—	—	—	99.43	—
Khorsheed and Ouis-2014 system	WRR	71.51	95	95	97.73	95	92	91.04
	CRR	—	—	—	—	—	—	—
Awaida and Khorsheed-2012 system‡	WRR	—	—	—	—	—	—	—
	CRR	—	—	—	—	—	—	96.65
UPV-2013†	WRR	97.0	99.6	99.7	99.8	99.8	99.8	99.3
	CRR	99.4	99.9	99.9	100	100	99.9	99.8

(Continued)

Table 9.1.   (*Continued*)

System/Size		6	8	10	12	18	24	Mean
UPV-2014 (with vertical repositioning)	WRR	98.84	98.87	98.88	98.88	98.87	98.85	98.86
	CRR	99.97	99.97	99.98	99.98	99.97	99.97	99.97
UPV-2014 (without vertical repositioning)	WRR	99.78	99.80	99.88	99.87	99.87	99.84	99.84
	CRR	99.96	99.96	99.98	99.98	99.97	99.97	99.97
Jiang et al.-2015 system	WRR	91.76	—	—	97.33	—	96.89	—
	CRR	98.53	—	—	99.50	—	99.47	—
Adhitama et al.-2014 system	WRR							
	CRR							95.16
KacemEchi et al.-2014 system	WRR	—	—	—	—	—	78.2	—
	CRR	—	—	—	—	—		—

Notes: *Evaluated with Set 6.
†Evaluated with Set 5.
‡Evaluated with 14,418 images.

Table 9.2.   Multisize "Arabic Transparent" word recognition results.

System/Size		6	8	10	12	18	24	Mean
SID systems — ICDAR 2013	WRR	93.80	97.28	96.84	96.54	96.14	96.70	96.22
	CRR	99.47	99.78	99.82	99.81	99.79	99.83	99.75
UPV–BHMM systems — ICDAR 2013	WRR	96.71	99.50	99.78	99.90	99.90	99.92	99.29
	CRR	99.41	99.94	99.97	99.99	99.98	99.98	99.88
THOCR 1 system — ICDAR 2013	WRR	40.68	66.69	78.86	85.46	86.74	86.67	74.18
	CRR	93.29	98.40	99.01	99.25	99.28	99.29	98.09
THOCR 2 system — ICDAR 2013	WRR	67.40	86.85	93.37	94.64	95.37	95.50	88.86
	CRR	94.99	98.65	99.28	99.46	99.54	99.57	98.58
Siemens System — ICDAR 2013	**WRR**	**99.45**	**99.86**	**99.92**	**99.85**	**99.96**	**99.88**	**99.82**
	CRR	**99.93**	**99.98**	**99.99**	**99.98**	**100**	**99.98**	**99.98**

in a multisize context as in the second and first protocols of the ICDAR 2011 and ICDAR 2013 competitions, respectively (one system for all font sizes).

Table 9.2 gives the results for the multisize "Arabic Transparent" word recognition systems. Most of the systems had good results for character recognition — above 98%, while word recognition rates from 74.18% for the THOCR 1 system-ICDAR 2013 to 99.82% for the Siemens System-ICDAR 2013. The Siemens System-ICDAR 2013 thus had the best character and word recognition rates of all the published multisize "Arabic Transparent" systems.

9.7.3 *Multisize DecoTypeNaskh Word Recognition Results*

The systems in this category were all evaluated using images from Set 6 of APTI generated using the "DecoTypeNaskh" font. Each system was tested in a mono-size context as in the second protocol of the ICDAR 2013 competition.

Table 9.3 summarizes the results achieved by the mono-size "DecoTypeNaskh" word recognition systems. Most systems had slightly worse results for word recognition compared to the mono-size "Arabic Transparent" results except for UPV–BHMM systems — ICDAR 2013 and the Siemens System — ICDAR 2013. This is due to the complexity

Table 9.3. Mono-size "DecoTypeNaskh" word recognition results.

System/Size		6	8	10	12	18	24	Mean
SID systems — ICDAR	WRR	64.12	76.99	80.61	81.40	86.88	86.81	79.47
2013	CRR	94.05	96.65	97.36	97.77	98.46	98.52	97.14
UPV–BHMM	WRR	85.57	92.15	93.23	93.53	93.55	93.81	91.97
systems — ICDAR 2013	CRR	97.16	98.47	98.71	98.77	98.76	98.81	98.45
THOCR 1 system —	WRR	5.42	44.93	57.09	58.33	60.14	58.49	47.40
ICDAR 2013	CRR	72.40	92.49	94.65	94.92	95.11	95.04	90.77
THOCR 2 system —	WRR	17.00	61.84	69.89	71.09	72.64	72.07	60.76
ICDAR 2013	CRR	75.99	92.65	94.62	94.85	95.24	95.02	91.40
Siemens System —	**WRR**	**98.82**	**99.20**	**99.24**	**99.72**	**99.75**	**99.37**	**99.35**
ICDAR 2013	**CRR**	**99.83**	**99.87**	**99.90**	**99.96**	**99.97**	**99.93**	**99.91**

of the writing morphology of these fonts, which are rich in ligatures and overlaps between the characters. Siemens Systems — ICDAR 2013 had the best result, averaging 99.35% for word recognition and 99.91% for character recognition, followed by UPV–BHMM systems — ICDAR 2013, with an average of 91.97% for word recognition and 98.45% for character recognition.

9.7.4 *Diwani Letter, Andalus, Arabic Transparent, Simplified Arabic, and Traditional Arabic Word Recognition Results*

The systems in this category were evaluated using APTI-generated images with the "Diwani Letter, Andalus, Arabic Transparent, Simplified Arabic, and Traditional Arabic" fonts. Each system was tested in a mono-size context as in the second protocol proposed in the ICDAR 2011 competition.

Tables 9.4–9.6 give the mono-font and mono-size system results evaluated using Andalus, Arabic Transparent, Simplified Arabic, Traditional Arabic, and Diwani Letter fonts. The UPV-2013 system, a newer version of the UPV–PRHLT–REC1–ICDAR 2011 system, had the best character recognition rates, which correlate with the complexity of the font used. Images generated with simple fonts like Andalus gave good results; however, complex fonts rich in overlaps and ligatures like Diwani Letter had poorer results.

Table 9.4.   IPSAR system-ICDAR 2011 results.

Font/Size		6	8	10	12	18	24	Mean
Andalus	WRR	13.9	35.7	65.6	73.8	69.5	64.5	53.8
	CRR	67.4	82.4	92.4	94.4	93.0	92.5	87.0
Arabic	WRR	29.9	40.0	73.2	74.9	65.9	69.1	58.8
Transparent	CRR	78.2	84.4	94.1	95.1	93.9	95.5	90.2
Simplified	WRR	30.8	39.8	73.2	75.5	66.2	68.6	59.0
Arabic	CRR	77.6	84.3	94.2	94.9	93.1	94.4	89.8
Traditional	WRR	4.6	3.4	46.7	55.1	52.9	50.4	35.5
Arabic	CRR	49.8	49.2	85.9	88.5	87.5	88.3	74.9
Diwani Letter	WRR	9.7	3.3	39.9	55.8	49.5	64.0	37.0
	CRR	60.1	48.3	83.4	89.1	91.7	92.6	77.5

Table 9.5.   UPV–PRHLT-REC1-ICDAR 2011 results.

Font/Size		6	8	10	12	18	24	Mean
Andalus	WRR	94.1	75.5	81.1	83.6	83.9	85.0	83.8
	CRR	98.9	94.8	96.1	96.7	96.7	97.0	96.7
Arabic	WRR	94.7	78.2	78.9	81.8	83.1	83.8	83.4
Transparent	CRR	99.0	95.2	95.5	96.1	96.2	96.1	96.4
Simplified	WRR	57.6	38.3	43.6	43.5	42.9	46.2	45.4
Arabic	CRR	89.3	81.9	84.3	83.6	83.5	85.0	84.6
Traditional	WRR	57.6	38.3	43.6	43.5	42.9	46.2	45.4
Arabic	CRR	89.3	81.9	84.3	83.6	83.5	85.0	84.6
Diwani Letter	WRR	61.7	27.7	30.9	31.6	76.4	35.1	43.9
	CRR	90.9	75.8	77.8	78.1	94.9	79.6	82.8

Table 9.6.   UPV-2013 Mono-font and mono-size character recognition results.

Font/Size		6	8	10	12	18	24	Mean
Andalus	CRR	99.1	99.8	99.9	99.9	100	100	99.8
Arabic Transparent	CRR	99.4	99.9	99.9	100	100	99.9	99.8
Simplified Arabic	CRR	99.5	99.9	99.9	100	100	100	99.9
Traditional Arabic	CRR	93.6	98.7	99.5	99.7	99.8	99.8	98.5
Diwani Letter	CRR	90.0	92.8	93.3	93.8	93.9	94.1	93.0

9.7.5 *Arabic Character Recognition Results*

The systems in this category's character recognition were assessed using images from APTI. Table 9.7 gives the results of the Adhitama *et al.*-2014 systems. The character recognition results are much higher with regular or simple fonts. Among six fonts, DecoTypeThuluth and DecoTypeNaskh fonts scored lowest performance. This might be because of the complex structure of the Arabic font, such as overlaps and ligatures. The Adhitama *et al.*-2014 system's character recognition rate was 98.2% with Traditional Arabic (simple font) and 90.8% with DecoTypeThuluth (rich with ligatures).

The aforementioned results show the improvement of postprocessing using the Levenshtein distance. The postprocessing method effectively raises up the word recognition. The improvement could be achieved up to 15% compared with the normal method.

9.7.6 *Multifont and Multisize Arabic Word Recognition Results*

The systems in this category were evaluated using APTI-generated images using 10 Fonts. Each system was tested in the multifont and multisize context of the third protocol of the ICDAR 2013 competition (one system for all fonts and font sizes).

Table 9.7.   Adhitama *et al.*-2014 character recognition system results.

Font/System	Adhitama *et al.* (2014)	
	Without postprocessing	**With postprocessing**
DecoTypeThuluth	75.4	**90.8**
DecoTypeNaskh	79.4	**92.6**
Simplified Arabic	82.6	**95.7**
Traditional Arabic	83.4	**98.2**
Tahoma	82.8	**96.5**
Andalus	80.5	**97.2**
Mean	80.68	**95.16**

Tables 9.8 and 9.9 present the multifont and multisize results of the Siemens-ICDAR 2013 and THOCR 3-ICDAR 2013 systems. Both have high character recognition rates; however, the Siemens-ICDAR 2013 system comes out top, averaging 99.07% for word recognition and 99.84% for character recognition (Table 9.8 with the WRR and CRR in bold). Although the results are very good, the text recognition of images

Table 9.8. Multifont and multisize Siemens-ICDAR 2013 word recognition system results.

Font/Size		6	8	10	12	18	24	Mean
Advertising Bold	WRR	99.86	99.96	99.97	99.97	99.96	99.95	99.95
	CRR	99.98	100	100	100	99.99	99.99	99.99
Andalus	WRR	98.93	99.88	99.92	99.91	99.92	99.76	99.72
	CRR	99.85	99.98	99.99	99.99	99.99	99.96	99.96
Arabic Transparent	WRR	99.57	99.92	99.99	99.97	99.99	99.94	99.90
	CRR	99.95	99.99	100	100	100	100	99.99
M Unicode Sara	WRR	95.70	97.63	97.66	97.75	97.82	97.68	97.71
	CRR	99.28	99.59	99.60	99.61	99.62	99.60	99.60
Tahoma	WRR	99.65	99.94	99.97	99.98	99.97	99.96	99.91
	CRR	99.96	99.99	100	100	100	99.99	99.99
Simplified Arabic	WRR	99.30	99.90	99.94	99.95	99.95	99.85	99.82
	CRR	99.90	99.99	99.99	99.99	99.99	99.99	99.98
Traditional Arabic	WRR	96.16	99.33	99.77	99.68	99.78	99.70	99.07
	CRR	99.51	99.92	99.97	99.96	99.97	99.95	99.88
DecoTypeNaskh	WRR	97.17	99.25	99.16	99.18	99.15	98.83	98.79
	CRR	99.61	99.89	99.41	99.50	99.87	99.83	99.69
DecoTypeThuluth	WRR	96.35	99.24	99.92	99.92	99.44	99.27	99.02
	CRR	99.49	99.90	99.92	99.94	99.91	99.90	99.84
Diwani Letter	WRR	91.77	97.60	98.28	98.41	98.06	96.68	96.80
	CRR	98.70	99.64	99.72	99.74	99.68	99.44	99.49
Mean RR	WRR	97.64	99.27	99.46	99.47	99.40	99.16	99.07
	CRR	99.65	99.89	99.86	99.87	99.90	99.87	99.84

Table 9.9.   Multifont and multisize THOCR 3-ICDAR 2013 word recognition system results.

Font/Size		6	8	10	12	18	24	Mean
Advertising Bold	WRR	86.05	87.99	88.55	88.42	87.14	85.90	87.34
	CRR	97.54	97.98	98.09	98.06	97.83	97.70	97.87
Andalus	WRR	71.70	91.10	94.28	95.88	97.09	96.61	91.11
	CRR	90.51	98.11	99.00	99.42	99.67	99.54	97.71
Arabic Transparent	WRR	47.18	76.56	92.71	94.24	93.99	94.40	83.18
	CRR	79.48	93.12	98.98	99.32	99.22	99.27	94.90
M Unicode Sara	WRR	38.57	55.89	76.51	77.97	80.66	80.04	68.27
	CRR	82.86	91.21	97.12	97.52	97.87	97.70	94.05
Tahoma	WRR	61.26	85.46	85.78	86.34	84.21	82.56	80.94
	CRR	92.84	98.52	98.52	98.66	98.78	97.81	97.52
Simplified Arabic	WRR	42.61	82.76	91.69	91.12	91.62	91.13	81.82
	CRR	82.76	95.45	98.74	98.64	98.60	98.49	95.45
Traditional Arabic	WRR	10.39	34.98	53.57	57.29	68.01	69.46	48.95
	CRR	67.06	80.59	88.77	91.01	93.83	94.42	85.95
DecoTypeNaskh	WRR	14.75	38.19	47.49	47.68	52.09	50.96	41.86
	CRR	69.65	82.69	86.96	88.03	89.34	89.16	84.31
DecoTypeThuluth	WRR	12.44	26.97	39.45	48.22	54.11	53.06	39.04
	CRR	69.26	78.81	83.97	87.71	90.06	89.55	83.23
Diwani Letter	WRR	5.21	19.52	28.30	31.45	92.74	33.20	35.07
	CRR	53.86	74.70	80.02	82.26	99.17	83.31	78.89
Mean RR	WRR	40.75	62.00	69.83	71.86	80.17	73.73	65.76
	CRR	79.42	89.71	93.02	94.06	96.44	94.70	90.99

generated with fonts like "Diwani Letter" and "M Unicode Sara" needs improvement.

9.7.7 *Arabic Font-identification Results*

Table 9.10 presents the font-identification results of the systems evaluated using APTI images generated in 10 fonts. The results were good overall, with the exception of the "Arabic Transparent" and "Simplified Arabic"

Table 9.10. Font-identification results using the APTI database {(A) Andalus, (B) Arabic Transparent, (C) AdvertisingBold, (D) Diwani Letter, (E) DecoTypeThuluth, (F) Simplified Arabic, (G) Tahoma, (H) Traditional Arabic, (I) DecoTypeNaskh, (J) M Unicode Sara}.

System/Fonts	A	B	C	D	E	F	G	H	I	J	Mean
Ahmad et al.-2015 system†	99.80	93.53	—	98.27	—	98.13	—	95.20	—	—	96.99
Slimane et al.-2013 system* (10 classes)	99.9	80.8	99.7	99.6	99.4	67.0	99.8	99.7	99.0	99.9	94.5
Slimane et al.-2013 system* (9 classes)	99.8	98.7	99.7	99.6	99.3	98.2	99.7	99.1	97.3	99.8	99.1
Nicolaou et al.-2014 system (10 classes)‡	—	—	—	—	—	—	—	—	—	—	94.27
Nicolaou et al.-2014 system (9 classes)‡	—	—	—	—	—	—	—	—	—	—	99.57
Slimane et al.-2013 system (10 classes)‡	100	87.27	100	99.72	99.86	75.94	99.51	99.23	96.92	100	95.85
Slimane et al.-2013 system (9 classes)‡	100	98.95	100	99.72	99.86	98.53	99.51	98.95	96.92	100	99.24

Notes: *Evaluated at the word level.
†Evaluated with 3,000 word images.
‡The Nicolaou et al.-2014 and Slimane et al.-2013 systems were evaluated at the line level (6 word images by text line) using the same data.

fonts, which are very similar. In some tests, these two fonts are considered as 1 font, and the system is tested with 9 font classes. In the final evaluation category (with 9 font classes), the best identification rates were 99.1% and 99.57%, respectively, with the word-based Slimane *et al.*-2013 system and the line-based Nicolaou *et al.*-2014 system.

In the category with 10 fonts, the best identification rates of 94.5% and 95.85%, respectively, were with the word-based Slimane *et al.*-2013 system and the line-based Slimane *et al.*-2013 system.

The Ahmad *et al.*-2015 system was developed with 5 fonts and evaluated with 3,000 word images for each font. The system performed well, with good results, for some fonts, equal to the best system results.

9.8 Conclusions and Recommendations

This chapter described the well-known APTI database used by more than 60 groups in the world. In addition, the chapter summarized the results when all the systems with this database were evaluated in organized competitions or in the literature. Many systems were evaluated using mono-font and mono-size protocols. System performance varies from one system to another and from the word to character level. For the multifont and multisize/mono-size protocols, only a few systems had good results over all fonts. All the results only came with plain writing style, although APTI has been developed with three other writing styles (bold, italic and, bold and italic).

Based on the overall results outlined in this chapter, it is recommended that researchers:

- Continue improving their text recognition, word segmentation, and font-identification systems, and share their results on APTI with the plain writing style.
- Work with other writing styles for more challenging and variability in the data.
- Participate in competitions organized with APTI to compare systems in blind mode and share the results.

References

1. A.M. AL-Shatnawi, S. AL-Salaimeh, F.H. AL-Zawaideh, and K. Omar, "Offline Arabic text recognition: An overview," *World of Computer Science and Information Technology Journal* (*WCSIT*), vol. 1, no. 5, pp. 184–192, 2011.

2. J.H. AlKhateeb, J. Ren, J. Jiang, and H. Al-Muhtaseb, "Offline handwritten Arabic cursive text recognition using hidden Markov models and re-ranking," *Pattern Recognition Letters*, vol. 32, no. 8, pp. 1081–1088, 2011.

3. F. Slimane, R. Ingold, S. Kanoun, A.M. Alimi, and J. Hennebert, "A new Arabic printed text image database and evaluation," *ICDAR*, pp. 946–950, 2009.

4. F. Slimane, R. Ingold, S. Kanoun, A.M. Alimi, and J. Hennebert, *Database and Evaluation Protocols for Arabic Printed*. Fribourg, Switzerland, DIUF-University of Fribourg, 2009.

5. S. Yousfi, S.-A. Berrani, and C. Garcia, "ALIF: A dataset for Arabic embedded text recognition in TV broadcast," *CBDAR Workshop @ ICDAR*, pp. 1221–1225, 2015.

6. O. Zayene, J. Hennebert, S. Masmoudi Touj, R. Ingold, and N. Essoukri Ben Amara, "A dataset for Arabic text detection, tracking and recognition in news videos — AcTiV," *ICDAR*, pp. 996–1000, 2015.

7. A. AbdelRaouf, C.A. Higgins, T. Pridmore, and M. Khalil, "Building a multimodal Arabic corpus (MMAC)," *International Journal on Document Analysis and Recognition*, vol. 13, no. 4, pp. 285–302, 2010.

8. A. Mezghani, S. Kanoun, M. Khemakhem, and H. El Abed, "A database for Arabic handwritten text image recognition and writer identification," *ICFHR*, pp. 399–402, 2012.

9. F. Kallel Jaiem, S. Kanoun, M. Khemakhem, H. El Abed, and J. Kardoun, "Database for Arabic printed text recognition research," *ICIAP*, pp. 251–259, 2013.

10. F. Slimane, S. Kanoun, H. El Abed, A.M. Alimi, R. Ingold, and J. Hennebert, "ICDAR 2011–Arabic recognition competition: Multi-font multi-size digitally represented text," *ICDAR*, pp. 1449–1453, 2011.

11. F. Slimane, S. Kanoun, H. El Abed, A.M. Alimi, R. Ingold, and J. Hennebert, "ICDAR2013 competition on multi-font and multi-size digitally represented Arabic text," *ICDAR*, pp. 1433–1437, 2013.

12. M. Khorsheed, "Offline recognition of omnifont Arabic text using the HMM ToolKit (HTK)," *Pattern Recognition Letters*, vol. 28, no. 12, pp. 1563–1571, 2007.

13. A. Giménez and A. Juan, "Embedded Bernoulli mixture HMMs for handwritten word recognition," *ICDAR*, pp. 896–900, 2009.

14. A. Giménez, I. Khoury, and A. Juan, "Windowed Bernoulli mixture HMMs for Arabic handwritten word recognition," *ICFHR*, pp. 533–538, 2010.

15. A. Graves, M. Liwicki, S. Fernandez, R. Bertolami, and H. Bunke, "A novel connectionist system for unconstrained handwriting recognition," *IEEE Transactions on Pattern Analysis and Machine Intelligence*, vol. 31, no. 5, pp. 855–868, 2009.

16. A. Graves, "Supervised sequence labelling with recurrent neural networks," *PhD Dissertation*, München, Germany, Technische Universität München, 2008.

17. A. Giménez, I. Khoury, J. Andrés-Ferrer, and A. Juan, "Handwriting word recognition using windowed Bernoulli HMMs," *Pattern Recognition Letters*, vol. 35, no. 1, pp. 149–156, 2014.

18. O. Zayene, "Contribution à la reconnaissance de l'ecriture arabe trés basse résolution," *Master's Thesis*, Sousse, Tunisia, Ecole Nationale d'Ingénieurs de Sousse (ENISo), 2012.

19. F. Slimane, S. Kanoun, A.M. Alimi, R. Ingold, and J. Hennebert, "Gaussian mixture models for Arabic font recognition," *ICPR*, pp. 2174–2177, 2010.

20. F. Slimane, J. Hennebert, S. Kanoun, A.M. Alimi, and R. Ingold, "A new baseline estimation method applied to Arabic word recognition," *DAS* (Short Paper), 2012.

21. F. Slimane, R. Ingold, A.M. Alimi, and J. Hennebert, "Duration models for Arabic text recognition using hidden Markov models," *CIMCA*, pp. 838–843, 2008.

22. F. Slimane, S. Kanoun, J. Hennebert, R. Ingold, and A.M. Alimi, *Benchmarking Strategy for Arabic Screen-Rendered Word Recognition*. London, Springer-Verlag, 2012.

23. B. Su and X. Ding, "Linear sequence discriminant analysis: A model-based dimensionality reduction method for vector sequences," *ICCV*, pp. 889–896, 2013.

24. A. Rosenberg, "Using SIFT descriptors for OCR of printed Arabic," *Master Report*, 2012.

25. I. Ahmad, S. A. Mahmoud, and G. A. Fink, "Open-vocabulary recognition of machine-printed Arabic text using hidden Markov models," *Pattern Recognition*, vol. 51 (issue C), pp. 97–111, 2015.

26. M. Khorsheed and S. Ouis, "Hidden Markov model based recognition engine using a novel feature extraction approach," *ICSAI*, pp. 225–229, 2014.

27. S.M. Awaida and M.S. Khorsheed, "Developing discrete density hidden Markov models for Arabic printed text recognition," *CyberneticsCom*, pp. 35–39, 2012.
28. I. Khoury, A. Giménez, A. Juan, and J. Andrés-Ferrer, "Window repositioning for printed Arabic recognition," *Pattern Recognition Letters*, vol. 51, pp. 86–93, 2015.
29. Z. Jiang, X. Ding, L. Peng, and C. Liu, "Exploring more representative states of hidden Markov model in optical character recognition: A clustering-based model pre-training approach," *International Journal of Pattern Recognition and Artificial Intelligence*, vol. 29, no. 03, pp. 1550014-(1–29), 2015.
30. P. Adhitama, S.H. Kim, and I.S. Na, "Lexicon-driven word recognition based on Levenshtein distance," *International Journal of Software Engineering and Its Applications*, vol. 8, no. 2, pp. 11–20, 2014.
31. A. Kacem Echi, I. Ben Cheikh, and A. Belaïd, "Collaborative combination of neuron-linguistic classifiers for large Arabic word vocabulary recognition," *International Journal of Pattern Recognition and Artificial Intelligence*, vol. 28, no. 1, pp. 1453001-(1–39), 2014.
32. P. Adhitama, S. Hyung Kim, and I. Seop Na, "Arabic character segmentation using horizontal projection and sliding window," *KISM*, 2013.
33. A. Nicolaou, F. Slimane, V. Märgner, and M. Liwicki, "Local binary patterns for Arabic optical font recognition," *DAS*, pp. 76–80, 2014.
34. F. Slimane, S. Kanoun, J. Hennebert, A.M. Alimi, and R. Ingold, "A study on font-family and font-size recognition applied to Arabic word images at ultra-low resolution," *Pattern Recognition Letters*, vol. 34, no. 2, pp. 209–218, 2013.
35. A. Dempster, N. Laird, and D. Rubin, "Maximum likelihood from incomplete data via the EM algorithm," *Journal of the Royal Statistical Society, Series B*, vol. 39, no. 1, pp. 1–38, 1977.

Index